Proficiency Testbuilder

Mark Harrison

Heinemann

Heinemann English Language Teaching
A division of Reed Educational and Professional Publishing Limited
Halley Court, Jordan Hill, Oxford OX2 8EJ

OXFORD MADRID FLORENCE ATHENS PRAGUE
SÃO PAULO MEXICO CITY CHICAGO PORTSMOUTH (NH)
TOKYO SINGAPORE KUALA LUMPUR MELBOURNE
AUCKLAND JOHANNESBURG IBADAN GABORONE

ISBN 0 435 24063 3 (with key)
0 435 24062 5 (without key)

Designed by Giles Davies

The publishers would like to thank:
Judith Ash; Roger Johnson; Andrew Walters - Hambakis
school; Karin Kopp and Gisela Szpytko of AngloWorld, Oxford;
Anthea Bazin of Oxford Academy, Oxford; Agnes Zimmer; Piotr
Ponikiewski; Juha Sorsa.
Photos: David Beard, ZoëYoud, Kate Melliss and family,Thorpe
Park.

The author and publishers would like to thank the following for
permission to reproduce their material:
Cohen, Grosberg and Zingen, ' The Americans; The Money
Game' by Alistair Cooke © 1980, Penguin (p115); Margaret
Coles, ' How to tame problem people', as appeared in Sunday
Telegraph, 28 February 1993 (p102); Education Guardian
extracts from: 'Cost of pop's vast army' (p126) and 'Rock's
roaring bull goes grey' (p126); Sebastian Goetz extracts from
'Chilly thrills of Davy Jones' locker' in The Times, Features
section, 13 March 1993 (p71); Hampstead and Highgate
Express/Guy Somerset extracts from interview with David
Feingold in Hampstead and Highgate Express,19 March 1993
(p62); Harper Collins Publishers Ltd extracts from 'Point of
Departure' by James Cameron for Grafton Books 1969 (p40);
The Independent: 'Obituary of William Shawn', by Anthony
Bailey in Gazette,10 December 1992 (p104); extracts from
'Mark Lawson Sums Up', by Mark Lawson in Independent
magazine, Home Thoughts section,18 July 1992 (p12); extracts
from 'To hell and back', by Caroline McGhie, 28 March 1993
(p94); extracts from 'Taxi History', by Reggie Nadelson,12
December 1992 (p20); extracts from 'Honest Opinions', by Kat
Thurston, 30 July 1992 (p53); extract from 'John Walsh clears
his desk', by John Walsh, Independent magazine, Home
Thoughts section, 16 January 1993 (p94); extract from 'They'd
work for nothing to get through the door', by Martin Wroe,17
February 1993 (p62); IPC Magazines, extract from '20 Ways -
How to get on well at work', Woman's Own magazine, 9
September 1991 (p94); Italian Trade Centre - Government
Agency, extracts from 'About Italian tomatoes', by Antonio
Carluccio (p77); Collected Short Stories by Michael McLaverty,
published by Poolbeg Press Ltd, Dublin (p101); Chris
Middleton, extract from article on theme parks, Homes and
Savings magazine, Summer 1992 (p126); National Magazine
Company Ltd, extract from 'Start being childish', by Rebecca
Adams (p41), and 'The travel bores', by Samantha Norman,
(p82), (SHE magazine, October 1992 and Cosmopolitan,
September 1991 [British editions] respectively); National Peanut

Council of America advertisement (p34); The New Yorker,
extract from, 'History denied - Talk of the town', reprinted by
permission ©1993 The New Yorker Magazine, Inc.(p14);
Newspaper Publishers Association Ltd, television
advertisement, 'You know how it is.... flip channels for
something - anything - to watch instead', (p62); Nissan
advertisement, Infiniti Division of Nissan Motor Corporation,
USA. (p34); Peters, Fraser and Dunlop Group Ltd, extract from,
'Unreliable Memiors', by Clive James reprinted by permission
(p10); Reuters Ltd, extract from, 'The power of news: the history
of Reuters', by Donald Read, (p48); The Scottish Tourist Board,
extracts from 'Undiscovered Scotland' brochure (STB, 1992)
(p34); Sunday Telegraph, © Megan Tresidder, extract from
interview with David Mellor, 'Still fun after the ministry', 7
February 1993 (p62); Times Newspapers Ltd: advertisement
headings (p62); 'Down with video', (Viewpoint, 1 March 1993)
by Susan Elkin (p42); 'Painting the town green - colour
blindness', by Gerald Haigh © Times Newspapers Ltd. 4
December 1992,(p25); William Heinemann Ltd: extract from
'Storm country', by Pete Davies (p69); extract from 'All played
out' by Pete Davies (p126); extract from 'Travels with Charley'
by John Steinbeck (p70); © UCLES/K&J (p128).

Recording acknowledgements:
Robert Opie, Ispo Facto, (BBC1, 2 December 1992), (p167);
Peter MacDiarmid, freelance photographer, 'Job Bank', (BBC 2,
16 March 1993) (p168); Hilary Kingsley, 'The importance of
soap', (BBC Radio 2, interview, 7 March 1993) (p172);
Gerald Marks, Mitchell Parish, Ann Rennell, 'Return to Tin Pan
Alley', (BBC Radio 3: 20's Season, 11 March 1993) (p169);Bill
Romme (Dept. of Biology, Fort Lewis College, Colorado, USA),
Tomorrow's World, 'Forest fires in Yellowstone Park', (BBC1, 2
December 1992) (p169); Horizon, 'The Iceman', (BBC2, 8
March 1993) (p172); Ray Gosling, 'Gosling on the High Street:
the history of Boots the Chemist', (BBC Radio 4, 30 December
1992) (p173); Jon Anderson (Columbia-Tristar), Malcolm Bird
(Radio Newcastle), 'Media File: English Time', (BBC2, 17 March
1993) (p174); Professor Martin A. Conway (Lancaster
University), Penny Mansfield (One plus One- Marriage and
Partnership research) and producer of Johnnie Walker show for
'The A.M Alternative', (BBC Radio 5, 1 February 1993) (p173);
Alan Horrox/Tetra Films Ltd, 'Ocho Rios - Junior Georgraphy',
(Channel 4, March 1993) (p170); LBC Radio: Travel and
Weather reports (23 March 1993) (p167); Curtain Mill
advertisement (p171); Eurokitchen advertisement (p171).
Airforce/Southern Business Group, 'Thank you...' advertisement
(p171);CTSS Advertising/Carphone Warehouse, 'Informed
decision...' (p171); Porter Agency/Trafficmaster advertisement
(p171);Sarah Williams, interview (LBC, 25 February 1993)
'Working for yourself'. (p170)

Cassettes Produced by James Richardson at Studio AVP

Photograph acknowledgements: Camera Press/Philip North
Combes (p93); The Independent/Robert Hallam (p125);/Geraint
Lewis (p93);/Nicholas Turpin (p61,p93); The Kobal Collection
(p61); Life File (p33); Retna Pictures/Paul Slattery (p125); Rex
Features/Nils Jorgensen (p61); Depth Charge/Thorpe Park
(p125)

Commissioned photography by Chris Honeywell (p33)

Printed and bound in Great Britain by The Bath Press, Bath

97 98 10 9 8 7 6

CONTENTS

Book cassette pack

INTRODUCTION 4

TEST ONE

PAPER 1	SECTION A	6
Further Practice		8
PAPER 1	SECTION B	10
Further Practice		15
PAPER 2		17
Further Practice		18
PAPER 3	SECTION A	20
Further Practice		23
PAPER 3	SECTION B	25
Further Practice		28
PAPER 4		30
Further Practice		32
PAPER 5		33
Further Practice		35

TEST TWO

PAPER 1	SECTION A	37
Further Practice		39
PAPER 1	SECTION B	40
Further Practice		43
PAPER 2		45
Further Practice		46
PAPER 3	SECTION A	48
Further Practice		51
PAPER 3	SECTION B	53
Further Practice		56
PAPER 4		58
Further Practice		60
PAPER 5		61
Further Practice		63

TEST THREE

PAPER 1	SECTION A	65
Further Practice		67
PAPER 1	SECTION B	69
Further Practice		72
PAPER 2		74
Further Practice		75
PAPER 3	SECTION A	77
Further Practice		80
PAPER 3	SECTION B	82
Further Practice		85
PAPER 4		88
Further Practice		91
PAPER 5		93
Further Practice		95

TEST FOUR

PAPER 1	SECTION A	97
Further Practice		99
PAPER 1	SECTION B	101
Further Practice		105
PAPER 2		107
Further Practice		108
PAPER 3	SECTION A	110
Further Practice		113
PAPER 3	SECTION B	115
Further Practice		118
PAPER 4		120
Further Practice		123
PAPER 5		125
Further Practice		127

Sample answer sheets – Papers 1 and 4 128

KEY AND EXPLANATION 129

LISTENING SCRIPTS 167

Assessment criteria – Papers 2 and 5 176

THE PROFICIENCY TESTBUILDER

The Proficiency Testbuilder is more than a book of Practice Tests. It is designed not only to enable students to practise doing tests of exactly the kind they will encounter in the exam itself, but also to provide them with valuable further practice, guidance and explanation. This will enable them to prepare thoroughly for the exam and increase their ability to perform well in it.

The Proficiency Testbuilder contains:

Four complete Practice Tests for the Cambridge Certificate of Proficiency in English

These tests reflect the level and types of question to be found in the real exam.

Further Practice and Guidance pages

These follow each paper or section of paper of each test.
For Reading Comprehension, Use of English and Listening Comprehension, they contain exercises, questions and tips directly related to each paper or section.
These encourage students to draw their own conclusions as to what the answers in the test should be. Their step-by-step approach enables students to develop and apply the right processes when answering questions in the exam.
For Composition and for Use of English Section B they contain suggestions and assessments of authentic sample compositions and summaries.
For Interview, there is practice in talking about pictures and passages, exercises for vocabulary development and suggestions for useful language.

Key and Explanation

This contains full explanations of every answer in the Tests and Further Practice and Guidance pages, together with a great deal of further information relevant to them. For questions where candidates must choose from a number of options, there are highly detailed explanations not only of the correct choice but also of why the other choices are incorrect. There is also a guide to examiner's assessment criteria for papers 2 and 5 on page 176.

How to use the Proficiency Testbuilder

Teachers and Students who have the edition with key can use the book in these ways:

● Simply follow the instructions

Clear directions are given as to the order in which to do things, enabling you to work through the book page by page. If you do this, you:

1 Complete the whole of or a section of each Paper, perhaps under exam conditions.

2 Complete the Further Practice and Guidance page or pages which follow this.

3 Return to the relevant part of the test and check, and possibly change, the answers given, as a result of what has been learned from doing the Further Practice.

● Vary the order

You may wish to do some of the Further Practice and Guidance pages before answering the questions to which they apply or immediately after them, rather than completing the whole paper or section first. In addition, teachers may wish to do the Further Practice and Guidance pages as discussion or pairwork, or ask students to prepare them before class.

The Certificate of Proficiency

PAPER 1: Reading Comprehension (1 hour)

SECTION A: 25 multiple-choice questions in which candidates must choose which one of four words or phrases correctly completes a gap in a sentence.

SECTION B: 3 passages on which a total of 15 multiple-choice questions are asked. Candidates write their answers on a separate answer sheet.(see sample on page 128).

PAPER 2: Composition (2 hours)

Two compositions to be written from a choice of topics. Each of the choices is for a composition of up to 350 words in length, except for one, which is 250-300 words long. Candidates write their compositions on paper provided.

Note: In this book, four choices are given. In the exam, there is a fifth choice relating to the three books which candidates have the option of reading. These books are specified in the examination regulations each year and candidates may write about one of them. As the books set change from year to year, this option is omitted in this book.

PAPER 3: Use of English (2 hours)

SECTION A:
1   A short passage with 20 gaps, each of which must be filled with one word.
2   A number of sentences that must be completed so that they mean the same as those printed above each one.
3   A number of sentences with gaps that must be filled with a phrase.
4   A number of sentences which must be rewritten using a word printed below each one.

SECTION B: A passage followed by
1   Up to 15 questions that must be answered with a phrase or sentence, with no choices given.
2   A question requiring a summary of the whole passage or part of it, 70-90 words in length. Candidates write their answers on the question paper.

PAPER 4: Listening Comprehension (about 30 minutes)

A cassette recording of (usually) four pieces, each of which is heard twice. There may be one speaker or more than one. A variety of accents are heard and speech is close to or at the speed of native speakers. Pieces include broadcasts, interviews, conversations, announcements, talks, etc.

Question types include filling in information, completing sentences, answering multiple-choice questions, indicating whether statements are true or false or whether certain views are expressed, matching, etc. Candidates are tested on their understanding of facts and information and the attitudes and opinions of speakers. Candidates are given 10 minutes at the end to transfer their answers onto a separate answer sheet.(see sample on page 128).

PAPER 5: Interview (15-20 minutes)

There are usually three parts, all of which relate to a common topic.
1   Candidates are shown and asked questions about one or more photographs. This may lead to discussion of the topic.
2   Candidates are shown and asked questions about one or more short passages.
3   Candidates are shown further material as the basis for a discussion of the topic.
The interview may be done individually, in pairs or in groups of three. When done individually, the candidate speaks only to the examiner; when done in pairs or groups of three candidates speak both to each other and to the examiner and a second examiner may be there to assess the interview.

In addition, candidates may choose to talk about one of the set books.

TEST ONE

PAPER 1   READING COMPREHENSION   1 hour

SECTION A

In this section you must choose the word or phrase which best completes each sentence. Indicate the letter A, B, C, or D against the number of each item 1 to 25 for the word or phrase you choose.

1 Following a lengthy power .... he became the Chairman of the company.

   A strife   B struggle   C rivalry   D confrontation

2 He proved to be distinctly .... to working in a position of responsibility.

   A incompatible   B inapt   C unfit   D unsuited

3 The passengers demanded .... for the loss of their luggage on the journey.

   A refund   B subsidies   C compensation   D proceeds

4 When questioned by the press, the Minister .... to discuss the matter.

   A rejected   B retracted   C declined   D denied

5 As the game went on, she .... in confidence.

   A rose   B grew   C advanced   D lifted

6 When I first came to this country, I only .... staying for a short time.

   A predicted   B envisaged   C forecast   D supposed

7 I gave them .... time to make a decision so I don't know why they still haven't replied.

   A spacious   B lavish   C extensive   D ample

8 What are the main .... of this illness?

   A traces   B symptoms   C emblems   D tokens

9 Money .... to be a problem after he had made his first successful film.

   A ceased   B discontinued   C terminated   D halted

10 Nobody would .... any tears if these terrible schemes were abandoned.

   A pour   B leak   C spill   D shed

11 She is so .... on getting to the top of her profession that she never lets anything get in her way.

   A willing   B desperate   C eager   D intent

12 There was little we could do .... registering a formal complaint.

   A beyond   B further   C over   D beside

13 .... every effort has been made to ensure that the details in this brochure are correct, the company cannot accept responsibility for any late changes.

   A Even so   B While   C Nevertheless   D Whereas

14 Unpopular government policies have given .... to widespread public discontent.

    A grounds   B rise   C cause   D consequence

15 Having never been in the country before, I was initially confused .... the value of each coin.

    A as for   B as with   C as of   D as to

16 She went into the bathroom and .... her face with cold water to wake herself up.

    A splashed   B scattered   C squirted   D sprinkled

17 Much of what he said had little .... to the issue we were discussing.

    A concern   B accordance   C relevance   D involvement

18 His personal problems seem to have been .... him from his work lately.

    A disrupting   B disturbing   C distracting   D dispersing

19 It was a terrible experience and it put her .... flying forever.

    A off   B out   C away   D through

20 He is a bad-tempered man who has a tendency to .... his problems out on other people.

    A let   B put   C get   D take

21 The captain's magnificent performance .... an example to the rest of the team.

    A set   B gave   C made   D laid

22 When I got back, they had eaten the whole cake and just a few .... were left on the plate.

    A grains   B drops   C crumbs   D shreds

23 Until a .... agreement has been reached, I am not committed to accepting the offer.

    A hard   B stable   C firm   D settled

24 She said that she .... the opportunity to show that she could play a serious film role.

    A greeted   B rejoiced   C welcomed   D cheered

25 I'll .... round to replying to their letter as soon as I have time, but I'm too busy at the moment.

    A get   B come   C go   D turn

Before you check your answers to this section of the test, go on to pages 8 and 9.

WORD SETS

Some of the questions in this part of the test require you to choose from words which are related in meaning. The numbers of the exercises below refer to questions 1–4 of the test on page 6, which are questions of this type.

In each of these exercises, choose from the list of words at the top which one best fits into each gap. All of the words are related in meaning. This may help you to choose the correct option in the test and to check or learn about the differences between related words, in terms of meaning, usage and structure.

1 | *competition   row   confrontation   strife   rivalry   controversy   struggle* |

  a Following a period of intense political ...., the country is now much more settled.

  b A .... has broken out between the major parties over the government's new tax measures.

  c Three candidates were in .... for the party leadership.

  d Their .... began when they were both ambitious junior politicians.

  e Following the leader's death, there was a bitter .... for control of the party behind the scenes.

  f Ministers are anxious to avoid a .... with union leaders.

  g The new education policy has caused considerable ...., with opinion strongly divided.

2 | *incompatible   unsuited   unfit   inapt   incongruous   wrong   inconvenient* |

  a The contaminated water was declared .... for human consumption.

  b She made several .... remarks which embarrassed everyone.

  c Surrounded by old buildings, the new office block looks completely ....

  d It was .... for me to talk to her because I was busy at the time.

  e She decided that the job was .... for her and that she wouldn't enjoy it.

  f His personality is .... to married life.

  g We couldn't share a flat because his lifestyle is .... with mine.

3 | *compensation   subsidies   rewards   bonuses   refund   receipts   proceeds* |

  a The .... of the collection will go to charity.

  b .... will be made to all those who bought tickets for the cancelled concert.

  c .... are frequently offered to anyone who gives useful information about the people who committed this kind of crime.

  d .... was offered to all those whose holidays had been cancelled by the company.

e .... are being offered to salesmen who exceed their targets.

f The film achieved record box-office ....

g Government .... for public transport have been cut.

4 | rejected   declined   dissented   retracted   defied   denied   disowned |

a She politely .... to reveal any further personal details.

b The minister .... his colleague's controversial remarks.

c In a statement, they .... being involved in anything illegal.

d All my suggestions were .... as totally unsuitable.

e Very few committee members .... from the general view.

f He .... the manager's orders and went ahead anyway.

g She later .... her accusations and apologized for making them.

Now check your answers to these exercises. When you have done so, decide whether you wish to change any of your answers to questions 1–4 in the test.
Then check your answers to the test.

SECTION B

*In this section you will find after each of the passages a number of questions or unfinished statements about the passage, each with four suggested answers or ways of finishing. You must choose the one which you think fits best. Indicate the letter A, B, C, or D against the number of each item 26–40 for the answer you choose. Give **one answer only** to each question. Read each passage right through before choosing your answers.*

FIRST PASSAGE

During the long vacation I was accepted as a trainee bus conductor. I found the job fiercely demanding even on a short route with a total of about two dozen passengers. I pulled the wrong tickets, forgot the change and wrote up my log at the end of each trip in a way that drew hollow laughter from the inspectors. The inspectors were likely to swoop at any time. A conductor with
5   twenty years' service could be dismissed if an inspector caught him accepting money without pulling a ticket. If a hurrying passenger pressed the fare into your hand as he leapt out of the back door, it was wise to tear a ticket and throw it out after him. There might be a plain-clothes inspector following in an unmarked car.
    I lasted about three weeks all told. The routes through town were more than the mind could
10   stand even in the off-peak hours. All the buses from our depot and every other depot would be crawling nose to tail through the town while the entire working population of Sydney fought to get aboard. It was hot that summer: 100° Fahrenheit every day. Inside the bus it was 30° hotter still. It was so jammed inside that my feet weren't touching the floor. I couldn't blink the sweat out of my eyes. There was no hope of collecting any fares. At each stop it was all I could do to reach
15   the bell-push that signalled the driver to close the automatic doors and get going. I had no way of telling whether anybody had managed to get on or off. My one object was to get that bus up Pitt Street.
    In these circumstances I was scarcely to blame. I didn't even know where we were, but I guessed we were at the top just before Market Street. I pressed the bell, the doors puffed closed,
20   and the bus surged forward. There were shouts and yells from down the back, but I thought they were the angry cries of passengers who had not got on. Too late I realized that they were emanating from within the bus. The back set of automatic doors had closed around an old lady's neck as she was getting on. Her head was inside the bus. The rest of her, carrying a shopping bag was outside. I knew none of this at the time.
25   When I at last cottoned on to the fact that something untoward was happening and signalled the driver to stop, he crashed to a halt and opened the automatic doors, whereupon the woman dropped to the road. She was very nice about it. Perhaps the experience had temporarily dislocated her mind. Anyway, she apologized to me for causing so much trouble. Unfortunately, the car behind turned out to be full of inspectors. Since it would have made headlines if a
30   university student had been thrown off the buses for half-executing a woman of advanced years, I was given the opportunity to leave quietly. Once again this failed to coincide with my own plans in the sense that I had already resigned. In fact, I had made my decision at about the same time as the old lady hit the ground.

26 What do we learn about the inspectors in the first paragraph?

    A They found the writer amusing.
    B They never wore uniforms.
    C They were feared by employees.
    D They distrusted older employees.

27 Why was the writer unable to do his job properly?

    A He wasn't tall enough.
    B The buses went too fast.
    C People avoided paying.
    D He couldn't move.

28 The old lady in the incident described

    A was injured.
    B fainted.
    C was dragged.
    D hit her head.

29 When the incident with the old lady happened,

    A the writer had already decided to give up the job.
    B the writer's employers wanted to avoid publicity.
    C the writer was offered the chance to continue.
    D the consequences were as the writer expected.

30 What is the writer's attitude now to the job?

    A He feels responsible for the incident that ended it.
    B He thinks that he was unfairly treated by the inspectors.
    C He is ashamed that he was incapable of doing it properly.
    D He believes that it was an impossible job to do well.

SECOND PASSAGE

A realization set in when I was flicking through two magazines on a recent flight in America. In the first – the airline's giveaway publication – there was an advertisement. 'Too Busy To Read Books?', it asked, perhaps a little perilously, given that the headline was only being seen by those with time to waste reading inflight magazines.

5   The sales line was that if you were a businessman too tied up with deals and meetings ever to open that status hardback weighing down your briefcase, then these nice people would do the eye-work for you. Every month, for a fee, they would fax you snappy A4 sheets, each encapsulating the main ideas in a bulky book connected with your profession. As well as a checklist of the central arguments, your proxies would provide a paragraph of comments for and

10 against the author's thesis. The benefit of this second service was that you could plausibly discuss the book with any cultural dinosaurs you bumped into who were still relying on reading.

I then turned to the second magazine. This had just been given a redesign, a face-lift. One of the innovations was the addition of a preface to the arts reviews, which boiled down diverse critical opinion to a thin stock of comment. This was surely another example of the same

15 phenomenon. Too harrassed to read the 600 words in which the critic dissects a new travel book? Well, then just read the preface and you'll find out that it's 'an excellent adventure by the great moaner of travel writing'.

It was apparent to me that I was witnessing the birth in the media of what might be called a *summary culture*. In addition to all the time-saving devices available in the modern world, it was

20 now possible to get someone else to do your reading for you. At the same (precious) time, the editors of the magazines you bought were tipping you the wink that they didn't really expect you to read it all.

In retrospect, this development was well telegraphed. Two years ago, a book called *Information Anxiety* was published in which the author argued that, with the coming of 24-hour television

25 news and newspapers which added new sections like a field adds new rabbits, people with wide general interests would become so battered by facts that they were eventually unable to assimilate any of them.

I remember the book well because, one Wednesday afternoon, I was rung up by a television researcher and asked to discuss *Information Anxiety* on a programme the following day. When I

30 replied – with an anxiety which would have delighted the creator of the thesis – that it would be impossible to read the book's 300 pages overnight, the researcher replied: 'Oh, we don't expect you to read it. I've boiled it down to two A4 sheets'. It can now be seen that in her answer was the solution to the crisis *Information Anxiety* described. Now, the magazine and the proxies I saw on the plane have followed the logic.

31 The writer felt that the headline of the advertisement

    A suggested that reading books was a waste of time.
    B was inappropriate in the circumstances.
    C was likely to appeal to those reading it.
    D was phrased in a rather peculiar way.

32 The advertisement implied that

    A businessmen only read certain types of book.
    B businessmen talk about books they have not read.
    C it is old-fashioned for businessmen to read books.
    D books for businessmen are longer than necessary.

33 What did the advertisement and the second magazine have in common?

    A They were both aimed at business people leading busy lives.
    B They both suggested that people rapidly become bored.
    C They were both aimed at people who are too busy to read books.
    D They both enabled people to discuss books they had not read.

34 What was the main argument of *Information Anxiety*?

    A People were beginning to have a narrower range of interests.
    B The media was expanding to an extent that was too great.
    C People were unable to retain much of any information they were given.
    D The media was giving people facts that contradicted each other.

35 The writer discovered from his conversation with the television researcher that

    A the service he later saw in the second magazine was available.
    B *Information Anxiety* described the services he later saw in the magazines.
    C *Information Anxiety* described a problem that was widely shared.
    D the service he later saw advertised in the first magazine was useful to him.

36 What is the writer's attitude to the *summary culture* he describes?

    A It is an inevitable development in the modern world.
    B It will have a culturally damaging effect.
    C It is unlikely to affect many people's reading habits.
    D It illustrates how lazy many people have become.

THIRD PASSAGE

To a passer-by, the familiar building on the corner of 77th Street in New York, which is a formal and inexpensive box, suggests very little about its occupant. To anyone who knows the nature of the Historical Society, however, who has ventured inside the bronze doors and climbed a flight of wide marble stairs to visit the stately library, closed behind tall doors, or has looked, even at
5 random, through one of the card catalogues along a back wall, it is the organization that first institutionalized the concept of historic preservation in New York.

The New York Historical Society is the mother of the city's cultural institutions. It .was founded in 1804 – sixty-five years before the American Museum of Natural History, sixty-six before the Metropolitan Museum of Art, ninety-one before the New York Public Library – at a
10 time when the nation was barely three decades old and only eccentrics were collecting American artefacts and ephemera. New York was a provincial town in 1804, and, as it grew, the Society, its self-appointed annotator, moved seven times to keep pace with its acquisitions before it settled on the sleepy Upper West Side and, in 1908, erected a pink granite building as a permanent home.

By this time, the city was old enough and big enough to have awakened to its own history. By
15 the 1890s, dozens of volumes had been published about New York, studying its origin and rise, celebrating its progress and its new fame. In 1899, a fat tome entitled 'The New Metropolis' was issued in commemoration of the city's growth; it ran to three hundred thousand words and included a thousand engravings. This historical-mindedness was part of a sudden rush to remember earlier times, to document a way of life that was disappearing, and to take stock before
20 the future took over. It was prompted by a mixture of civic pride and the imminent arrival of the millennium.

A century later, New York is in a similar frame of mind. The past seems to be a more reliable source of inspiration than the future for architects, moviemakers and fashion designers, and that historic preservation is a national passion. Many things in the Historical Society's collection have
25 acquired star status. The heart of the collection resides in the everyday and the commonplace, however, – in unsung glories like civic documents, scrapbooks and diaries, architectural drawings, street photographs and old books. Writers and scholars refer to these as 'our collective memory bank'. These are the things, they say, which are truly priceless.

37 What do we learn about the Historical Society in the first paragraph?

A It is difficult for most people to gain access to it.
B Its premises reveal nothing about it from the outside.
C Much of the collection it houses is disorganized.
D Few people are aware of where it is located.

38 When the Historical Society was founded

A it had difficulty acquiring objects for its collection.
B New York had already become a large town.
C few people collected objects concerning American life.
D Americans wanted there to be such an organization.

39 What change had taken place in New York by the 1890s?

A People had started to analyse the history of America.
B People were regretting the passing of a way of life.
C New Yorkers had become interested in the city's development.
D New Yorkers were worried about the way the city was changing.

40 Which of the following is true of the Historical Society now, according to the writer?

A It contains objects that were of little interest in the past.
B It provides creative people with useful information.
C It houses some objects that are worth a lot of money.
D It contains objects associated with famous people.

Before you check your answers to this section of the test, go on to pages 15 and 16.

A DETAILED STUDY

The questions on these pages will help you to make sure that you have chosen the correct options for the questions on the second text, on pages 12–13.

Question 31 *Look at the first paragraph of the text and answer these questions.*

1 Who will read the headline?

2 Will they have anything else to do?

3 Who is the headline aimed at?

Question 32 *Look at the second paragraph and answer these questions.*

1 Does the advertisement talk about businessmen's reading preferences?

2 Will its service allow businessmen to talk about books they haven't read?

3 Does it state that books for businessmen are large?

4 Does it state that books for businessmen are too big?

5 What is a 'dinosaur' in the context of the article?
  a a person who doesn't use modern methods
  b a businessman who is efficient
  c a person who has read a lot of books
  d a businessman you meet by chance

Question 33 *Look at the third and fourth paragraphs and answer these questions.*

1 In the context of the article, if you are 'harrassed' you
  a have little interest in something.
  b are too lazy to do something.
  c suffer from pressure to do something.
  d are not familiar with doing something.

2 Do the advertisement and the magazine both refer to discussing books?

3 Is the second magazine aimed specifically at business people?

Question 34 *Look at the fifth paragraph and answer these questions.*

1 Does it state that people's interests are changing?

2 Is the problem to do with the amount, the nature, or the accuracy of things that people are told?

3 Does it refer to information in general or to information from particular sources?

Question 35 *Look at the last paragraph and answer these questions.*

1 Did the researcher offer the main points of a book or of a review?

2 Did the advertisement or the second magazine offer a similar thing?

3 What did the researcher's offer enable him to do?

4 What did the researcher tell him about *Information Anxiety*?

Question 36 *Answer these questions about the article as a whole.*

1 Does the writer state in paragraph 4 that the services offered are similar to other things that progress has brought?

2 Does he state in the first three paragraphs a belief that people should read the whole of books?

3 Does he state anywhere that the services are of use to only a few people?

4 Does he seem to be critical of the services and the people using them?

Now check your answers to the questions on these pages. Then decide whether you wish to change any of the answers that you gave to the questions on the second passage, on pages 12–13.

Then check your answers to the questions on the second passage and to the other passages in the test.

PAPER 2 COMPOSITION 2 hours

*Write **two only** of the composition exercises. Your answers must follow exactly the instructions given. Write in pen, not pencil. You are allowed to make alterations, but make sure that your work is clear and easy to read.*

1   Describe a job that you would or would not like to have and explain what skills and type of personality are required for it. (About 350 words)

2   'We live in an age when anyone can be famous for fifteen minutes.' Do you think that fame is brief and too easily attained nowadays? (About 350 words)

3   'Imagine my surprise on seeing her again after all that time!' Use this as the first or last sentence of a story. (About 350 words)

4   Write a report about the ways in which the place where you live or come from has changed in recent years. Your report could cover some of the following points: (About 300 words)
     – population
     – transport
     – employment
     – entertainment
     – housing

Before you write your compositions, go on to pages 18 and 19.

PLANNING A COMPOSITION

*One of the questions in Paper 2 requires you to **describe** something or someone. Look at question 1 on page 17 and answer the following. This will help you to plan your composition for that question. It is advisable to practise each of the types of composition.*

1   Which job would you particularly like to do or not like to do?

....

2   Tick which of the following are requirements for that job and add any others that apply.

☐ ability to make your own decisions

☐ high level of efficiency

☐ ability to organize others

☐ academic qualifications

☐ ability to work as part of a team

☐ ability to work under pressure

☐ practical training

....

....

....

3   Tick those characteristics required of someone doing the job and add any others that apply.

☐ patience

☐ desire to help others

☐ sense of humour

☐ self-confidence

☐ ambition

☐ self-discipline

☐ friendly manner

....

....

4   If you have chosen a job you would like, tick which of the following are its advantages and add any others that apply.

☐ the salary

☐ the conditions

☐ the amount of travelling involved

☐ the variety of work involved

☐ the challenge

☐ the opportunity to meet people

☐ the chance to make your own decisions

....

....

....

....

5   If you have chosen a job you wouldn't like, tick which of the following are its disadvantages and add any others that apply.

☐ the salary

☐ the conditions

☐ the amount of travelling involved

☐ the hours worked

☐ the boredom/routine involved

☐ having to take orders

☐ having to deal with people all the time

....

....

....

....

Now use this information to write your composition. You may, of course, wish to choose a job that you find attractive in some ways and unattractive in others.

Then write one or more of the other compositions.

Now read through the following sample composition for question 1 on page 17. When you have done so, answer the questions that follow it.

Nowadays the decision for a career can be a complicated one. Centuries ago our anchestors lived strictly from nature – farming crops and hunting. Today one has to choose work from a wide range of different fields.

As our anchestors did, I would also like to work in the field that uses nature's own products. In today's industrial world it could be more difficult to find such job, but for a carpenter, the trees still provide the most of materials he works with. Putting wood together so that it makes a piece of furniture or more structural part of a building has always fascinated me.

To choose the right materials and joints for a particular work requires a lot of knowledge and skills that can only be gained by experience and studying. Each piece of woodwork needs its own special cuts and joints, and the only way to make it well is being patient and meticulous. Each measurement have to be very carefully made and the cuts have to be exactly in the right place, if you want your creation strong and good looking.

Today's carpenter also has to be a bit of an environmentalist, since the materials he uses come from the nature's diminishing resources. A lot of hard wood, like teak, can only be obtained from parts of the world where forests already are threathened. Although the rain forest still is the biggest provider of oxygen, every tree that is cut down can build up the risk for our well-being. Using Scandinavian wood is less risky, since there new trees are often planted to replace the cut ones.

A carpenter creates something that lasts and is useful perhaps even for next generations. He also makes things with his hands. These qualifications for a job I value the most.

1 Does the composition actually answer the question set or does it contain irrelevant parts, 'waffle' – writing that is simply intended to fill the space but does not really say anything – or 'padding' – writing that is repetitious in order to reach the required number of words?

2 Is the composition well-organized? Is it divided into paragraphs appropriately? Explain what each paragraph contains.

3 Are appropriate linking words and phrases used for connecting sentences and paragraphs? Give examples of some that are; if some are not, correct them.

4 Does it have a good range of appropriate vocabulary or is the vocabulary used mostly too simple? Give examples and correct any inappropriate or incorrect vocabulary.

5 Is there a good range of accurate structures forming sentences that are not very simple or are the structures used mostly too basic? Give examples and correct any incorrect structures or other mistakes.

6 Is the style appropriate for this type of composition?

Now check your assessment of and corrections to this sample composition.

PAPER 3   USE OF ENGLISH   2 hours

SECTION A

1   *Fill each of the numbered blanks in the passage with* **one** *suitable word.*

The first known taxi was an Egyptian water cab in about 4000 BC. In the 17th century, first in Paris,

then in London, there were horse-drawn hackneys and as (1) .... as 1623 London's

wherry-boat operators were already complaining that the hackneys (2) .... them of

their living.

Taxis soon came (3) .... government regulation. In 1800, in Paris, the cabriolet, a

speedy two-wheeled carriage (4) .... by a single horse, was dubbed the 'cab'

(5) .... in 1834, Joseph Hansom patented the Hansom Cab. Before the automobile

became the taxi (6) .... choice, there were a few eccentric efforts to improve

(7) .... the Hansom Cab, but (8) .... was Harry N. Allen who was the father

of the taxi cab. (9) .... his New York vehicles he imported the French *taxi-mètre*, which

(10) .... measure taxes, (11) .... 'fares', and the 'taxi cab' was born.

(12) .... as the men who made Hollywood were dreamers and entrepreneurs, so

(13) .... the men who made the taxis in America run. (14) .... them was John

Hertz, who got (15) .... the taxi business in 1907. After reading a University of Chicago

study that said yellow was the colour (16) .... easily spotted, he developed the Yellow

Cab. He was (17) .... for the purpose-built taxi and he (18) .... it affordable –

cabs had always (19) .... for rich folk. He organized Yellow Cab companies in other

towns, (20) .... New York City, and later set up the first car rental service.

2   *Finish each of the following sentences in such a way that it is as similar as possible in meaning to the*
sentence printed before it.
Example: She said that he was a brilliant musician.
Answer: She described *him as a brilliant musician.*

a   Installation of a new computer system is currently taking place at our head office.

A new computer system ....

b   I only realized the full implications of what had happened some time later.

It wasn't ....

c   We can only invite a limited number of people.

There is ....

d Nobody could have done anything to prevent the problem from arising.

Nothing that ....

e You can be highly intelligent but not have much common sense.

Having ....

f I was just about to phone her office when she finally arrived.

I was on ....

g He has been put in charge of re-organizing the department.

He has been made ....

h She listened to a recording of the piece and worked out how to play it.

She taught ....

3 *Fill each of the blanks with a suitable word or phrase.*
Example: She had difficulty *making up her* mind which one to buy.

a As .... its sales decreasing substantially, the shop was
forced to close.

b Why didn't you ask me for help? I .... advice.

c I can't .... all that washing up now, I just want to sit down
and take it easy.

d We might .... wait and see what happens before we make
a decision.

e Just when it looked .... lose, they made an astonishing
comeback and won.

f Am .... amount now or can I pay some now and the rest later?

4 *For each of the sentences below, write a new sentence* **as similar as possible in meaning to the original** **sentence**, *but using the word given. This word* **must not be altered** *in any way.*

Example: She paid no attention to his warning.
            notice
Answer: *She took no notice of his warning.*

a It was discovered that the fire in the building had been started deliberately.
set

....

b The letter reached me even though it was wrongly addressed.
way

....

c She wasn't forced to resign, it was her own decision.
accord

....

d My situation and yours are completely different.
comparison

....

e I got bored with the film half-way through.
interest

....

f He said that he didn't deserve such a high honour.
worthy

....

g I didn't feel like doing anything energetic.
mood

....

h She must have been offended by something I said.
exception

....

Before you check your answers to this section of the test, go on to pages 23 and 24.

FILL IN THE MISSING WORD

Look again at question 1 of this test on page 20 and then choose which one of the four options below fits into each of the twenty gaps there. You may wish to change some of the answers you gave in the test after you have done this. However, if an answer that you gave in the test is not among the choices here, this does not necessarily mean that it is wrong.

1 **A** soon   **B** long   **C** early   **D** well

2 **A** took   **B** replaced   **C** stole   **D** robbed

3 **A** about   **B** under   **C** for   **D** above

4 **A** drawn   **B** grabbed   **C** fetched   **D** run

5 **A** and   **B** but   **C** also   **D** afterwards

6 **A** to   **B** for   **C** as   **D** of

7 **A** up   **B** on   **C** for   **D** at

8 **A** then   **B** it   **C** at   **D** there

9 **A** For   **B** As   **C** Along   **D** To

10 **A** should   **B** would   **C** could   **D** did

11 **A** or   **B** and   **C** otherwise   **D** thus

12 **A** Like   **B** Just   **C** Also   **D** So

13 **A** were   **B** did   **C** could   **D** had

14 **A** Among   **B** Along   **C** According   **D** Aside

15 **A** for   **B** into   **C** with   **D** on

16 **A** most   **B** well   **C** so   **D** such

17 **A** responsible   **B** originator   **C** manufacturing   **D** successful

18 **A** caused   **B** let   **C** made   **D** produced

19 **A** been   **B** limited   **C** gone   **D** afforded

20 **A** as   **B** like   **C** with   **D** apart

Now check your answers to these questions and to question 1 of the test on page 20. Then go on to page 24.

COMPLETE THE SENTENCES

Look again at question 2 of this test on page 20 and then decide which one of the four options below for each question there is correct. You may wish to change some of the answers you gave in the test as you do so. However, if an answer that you gave in the test is not among the choices here, this does not necessarily mean that it is wrong.

a 1   is currently being installed at our head office.
   2   is installed currently at our head office.
   3   is at our head office installed currently.
   4   is currently at our head office being installed.

b 1   until some time later then I realized the full implications of what had happened.
   2   that I realized the full implications of what had happened until some time later.
   3   my realization of the full implications of what had happened until some time later.
   4   until some time later that I realized the full implications of what had happened.

c 1   limitation on the number of people we can invite.
   2   limited number of people we can invite.
   3   a limit to the number of people we can invite.
   4   a limit for how many people we can invite.

d 1   anybody could have done had prevented the problem from arising.
   2   nobody did would have prevented the problem from arising.
   3   anybody could have done would have prevented the problem from arising.
   4   would have prevented the problem from arising anybody could do.

e 1   high intelligence doesn't mean that you have common sense.
   2   highly intelligent is nothing to do with common sense.
   3   high intelligence doesn't mean to have common sense.
   4   high intelligence doesn't mean common sense.

f 1   the way to phoning her when she finally arrived.
   2   the point of phoning her when she finally arrived.
   3   the verge to phone her when she finally arrived.
   4   the moment to phone her when she finally arrived.

g 1   the responsible for re-organizing the department.
   2   the one for re-organizing the department.
   3   into re-organizing the department.
   4   responsible for re-organizing the department.

h 1   herself how to play the piece by listening to a recording of it.
   2   from a recording of the piece how to play it.
   3   to play the piece from listening to a recording of it.
   4   herself to play the piece with listening to a recording of it.

Now check your answers to these questions and to question 2 of the test on page 20.
Then check your answers to questions 3 and 4 of the test on pages 21 and 22.

SECTION B

Read the following passage, then answer the questions which follow it.

Colour Blindness

When I took my art exam many years ago, for one paper we sat in a circle and painted a group of objects set before us in the centre. Among them was a lovely sponge cake, cut to reveal its colour and texture. As I struggled to capture it, mixing and applying paint, the invigilator came several times to watch me. Afterwards, he took me to one side. 'Why did you paint the cake green?' he
5 asked. I groaned, realizing that once again I had been handicapped by what I was beginning to call 'my colour blindness'.

A couple of years later, the Army agreed that I had a problem and reacted by banning me from just about every trade except that of clerk. Two years after that, working in the sales office of a steelworks, I consistently made a hash of a multi-colour graph of production which I had to keep
10 up to date. The management were not pleased when the lines changed colour from one week to the next.

Defective colour vision – a more accurate description than 'colour blindness' – is hereditary and caused by faults in the retina at the back of the eye. About 8 per cent of men and 0.4 per cent of women have it. It takes several forms and varies from slight to severe, but it almost always
15 operates in the red to green part of the spectrum. This means, simply, problems distinguishing between colours within that range. It is not just a matter of misnaming colours. People always ask me 'What do you call green if you can't see it?' Or they hold up a green tie and say 'What colour is this then?' These are, to me, meaningless questions at which I can only shrug and stammer helplessly.
20 Think of it more as a matter of colour matching. Give me lots of bits of red and green cloth of different shades and ask me to find one which matches a particular green tie and I will always fail. Most of them will look exactly the same to me and I will stare and pick helplessly at them. Left to myself I am likely to appear in all sorts of bizarre shirt–tie–jacket combinations.

Disability, of course, it is not. Irritant, though, it most certainly is – and there are, of course,
25 many jobs from which the colour-defective applicant is automatically barred. Think, for example, of how a good lawyer might treat the testimony of a colour-defective policeman. 'What colour did you say his jacket was, officer? The same as this one I am holding up, was it? Or this one over here?' And how would you feel about taking a ferry at night with a captain who was unable to tell the difference between the port and starboard lights of an oncoming ship?
30 Now consider the colour-defective young child in the classroom, doing colour matching and naming activities. One teacher has described giving a class coloured cards and sending them off to find things in the environment that matched. Were I asked to do that today, I would joke and con my way through. At six, however, I would have been bewildered.

Then, of course, there are colour-coded reading schemes and coloured maps. Any multi-
35 coloured map will contain several shades which, to the colour-defective child, are indistinguishable from each other and the fact that he *knows* they must, in fact, be different only adds to his annoyance.

The point is not that the child can be cured or that the whole classroom regime should be changed. All I want, from the strength of 55 years of living with the problem, is to speak up for all
40 pupils and students with defective colour vision and ask simply that their teachers be aware of the problem. Any class of 30, after all, is likely to have a boy with poor colour vision in it. Any school of 300 could have 10 boys and a girl. It might help some of these children, too, if their teacher could talk to them and help them understand that their frustration has a genuine cause.

a Why did the writer groan when the invigilator asked him about his painting?

....

....

b What was the writer's problem with the graph at the steelworks?

....

....

c   Why does the writer put 'colour blindness' in inverted commas in the article?

....

....

d   What misunderstanding do people have about colour-defective vision?

....

....

e   Explain in your own words how the writer reacts to questions people ask him about colours.

....

....

f   Explain the phrase 'I will stare and pick helplessly at them'. (line 22)

....

....

g   What is meant by the phrase 'left to myself'? (line 22–23)

....

....

h   Explain in your own words why a colour-defective policeman might have problems.

....

....

i   Explain in your own words why it is undesirable for a colour-defective person to be a ferry captain.

....

j   What does the writer say that he has in common with a colour-defective young child?

....

....

k   In what ways does the writer differ from a colour-defective young child?

....

....

l   What particularly annoys colour-defective children at school?

....

....

m What does the writer imply about the number of children likely to have colour-defective vision?

....

....

n What does the writer suggest to teachers about pupils and students with colour-defective vision?

....

....

o In a paragraph of 70–90 words, summarize the problems caused by colour-defective vision that the writer describes.

....

....

....

....

....

....

....

....

....

....

....

Before you check your answers to this section of the test, go on to pages 28 and 29.

ANSWERING THE QUESTIONS – GENERAL NOTES

When answering the questions in this part of the paper it is important to remember the following:

– You often do not have to write complete sentences. Sometimes it may be necessary to do so, especially when a longer answer is required, but many of the questions can be answered with a phrase, and perhaps a short phrase. If you write more than is required, you may make unnecessary mistakes.

– There is often more than one element to answers, with a mark given for each element. Make sure that you have given a full answer and not left out anything relevant.

A DETAILED STUDY

Many of the questions in this part of the paper test detailed comprehension of parts of the text. To answer them well, it is a good idea to follow this procedure:

– locate the relevant part of the text

– decide **exactly** what is stated there

– decide whether there is **more than one aspect** to the answer; this may not be the case but make sure that you have not failed to include something that is part of the answer

– work out how to phrase your answer. It may be necessary to write a full sentence and the answer may be fairly complicated. However, it may be possible to answer with a fairly simple phrase or sentence. Do not feel that you have to be elaborate. You may spoil an answer that might otherwise be correct by trying to write something unnecessarily complicated.

Look at question a

1   You might groan because you are
   a   surprised
   b   unhappy
   c   pleased
   d   impressed

2   What was the writer aware of at this time in his life?

Look at question b

What did the graph consist of?

Look at question d

1   Does the writer give the correct name for every colour?

2   Is the writer unable to identify every colour correctly?

Look at question i

What might a ferry captain have to decide about an oncoming ship?

Look at questions j and k

If you are 'bewildered', you are
   a   angry
   b   puzzled
   c   unaware
   d   frightened

Look at question l

Why has the writer put the word *knows* (line 36) in italics?

Now check your answers to these questions and decide whether you wish to change any of the answers you gave in the test. If you have phrased anything you wrote in the test differently from the choices given on these pages, this does not necessarily mean that you answered incorrectly in the test.

Then check your answers to questions a–n of Section B of the test on pages 25–27.

WRITING A SUMMARY – GENERAL NOTES

When you are writing your summary, it is important to remember the following:

– You must keep to the limit on the number of words specified in the paper.

– You are not writing a composition, and, since you are restricted to a relatively small number of words, it is advisable to keep the language that you use fairly simple and the sentences relatively brief. If you write long, elaborate sentences, you will not be able to cover all the relevant points in the required number of words and you may make unnecessary mistakes trying to do something you are not required to do.

– This part of the paper requires you to briefly summarize **all the relevant points** in the passage relating to the aspect of it you are asked about. It may relate only to specific paragraphs or a specific section, it may relate to various different parts, or it may relate to the passage as a whole. You are required to include all the relevant points and so it is important to make sure that you do not leave out anything that is relevant.

For the summary in this test, decide which of the following are relevant and therefore must be included. Tick the box next to each point that should be included.

1 being unable to paint food properly

2 being inefficient at certain jobs

3 being restricted to one job in the Army

4 being incompetent in a steelworks

5 having a problem that affects men more than women

6 being asked impossible questions by other people

7 being unable to dress appropriately

8 knowing that you cannot call it a disability

9 being unable to get certain jobs

10 being inefficient as a policeman

11 being incompetent as a ferry captain

12 being unable to take part in certain classroom activities

13 being frustrated as a child

14 knowing as a child that you have a problem

15 receiving no understanding or help from teachers

16 being in a minority at school

Now look again at your summary and decide whether you wish to change anything. Then check your answers to this exercise and to the summary on page 27.

PAPER 4 LISTENING COMPREHENSION about 30 mins

PART ONE

You will hear a local radio station's morning traffic and weather reports.
For questions 1–10, fill in the information given in the reports.

You will hear the piece twice.

Traffic		Weather

Road	Reason for problem
M3	*accident*
A40	*broken-down coach*
	1 ....
M1	2 ....
M4	3 ....
A107	4 ....
A374	5 ....

Weather

At the moment it is a very **6** ....

morning.

Later in the morning there will be a fair

amount of **7** ....

In the afternoon it will become **8** ....

and **9** ....

everywhere.

It is usually **10** ....

at this time of year.

PART TWO

You will hear a discussion about violence in films and on television.
For questions 11–18, write YES in the boxes next to those views which are expressed in the discussion and NO in the boxes next to those views which are not expressed.

You will hear the piece twice.

11 Films depicting violence tend to be of lower quality than other types. ☐

12 Stories in the past pretended that life was better than it really was. ☐

13 America used to be a more dangerous place than it is now. ☐

14 Violence should be regarded in the same way as diseases of the past. ☐

15 Boredom is one of the causes of violent crime. ☐

16 Film-makers make excuses for the amount of violence in their films. ☐

17 Reports of real violence contribute to making people violent. ☐

18 Most people have decent moral principles. ☐

PART THREE

You will hear an interview with someone who collects certain objects. For questions 19–23, choose the most appropriate answer, A, B, C, or D and write your choice in the box provided below each question.
You will hear the piece twice.

19 What is Robert's main reason for collecting what he collects?

    A regret about the passing of time
    B interest in social history
    C fascination for advertising
    D interest in people's shopping habits

Answer:

20 He doesn't buy a product for his collection if

    A it is very expensive.
    B he dislikes the design of it.
    C he doesn't wish to consume it.
    D its design hasn't changed.

Answer:

21 What made him start this collection?

    A Other children he knew had collections.
    B His mother encouraged him to do so.
    C He was unable to find enough stones to collect.
    D It was something he could collect forever.

Answer:

22 What is his attitude towards his collection?

    A He admits it is a rather ridiculous thing to do.
    B He feels it is his duty to continue with it.
    C He accepts that others have more important pursuits.
    D He believes it is different from other dedications.

Answer:

23 What does he think is the main problem of his collection?

    A It is impossible ever to complete it.
    B It takes up too much of his time.
    C Other people do not take it seriously.
    D He would like to give it up but cannot.

Answer:

PART FOUR

You will hear a professional photographer talking about his work. For questions 24–33, complete the notes.
You will hear the piece twice.

THE PHOTOGRAPHER
Exact nature of job:
24 ....
Department that contacts him:
25 ....
Main focus when working:
26 ....
First photography work: 27 ....
Does his own: 28 ....

THE PROFESSION
Qualifications required:
29 ....
Subject of courses available:
30 ....
Useful reference books: 31 ....
32 ....
Personality requirement:
33 ....

Before you check your answers to Part 4 of the test, go on to page 32.

FACTS AND INFORMATION

Some of the pieces in the listening test require you to understand and identify certain facts or pieces of information. You may be required to put missing information or details into notes, tables, or incomplete sentences or phrases. Your answer may be **one word** or a **short phrase**.

Listen again to Part 4 of the test on page 31 and answer these questions. This will give you further practice in answering this type of question and enable you to check the answers that you gave in the test.

1   Is he permanently employed by anybody?...

2   What kind of pictures does he take?...

3   Which newspaper does he work for regularly? ....

4   Which department of it does he work for? ....

5   Who runs that department? ....

6   What **doesn't** he have to think about when he's working? ....

7   What did he learn at school? ....

8   Where did he first work after school?..

9   What kind of photographs did he take there? ....

10 Who did he work for after that?..

11 Who found him employment after that?..

12 What does he always do himself at the office? ....

13 What can he have done for him at the office? ....

14 What did he get at school?..

15 What does the college in Manchester offer?...

16 Where can you get the addresses of papers?

   A ....   B ....

17 Which body gives advice?...

18 What is required to be a successful photographer, apart from personal qualities?

   A ....   B ....   C ....

Now check your answers to the questions on these pages. When you have done so, decide whether you wish to change any of the answers you gave in Part 4 of the test on page 31.

Then check your answers to Part 4 of the test and then to Parts 1, 2, and 3 on pages 30–31.

PAPER 5 INTERVIEW

1 *Look at one or more of these photographs and answer the questions that follow them.*

What's happening in each picture?
Describe the people. What kind of people are they?
Describe the places where they are.
What do you think is the purpose of each photograph?
How is each photograph trying to achieve these purposes?

How many kinds of advertising are there?
Do you think that advertising on television is more effective than in magazines or newspapers?
What kind of ideas do advertisers try to communicate?
Are there any restrictions on advertisers in your country?

2 *Read one or more of these passages and then answer the questions that follow them.*

a How long does a car stay new? For the creators of the *Infiniti J30*, it isn't simply a question of time, but rather a matter of style, engineering and, dare we say, emotion. It's definitely not a car that years from now you'll say 'What was I thinking about.' The *J30* echoes the good design thinking of the past. At the same time, it gives us a glimpse of what will be. In terms of luxury, performance, even responsibility.

b Don't, whatever you do, tell your kids that a peanut butter sandwich contains higher levels of protein than milk, beef, chicken, turkey or white fish. Never mention to them that it's a rich source of Vitamin E or that it contains calcium, which is good for teeth and bones. Never pass comment on the other twelve essential vitamins and minerals you'll find in peanut butter. Never let on that it has more fibre than cabbage, potatoes or carrots. If you do, knowing what kids are like today, they'll go and eat something which isn't as good for them.

c The Northern Islands of Scotland have an elemental quality; soaring skies and vivid luminous light, beloved of photographers and painters. The stone from which much of the land mass is forged is among the oldest in the world. Time has little meaning in this part of the world; people's lives are geared to nature and the seasons and the effect of this is to ease away the cares of the modern world. Life in the islands may move slowly, but there's an extraordinary variety of things to see.

What ideas is each advertisement trying to communicate?
How does it communicate these ideas?

3 *Do one or more of these tasks. If you are working with others, discuss them together.*

a Imagine that you are going to do a television or newspaper advert for one of the following. What kind of advert would you produce and why?

- a washing powder
- a shampoo
- a family car
- a make of jeans
- a watch
- a breakfast cereal
- a hi-fi system

b You know how it is. You're just settling in nicely to the big movie on TV when all of a sudden the hero freezes in mid-action. Oh no, it's the adverts again. Quick, where's the remote control? Flip channels for something – anything to watch instead.

Do you like the commercials on TV or do they irritate you?
What are the TV commercials like in your country?
Describe a TV commercial that you think is particularly effective/poor. Why is it effective/poor?

c 'We are all influenced by advertising.'
In what ways does advertising influence people?
Describe an advert that you particularly like/don't like. Give reasons.
What products have you bought/not bought because of the way they are advertised?

TALKING ABOUT YOURSELF

The interview may begin with the examiner asking you questions about yourself. This is mainly intended to begin the interview in a relaxed and friendly way, but it will help to create a favourable overall impression if you can answer such questions naturally, fluently, and without excessive hesitation.

However:

– the examiner is not expecting to hear your entire life story!
  Keep your answers reasonably brief and keep to the point.

– **do not** prepare a fixed speech, learn it by heart and repeat it! The examiner will detect this immediately, especially because it will not sound natural, and you cannot be sure exactly what questions you will be asked.

With a partner, ask and answer questions about the following:

– where you are currently living (your home)
– where you are currently living (the town/city/village/region)
– where you come from (if different)
– what your current occupation is
– what your current occupation involves
– what you did before that (if applicable)
– why you are taking the exam (no particular reason needed)
– what your aims for the future are

TALKING ABOUT PICTURES

When you are describing a picture, it is essential to know what the various parts of a picture are called.

Look at this list of phrases describing the various parts of a picture. Then look again at each of the three photographs on page 33 and complete the sentences about them using appropriate phrases from the list.

in the foreground
in the background
on/to the right; on the right-hand side
on/to the left; on the left-hand side
at the top
at the bottom
in the middle
in the top right-hand corner

in the top left-hand corner
in the bottom right-hand corner
in the bottom left-hand corner
in front of someone/something
behind someone/something
next to/beside someone/something
between someone/something and ...

Picture one

1 .... of the picture, there is a woman leaning on a computer

  screen, which is .... of the picture.

2 .... of the picture, there is a sign partly covered by some files.

3 ...., there is a noticeboard and another desk, which are

  .... the woman.

4 Scissors, a stapler and a telephone are .... of the picture.

5 There is a container with pens and pencils in it _____ of the picture.

6 _____ of the picture, _____, there is a white flowerpot with a plant in it.

7 There is a mug _____ the telephone and the keyboard.

8 The desk is _____ the woman.

Picture two

1 A man and a woman are _____ of the picture.

2 There is a fireplace in the wall _____ the two people.

3 _____ of the picture, there are some shelves and some plants.

4 _____ of the picture, _____, there is a hat hanging on the wall.

5 _____, there is a table with breakfast things and newspapers on it.

6 _____, there is a shelf with some books and a toy animal on it.

7 There is a letter _____ a white jug and a jar.

8 _____ of the picture, _____, there is a plant in a white pot.

Picture three

1 There is a woman holding a pizza _____ of the picture.

2 _____, there is a table with food, glasses and plates on it.

3 The children are sitting _____ each other.

4 The children have plates _____ them.

5 The boy is sitting _____ the two girls.

6 There is a plate of fruit _____ of the picture.

7 _____ of the picture, there is part of a noticeboard with postcards on it.

8 _____ there is a building/tower leaning to one side.

Now check your answers to these questions.

TEST TWO

PAPER 1   READING COMPREHENSION   1 hour

SECTION A

In this section you must choose the word or phrase which best completes each sentence. Indicate the letter A, B, C, or D against the number of each item 1 to 25 for the word or phrase you choose.

1 The film is .... based on a true story, but most of it is fiction.

   A loosely   B casually   C faintly   D lightly

2 Unfortunately, the clerk .... to tell me that the ticket I bought was not valid before 9 am.

   A ignored   B disregarded   C omitted   D missed

3 It was with .... regret that we left the village in which we had lived happily for so many years.

   A deep   B full   C keen   D passionate

4 Joan has always had a tendency to .... the importance of minor problems.

   A overrate   B exaggerate   C multiply   D heighten

5 They started the business in .... of making a lot of money quickly, but things didn't work out that way.

   A expectation   B belief   C certainty   D likelihood

6 Police have not revealed the .... details of the case.

   A full   B total   C whole   D sheer

7 She set .... to write a short novel, but it got longer and longer as she wrote it.

   A up   B in   C out   D about

8 In .... of value for money, this is the best car I've ever bought.

   A sense   B light   C terms   D regards

9 The cast .... several times and then left the stage to wild applause.

   A bowed   B ducked   C crouched   D stooped

10 Competition winners will be selected at .... from a bag containing all correct entries.

   A muddle   B random   C fluke   D disarray

11 The pilot spoke to the passengers to .... their fears when the plane entered a storm.

   A allay   B deter   C soothe   D placate

12 Then he started out on what .... to be a very eventful journey.

   A proved   B arose   C turned   D developed

13 I think you're being .... pessimistic and that you'll do better than you expect.

    A additionally   B abundantly   C unduly   D worthlessly

14 Losses have forced the company to .... 1000 of its workers.

    A lay off   B take away   C set apart   D lose out

15 She .... being treated as an inferior at work.

    A exasperates   B resents   C enrages   D embitters

16 She seemed to be .... to losing and didn't make much effort.

    A acceptable   B resigned   C compromised   D content

17 I don't know why you have to make such a .... about such a trivial matter.

    A fuss   B sensation   C trouble   D stir

18 I'd like to start my own business, but I'm not sure how to .... about it.

    A come   B bring   C go   D see

19 She often appears not to care about her work, but appearances can be ....

    A cunning   B deceitful   C deceptive   D insincere

20 In .... to them, it wasn't their fault that the party went so badly.

    A fairness   B justice   C recognition   D sympathy

21 Brian isn't keen on exercise, but he isn't .... to the occasional walk.

    A averse   B unwilling   C reluctant   D contrary

22 It is difficult to decide on the best .... of action in these circumstances.

    A measure   B course   C process   D policy

23 He has been with the company for 30 years, but the management has now decided to .... with his services.

    A discard   B dispense   C disuse   D dismiss

24 Ruth is .... to give up immediately when faced with any problem.

    A habitual   B subject   C susceptible   D apt

25 The government is making every effort to .... an economic crisis.

    A hinder   B avert   C impede   D swerve

Before you check your answers to this section of the test, go on to page 39.

WORK IT OUT

*Some of the questions in this section require you to decide which of the words fits **in the** **context**. The words may all mean the same, but only one can be used in the context of the sentence. The numbers below refer to questions 1–3 of the test, on page 37, which are questions of this type. Read each of the sentences, which show contexts in which the options are used. They may help you to answer the questions they refer to.*

1 **a** I can tell you something which is loosely connected with what you're talking about.
   b He mentioned the possibility casually so I don't know how certain he was.
   c I can faintly remember the incident, but I can't recall any details.
   d She touched him lightly on the sleeve.

2 **a** You can ignore the parts of the form that don't apply to you.
   b I decided to disregard everything that didn't apply to me.
   c She omitted to enclose the documents I required.
   d She missed out some of the details so as not to upset him.

3 **a** He expressed his deepest sympathy for her at such a difficult time.
   b The project was undertaken with the full agreement of everyone concerned.
   c She has always taken a keen interest in current affairs.
   d He has a passionate commitment to caring for the poor.

THE PROCESS OF ELIMINATION

*Sometimes you need to decide which options **do not fit** in order to answer questions in this section. The numbers of the exercises below refer to questions 4–6 of the test.*

In each of the exercises, choose which of the four options given in the test best fits each gap. This may help you to eliminate some of the incorrect options in the questions they refer to, and to check or learn the differences between the options, in terms of meaning, usage and structures.

4 | overrated   exaggerated   multiplied   heightened |

   a Tension is .... throughout the film.

   b Reports of the situation have been .... in the press.

   c Everybody says he's a great actor, but I think he's ....

   d Theme parks have .... in recent years and there are now lots of them.

5 | expectation   belief   certainty   likelihood |

   a What is the .... of you being able to give me an answer this week?

   b Nobody can say with absolute .... what the outcome will be.

   c In .... of a fall in their value, he sold his shares.

   d She signed the contract in the .... that she was making the right decision.

6 | full   total   whole   sheer |

   a He later made a .... confession to the police.

   b The company's failure has been attributed to .... bad management.

   c She did the .... job in record time.

   d I am in .... disagreement with this proposal.

Now check your answers to these exercises. When you have done so, decide if you wish to change any of your answers to questions 1–6 in Section A. Then check your answers.

SECTION B

*In this section you will find after each of the passages a number of questions or unfinished statements about the passage, each with four suggested answers or ways of finishing. You must choose the one which you think fits best. Indicate the letter A, B, C, or D against the number of each item 26–40 for the answer you choose. Give **one answer only** to each question. Read each passage right through before choosing your answers.*

FIRST PASSAGE

Like almost everyone else who has ever had to move a great deal from place to place, I like to consider myself an authority on hotels. I am prepared to admit to being a hotel snob in a perverse way; I consider that after some five and a half circuits of the globe I am familiar with more wretched and abominable hotels than any other contender. I have debated this claim with many
5 travellers equally well versed in the global science of bad hotels, and I have usually been able to secure the decision on the recollection of some little-known but incontestably terrible place.

Darjeeling in mid-winter cold was a place of solitude and desolation. The hotel was probably, at that moment, the emptiest in all the world. It was a barren vacancy, an echoing cavernous place from which almost all sign of life had been removed. It had been built to accommodate hundreds
10 of guests; now there were only six. And had no sudden whim struck the controllers of our magazine some days before, there would have been nobody at all.

I bear no grudge against this place; I have known many hotels slightly worse. By the standards of some places, it was not unreasonable. It was merely abandoned; a vast lounge resounding bleakly to every footstep, vast lengths of freezing corridors, a deserted bar and an untended chill
15 pervading everything. It had the curious characteristic of being many degrees colder inside than the wintry open air. After a while we acquired the trick of leaving our thick coats in the hallway, to put on as we went in, plunging for meals in that deadly interior.

But the first morning there, at dawn I opened my eyes directly on the window and the shock of that tremendous view nearly bounced me out of bed. It was sensational; a soaring extravagant
20 horizon of enormous peaks, with the highest mountain in the world invisible only because the second-highest mountain in the world was in the way. It is customary to disparage the better known and generally praised aspects of famous beauty, to profess a sense of disappointment when confronted at last by the Taj Mahal or the Victoria Falls. Indeed, it may be that too much renown spoils the final experience. But on this day, this first Himalayan dawn, the impact of that
25 view so far surpassed anything I had foreseen that I stood trembling with cold at the window, staring at that fading achievement of rock and snow, as swiftly the clouds assembled and engulfed it before my eyes.

26 In what way does the writer consider himself different from other travellers?

  A He has travelled more extensively.
  B He has stayed in more bad hotels.
  C He is more particular about hotels.
  D He remembers more about his trips.

27 The writer was staying at the hotel in Darjeeling because

  A he wanted to be alone.
  B it was the biggest hotel there.
  C he had been sent there.
  D it had been recommended to him.

28 What did the writer think of the hotel?

  A He was depressed by the atmosphere there.
  B He was amazed by the size of the place.
  C He was disgusted by the temperature inside the place.
  D He was annoyed by the lack of service there.

29 What does the writer say about places famous for their beauty?

  A They are often less beautiful than they are said to be.
  B People often find something new to appreciate about them.
  C People often say they are less impressive than they are supposed to be.
  D They are often spoiled by the number of people visiting them.

30 When the writer woke on the first morning,

  A he was disappointed that he couldn't see the world's highest mountain.
  B he was too cold to appreciate the view of the mountains.
  C he was annoyed that the view of the mountains was obscured.
  D he was unprepared for the view he saw outside his window.

SECOND PASSAGE

Here is a confession: sometimes I have to succumb to the urge to slam doors. It's childish, I know, but it is exactly what I need when I don't want to be grown-up and talk about it.

Whether you're aged four or forty, being childish is usually considered to be a 'bad thing'. Toddlers, teenagers and people in their thirties are all liable to be told to 'act your age', 'grow up'
5 or 'stop being such a baby'. To say that someone is childish is to imply they are selfish, silly, insensitive, immature or embarrassing. But most of the things that we do as adults contain elements of childishness. If it's so childish to care about winning or losing a game, for example, why are the sports pages of every newspaper given over to describing just that?

We live in a culture which prizes self-restraint: childishness is equated with being ruled by
10 moods and emotions. But what we are critical of is often nothing more sinister or harmful than exuberance and unselfconscious self-expression. While there is a place for self-restraint, too much of it can be bad for you.

Many people say they feel guilty about being childish. 'It's a bit naughty, isn't it?' says one friend. 'I mean, we're supposed to be grown-up.' The fear of letting go prevents many of us from
15 indulging in the luxury of being childish. But satisfying our non-adult whims is not only about slamming doors, it is about having fun, letting off steam and letting go of some of the tension which has accumulated after days, weeks or years of sensible, mature, rational and responsible behaviour.

Being childish is about doing all the things you are no longer supposed to do now that you are
20 grown-up. But there is no need to consign childishness to the past. A writer friend of mine in his thirties has an array of children's toys beside his computer; a plastic helicopter, a car and a green and yellow frog. When work is going badly, he picks up the helicopter, flies it round the desk and practises crash landings. 'It stops me worrying about my work and gets my brain working again,' he says.
25 Playing is a state of mind and it's good for you. Research into ageing suggests that there is truth in the adage, 'You're only as old as you feel'. The people who enjoy old age most are those who allowed themselves time off from the responsibilities of adulthood when they were younger. It seems that people who know how to enjoy themselves in their 30s and 40s are better equipped to deal with the challenges of life at 70 and 80.
30 Whether you call it being childish or having fun, it need not be the preserve of the old or the young. Everyone needs it. After a day spent chasing clients, attending meetings, coping with office politics, buying groceries, collecting clothes from the dry cleaners, paying bills and juggling debts, most of us crave a breather from 'grown-upness'. We all need to have a place and a time where it's safe to drop the responsible, capable self for a moment and be looked after, irresponsible and
35 carefree. So next time you feel life getting on top of you, stamp your foot, giggle, pull some silly faces or slam a door.

31 What is the writer's reference to the sports pages of newspapers intended to illustrate?

   A how childish it is to be competitive in games
   B the difference between adult and childish interests
   C the fact that we are all childish to an extent
   D how important it is to be childish sometimes

32 According to the writer, how does the culture she lives in affect people's behaviour?

   A It inhibits people's behaviour.
   B It makes people behave selfishly.
   C It makes people unpleasant to each other.
   D It increases the desire to be childish.

33 What does the example of the friend who is a writer illustrate?

   A how guilty people feel about being childish
   B how much fun it is to be childish
   C how strangely some adults behave
   D how useful being childish can be

34 Research into the elderly has shown that

   A people who had few responsibilities when younger are happier in old age.
   B people feel free to behave more childishly when they reach old age.
   C people who are free of all responsibilities when older are happier.
   D people who behave childishly when younger are likely to be happy when old.

35 The writer's intention in the article is to

   A defend her own childishness.
   B regret the pressures of adulthood.
   C encourage childish behaviour.
   D criticize her own culture.

THIRD PASSAGE

The video wave has swept too far. It bears a large responsibility for the declining interest in reading among the young. If we don't do something to stem the tide, the reading impulse will soon be drowned.

5 The time-honoured way of improving reading is by reading fiction. Everyone, psychologists tell us, needs stories. Cavemen told them round their fires. Mythologies and folk stories have been passed between generations for centuries. Most of us are literate and in theory our fictional needs could be satisfied by reading.

But it's not so. Today's generation of average and below average school children rely on video, television and film. While many of these offerings may be harmless in themselves, they do nothing 10 to build up reading skills. They are replacing the consolidatory work which turns halting mechanical reading into the real thing. If some of the hours children spend watching television were devoted to reading, the population would be better educated.

Watching a story is a totally passive pastime. Someone else has made all the decisions about casting, set, clothing, facial expressions, tone and so on. Reading a story is an active partnership 15 between writer and reader. Ideas are sketched and the mind of the reader creates the rest.

Why is dramatized fiction usurping the written kind? It is because children whose reading is hesitant cannot readily identify and enjoy the plot. Watching something is easier. This is leading to a generation whose mental processes are too stultified. The problem is that many children read very slowly. I worry, for instance, about children who carry the same 100-word book about with them for 20 a fortnight. I meet them daily. They conscientiously decode a page or two in a class and about the same again for homework. It is hardly surprising that such children then declare that they find reading boring and prefer to watch television. Their difficulty is not reading the words – it is interpreting them. They need to be able to read fast enough to feed the mind's hunger for a story.

That means practice. Only by reading daily will a child become a strong and independent reader. 25 Parents need to be convinced of the importance of preventing their children from wasting their hours on inert viewing. Without the television the child is likely to turn to books for entertainment.

I used to think that filmed versions of enjoyable books were a spur to reading. I have changed my mind. Visual images drown the imagination. A dramatization, seen once, can spoil your reading for ever. Dramatized fiction is the literary equivalent of empty calories. It replaces the appetite for 30 real food. Children must have a nutritionally balanced reading diet.

36 What is the writer's main objection to the 'video wave'?

A It prevents children from learning how to read properly.
B It fails to provide children with enough good stories.
C It has replaced the reading of traditional stories.
D It exposes children to stories that they shouldn't see.

37 According to the writer, dramatized fiction is different from written fiction because

A it consists mainly of simpler stories.
B it concentrates more on action than on character.
C it does not contain as much detail.
D it does not require use of the imagination.

38 What tends to put children off reading fiction, in the writer's opinion?

A There are frequently words in it that they can't read.
B They lose interest because of their reading deficiencies.

C They are often required to do it for homework.
D The stories they are given take too long to develop.

39 What has the writer changed her opinion about?

A the importance for children of reading
B the influence of parents on children's reading
C the effect of filmed stories on children
D the power of children's imaginations

40 What is the purpose of the article?

A to analyse the differences between dramatized fiction and written fiction
B to criticize parents for failing to encourage their children to read
C to urge greater concentration on developing children's reading skills
D to encourage children to do more reading than watching television

Before you check your answers to this section of the test, go on to pages 43 and 44.

A DETAILED STUDY

The questions on these pages will help you to make sure that you have chosen the correct options for the questions on the first text, on page 40.

Question 26 *Look at the first paragraph of the text and answer these questions.*

1   How much travelling does the writer say he has done?

2   What does the writer mean by a 'hotel snob'?
   a   a person who hates hotels
   b   a person who has stayed in a lot of hotels
   c   a person who likes to stay in good hotels

3   What does the writer mean by 'perverse'?
   a   quiet
   b   opposite
   c   exaggerated

4   What does the writer particularly remember about his trips?

5   On what subject does the writer defeat other travellers in discussions? .

Question 27 *Look at the second paragraph and answer these questions.*

1   Which of these words is closest in meaning to 'solitude and desolation'?
   a   tranquility
   b   relaxation
   c   loneliness

2   Which adjective suggests that the hotel was big?

3   What is 'a whim'?
   a   a desire to please
   b   an impulsive idea
   c   a generous feeling
   d   a strong recommendation

Question 28 *Look at the third paragraph and answer these questions.*

1   If you 'bear no grudge', you have no
   a   interest
   b   anger
   c   opinion

2   Which adjective describes the size of the hotel?

3   If something is 'bleak', it is
   a   miserable
   b   annoying
   c   strange

4   Does the writer describe the hotel staff?

5   Why did they leave their coats in the hallway?

Questions 29 and 30 *Look at the final paragraph and answer these questions.*

1   What shocked the writer when he woke up?

2   Was he able to see the world's highest mountain?

3 Could he see any mountains when he got

up?..

4 If you 'disparage' something, you
   a exaggerate it.
   b criticize it.
   c ignore it.
   d concentrate on it.

   ....

5 Does the writer refer to people who have
   actually seen places of great beauty?

   ....

6 What is 'renown'?
   a fame
   b knowledge
   c contact

   ....

7 Was what he saw better than what he had
   expected?

   ....

8 Was he cold when he got up?

   ....

*Now check your answers to the questions
on these pages. Then decide whether you
wish to change any of the answers that
you gave to the first text, on page 40.
Then check your answers to this section
of the test.*

PAPER 2 COMPOSITION 2 hours

*Write **two only** of the composition exercises. Your answers must follow exactly the instructions given. Write in pen, not pencil. You are allowed to make alterations, but make sure that your work is clear and easy to read.*

1 Describe some of the current fashions in your country. (About 350 words)

2 'Modern technology does as much harm as good.' Do you agree? (About 350 words)

3 Describe an event that changed your attitude to something. (About 350 words)

4 You have been appointed to run a school or college club. Write a notice containing a programme of events for this club and explaining what these events will involve. (About 300 words)

Before you write your compositions, go on to pages 46 and 47.

PLANNING A COMPOSITION

*One of the questions in Paper 2 requires you to **give your opinions** on a certain subject. You may be asked whether you agree with a statement or not. It is important to know that you don't have to agree or disagree completely; you may prefer to present contrasting points of view.*

Look at question 2 on page 45 and answer the following. This will help you to plan your composition for that question. It is advisable to plan each of the types of composition.

1   Choose which of the following examples of modern technology you wish to include. Add any others that you wish to mention.

☐ television/satellite TV

☐ computers

☐ communications: telephones, fax machines, etc

☐ video recorders and cameras

☐ kitchen equipment

☐ air and other transport

☐ theme parks, funfairs, etc

....

....

....

....

....

2   Tick the advantages that you think any of them have and add any other advantages that you think apply.

☐ make our lives easier

☐ make things happen more quickly

☐ make things possible that were previously impossible

☐ enable us to enjoy life more

☐ make things available to more people than before

☐ make us more independent

☐ give us more free time

....

....

....

....

....

3   Tick the disadvantages that you think any of them have and add any others of your own.

☐ make us lazy

☐ make us lose our individuality

☐ are bad for health

☐ make the pace of life too fast

☐ make us selfish

☐ decrease personal contact with others

☐ are bad for the environment

....

....

....

....

Now use these ideas to write your composition. Remember that you do not have to be completely in favour of or against the statement, although it is perfectly acceptable if you are.

Then write one or more of the other compositions.

Now read through the following sample composition for question 2 on page 45. When you have done so, answer the questions that follow it.

If we think of the last 100 years, mankind has made great strides concerning technology. Progresses that, on the one hand, can can make life much easier or much more comfortable but, on the other hand, they complicate our lifes as well. Some hundred years ago, nobody could have imagined that one day a human being would be able to talk to somebody who – at the same time – lives at the other side of the world (I guess they weren't even convinced that the world was realy round) or that people would be able to fly to the moon.

Technological progress is great. But there is a big problem; the ethical progress of mankind didn't proceed as fast as the technological one, e,g, weapons. It is incredible how much time and money was/is spent on inventing and creating weapons. Very intelligent human beings waste their time thinking about how people are able to destroy each other most effectively. Unfortunately humanity didn't proceed a lot concerning how to live with each other in peace. We couldn't get rid of wars and we are still struggeling and fighting like our ancestors. Only the equipment has changed. Instead of clubs we use machine guns.

Or let's take an other example that shows some pros of modern technology as well. Nowadays doctors are able to cure diseases because of which people used to die half a century ago. By the help of gene-technology they even manage to eradicate them. If your heart doesn't work properly anymore, surgeons implant you an other one or an artificial heart. Life expectancy has increased a lot and medical progress relieves our lifes (especially when we are ill).

But, as a matter of fact, there are cons too. Medical men are able to prolongue one's life by the help of machines. In a few words, there is the ethical problem of euthenasia. And what about the abuse of gene-technology? Maybe in 200 years people won't be born anymore. They will be created 'in test tubes and uncorked' instead of born, like Aldous Huxley imagined it in is novel 'Brave New World'.

To cut a long story short it seems to me quite obvious that modern technology does much more harm than good. It made us able to destroy our environment, to pollute the air we breath, etc. Human beings are just not able to deal with the technological progress.

1   Does the composition actually answer the question set or does it contain irrelevant parts, 'waffle' – writing that is simply intended to fill the space but does not really say anything – or 'padding' – writing that is repetitious in order to reach the required number of words?

2   Is the composition well-organized? Is it divided into paragraphs appropriately? Explain what each paragraph contains.

3   Are appropriate linking words and phrases used for connecting sentences and paragraphs. Give examples of some that are; if some are not, correct them.

4   Does it have a good range of appropriate vocabulary or is the vocabulary used mostly too simple? Give examples and correct any inappropriate or incorrect vocabulary.

5   Is there a good range of accurate structures forming sentences that are not very simple or are the structures used mostly too basic? Give examples and correct any incorrect structures or other mistakes.

6   Is the style appropriate for this type of composition?

Now check your assessment of and corrections to this sample composition.

PAPER 3   USE OF ENGLISH   2 hours

SECTION A

1   *Fill each of the numbered blanks in the passage with **one** suitable word.*

The name of the news agency Reuters appears daily in thousands of newspapers and upon thousands of screens (1) .... over the world. (2) .... success over almost a century and a half has provided an institutional (3) .... of the power of news and its founder, Julius Reuter, (4) .... his fortune by recognizing this power.

He began (5) .... using carrier pigeons (6) .... forward stock-market and commodity prices from Brussels to Achen in Germany. In 1851, he moved to London and it was (7) .... that he launched his telegraph agency. (8) .... the end of the 1850s he had found success by (9) .... a standard for news gathering and distribution. Reuter set (10) .... to be 'first with the news', and often was. But above (11) .... he placed accuracy, and alongside accuracy he set impartiality in news distribution.

For over a hundred years, Reuters was the news agency of the British Empire. In the mid-twentieth century the British Empire faded (12) .... and Reuters (13) .... have faded with it, but (14) .... it made a new start, transforming (15) .... into an international institution. This transformation has been linked to the revolution (16) .... communications technology (17) .... possible by (18) .... microchip and it (19) .... supplies computerized economic news and information (20) .... screen to business people working increasingly within a global economy.

2   *Finish each of the following sentences in such a way that it is as similar as possible in meaning to the sentence printed before it.*

Example: She said that he was a brilliant musician.
Answer: She described *him as a brilliant musician.*

a   She didn't seem very enthusiastic about the idea.

She showed

....

b   I enjoy playing golf much more than watching it.

I much ....

c   It was only because I owed him a favour that I agreed to help him.

But ....

d   The news was so wonderful that we decided to have a celebration.

It was..

e   I was greatly relieved to hear that her condition was not serious.

It was with ....

f   'Why can't you do your work more carefully?' Helen's boss said to her.

Helen's boss criticized ....

g   I'd quite like to be able to have as much time off work as he does.

I wouldn't ....

h   He has strongly opposed government policy for many years.

He has been a ....

3   *Fill each of the blanks with a suitable word or phrase.*
    Example: She had difficulty *making up her* mind which one to buy.

a   I thought I was going to be late but I got there just .... catch the start
    of the film.

b   Could you pick me up from the station to .... having to queue for a taxi?

c   In .... hardly any tickets were sold, the event was cancelled.

d   I often listen to music as .... relaxing after a hard day at work.

e   Whereabouts on this form am .... my signature?

f   The receptionist gave me all the information I asked for – in fact she ....
    more helpful.

4 *For each of the sentences below, write a new sentence* **as similar as possible in meaning to the original sentence**, *but using the word given. This word* **must not be altered** *in any way.*

Example: She paid no attention to his warning.
          notice
Answer: *She took no notice of his warning.*

a The course emphasizes practical skills.
emphasis

....

b The meeting was rearranged shortly before it had been due to take place.
notice

....

c She'll always be angry that he let her down.
forgive

....

d I agreed to do the work because I understood that I would be paid for it.
understanding

....

e She is in danger of losing her job because of her attitude.
risk

....

f I think you should be tolerant of other people's weaknesses.
allowances

....

g There is very little chance of them winning the game.
highly

....

h I'm not trying to make you feel any worse about this.
wish

....

Before you check your answers to this section of the test, go on to pages 51 and 52.

FILL IN THE PHRASE

Look again at question 3 of this test on page 49, and then decide which of the four choices below for each question there best expresses the meaning of the sentence or the missing part of the sentence. You may wish to change some of the answers you gave in the test after you have done this. However, if an answer you gave in the test is not among the choices here, this does not necessarily mean that it is wrong.

a 1   I got there at about the time when the film was starting.
   2   I got there slightly after the start of the film.
   3   I got there long before the film started.
   4   I got there much too late for the start of the film.

b 1   because I will have to queue for a long time
   2   or is it necessary for me to queue
   3   or I'll have to queue
   4   so that I don't have to queue

c 1   Because it was possible that few tickets would be sold
   2   Just after the tickets went on sale
   3   If not many tickets had been sold
   4   Because not many tickets were sold

d 1   Listening to music enables me to relax.
   2   I listen to music when I'm feeling relaxed.
   3   I listen to music immediately I come home.
   4   The music I listen to has to be of a relaxing kind.

e 1   can I sign
   2   is it possible for me to sign
   3   is the best place to sign
   4   should I sign

f 1   The receptionist tried but failed to help me.
   2   The receptionist was as helpful as possible.
   3   The receptionist was reasonably helpful to me.
   4   The receptionist wasn't as helpful as I expected.

Now check your answers to these questions and to question 3 of the test on page 49.
Then go on to page 52.

REWRITE THE SENTENCES

Look again at question 4 of this test on page 50, and then decide in which of the following ways your answer to each of the questions there could begin. Sometimes only one choice is possible and sometimes more than one choice is possible. You may wish to change some of the answers you gave in the test when you have made your choice or choices. If the answer that you gave there does not begin with any of the choices, this does not necessarily mean that it is wrong.

a 1 The course makes
   2 The course places
   3 The emphasis
   4 The course puts
   5 Emphasis of

b 1 Notice of the meeting
   2 The meeting was rearranged
   3 It was without
   4 The notice for the meeting
   5 Without notice

c 1 She'll ever
   2 She'll never
   3 She won't ever
   4 She'll always
   5 She won't never

d 1 If I had been understanding
   2 I agreed to do the work
   3 It was my understanding
   4 Understanding to be paid
   5 My understanding

e 1 She will risk
   2 Her job
   3 Her attitude can
   4 The risk
   5 Her attitude is

f 1 Your allowances
   2 I think you should make
   3 You should let
   4 Without allowances
   5 I think you should have

g 1 They win
   2 They are highly
   3 Highly
   4 It is highly
   5 Chance that

h 1 I wish you
   2 It is not my wish
   3 I don't wish
   4 I wish I
   5 My wish is

Now check your answers to these questions and to question 4 of the test on page 50. Then check your answers to questions 1 and 2 of the test on pages 48 and 49.

SECTION B

Read this passage, then answer the questions which follow it.

Honest opinions

An artist friend of mine recently presented me with an enormous portrait of myself completely out of the blue. It was a real shock which rendered me speechless for several minutes as I fought for the right thing to say. The portrait was horrendous. I was so concerned not to offend my friend by revealing my true emotions that I went way over the top with vacuous flattery: I simply loved
5 it, the best painting I'd ever seen, I would treasure it forever. I silently knew that I could never live with it.

But this monstrous caricature moved into the flat and was here to stay. As I sat and stared at it (at me!) it began seriously to disturb me. Was this how I really looked? Did the artist really see me like this? My flatmate said there was something positively evil about it, and thought the artist
10 must hate me with a vengeance, while others thought it was a joke.

When I saw the photograph from which the portrait had been taken, I could vaguely see a resemblance. But I had looked like that only for the millisecond during which the camera shutter had been open; the artist had captured me in that form forever. I knew she was not trying for a literal likeness (the camera had done that, sort of) but was seeking to portray the essence of my
15 personality, or some characteristic of my inner soul. When I looked at my portrait I expected to recognize some part of me, but all I saw was this vile lump.

The problem I faced was what to do when the artist came round to the flat. After declaring dishonestly how much I loved it, how would I be able to explain its absence from my walls? How would she attract new commissions (which she desperately needed) if it wasn't prominently
20 displayed? How could I say I was so attached to it that I'd had to put it in the attic for future generations to find? Or should I bring it out just before her visit? Supposing I forgot one time? I would have to live that lie forever. That fear destroyed our friendship.

Now it has happened again. Another friend has just changed careers and taken up painting. I thought it my duty to support and encourage her (as good friends do). She suggested I
25 commission her to paint a picture of my mother's house, as I was stuck for a present for her birthday. When it eventually arrived it was a real horror. I knew my mother would hate it. It was totally unsympathetic to the feel and character of the little country cottage, all overgrown with rambling wild roses.

This friend had been to the cottage on many occasions and I thought she had shared in its
30 tranquil and timeless atmosphere. But she had chosen to portray it as a shocking confusion of violent and clashing colour. I tried to be objective and judge it as a work of art, but it was too personal; however I looked at it, it was my mother's home and the place where I had spent an idyllic childhood. I felt it was insensitive and insulting.

The dreaded moment came when she asked me what I'd thought of it. I um'd and ah'd and
35 played for time. I really tried to like it so that my critical appraisal could gush with sincerity. As I had been in this situation before, I was determined to be honest this time and not get tied up in knots of deceit. Then my friend asked me whether my mother liked the painting. I said I thought so, that it already had pride of place up on the wall. This was hardly critical, but not effervescent with praise either. She immediately went into a massive sulk that unleashed a string of pent-up
40 emotions about what a bad friend I was. She hasn't spoken to me since.

a How did the writer react when the portrait was presented to her and why did she react in this way?

....

....

b What does the writer mean by the phrase 'I went way over the top with vacuous flattery'? (line 4)

....

....

c   What explanations did other people give for the way the portrait looked?

....

....

d   To what does 'in that form' (line 13) refer?

....

....

e   What does the writer mean by 'sort of'? (line 14)

....

....

f   What had the artist attempted and not attempted to do in the painting?

....

....

g   Why was the writer worried about the artist visiting her and noticing that the painting was not displayed?

....

....

h   What did the writer consider telling the artist about the painting when she visited her?

....

....

i   What was 'that lie' (line 22) that the author would have to 'live forever'?

....

....

j   Why did the writer commission a painting of her mother's house?

....

....

k   Why did the writer have strong feelings about the cottage?

....

....

l   What is meant by the phrase 'played for time'? (line 35)

....

....

m What are the 'knots of deceit' mentioned in line 37?

....

....

n Explain the phrase 'had pride of place' (line 38)

....

....

o How did the artist react to the writer's comments and why did she react in this way?

....

....

....

p In a paragraph of 70–90 words, explain what the writer disliked about the two paintings.

....

....

....

....

....

....

....

....

....

....

Before you check your answers to this section of the test, go on to pages 56 and 57.

For general guidance on the questions for this part of the test, see Answering The Questions – General Notes on page 28.

EXPLAIN THE MEANING

In some questions in this part of the paper, you are asked to explain the meanings of certain phrases. These questions normally begin 'What is meant by the phrase …?', 'Explain the meaning of the phrase …', 'What does the writer mean by …?' and a reference to the line in which the phrase occurs.

These questions ask you to explain in your own words the meaning of a particular phrase, either in general terms or in the particular context of the text. There may be more than one part to be explained in this type of question.

This is not intended to be purely a test of your vocabulary. Even if you do not know the phrase or parts of it, you may be able to work it out from the context.

Look at question b

1 In the context, 'I went over the top' means:
   a I became excited
   b I exaggerated
   c I told lies
   d I became nervous

2 In the context, 'vacuous flattery' means:
   a invented excuses
   b guilty promises
   c weak praise
   d false compliments

Look at question l

In the context, 'I played for time' means:
   a I made a joke of it for a while
   b I delayed giving an answer
   c I said a lot of untrue things
   d I gave a lengthy answer

Look at question n

In line 38 'had pride of place' means:
   a was displayed in the most noticeable place
   b looked attractive where it had been hung
   c attracted compliments from those who saw it
   d looked better than others in the same room

EXPLAIN THE REFERENCE

Some questions in this section require you to explain what something in the passage refers to. This reference is to something mentioned earlier in the text, perhaps in the same sentence or paragraph or perhaps even earlier. The questions test whether you have understood the relationship between things that are mentioned in the passage and to answer them you must locate exactly what is referred to.

Look at question d

In line 13 'in that form' refers to:
   a the writer's appearance in the photograph
   b the artist's own style of painting
   c the shape of the portrait
   d the angle from which the portrait was painted

Look at question i

In line 22 'that lie' refers to:
   a the lie about giving the painting to her children
   b the lie that she thought the artist was good
   c the lie about where she had put the painting
   d the lie that she liked the painting.

Look at question m

In line 37 'knots of deceit' refers to:
a   the fear of telling the truth
b   the complicated lies she told the first artist
c   the problems caused by keeping silent
d   the false compliments she paid the second artist

Now check your answers to these questions and decide whether you wish to change any of the answers you gave in the test. If you have phrased anything you wrote in the test differently from the choices given on these pages, this does not necessarily mean that you answered incorrectly in the test.

Then check your answers to questions a–o of Section B of the test on pages 53–55.

WRITING A SUMMARY

For general guidance on writing the summary for this part of the test, see Writing a Summary – General Notes on page 29.

For the summary in this test, decide which of the following are relevant and therefore must be included. Tick the box next to each point that should be included.

FIRST PAINTING

1   she hadn't asked for it □

2   it made her look ugly □

3   it was disliked by other people □

4   she had only looked like that briefly □

5   it didn't reflect her personality □

6   it ruined her friendship with the artist □

SECOND PAINTING

1   her mother would dislike it □

2   it didn't capture the essence of the place □

3   it didn't make the place look peaceful □

4   the colours were inappropriate □

5   the colours didn't match each other □

6   she couldn't view it objectively □

Now look again at your summary and decide whether you wish to change anything.

Then check your answers to this exercise and to the summary on page 55.

PAPER 4   LISTENING COMPREHENSION   about 30 mins

PART ONE

You will hear an extract from a radio programme about the early days of popular songwriting in the USA.
For questions 1–10, *write T next to those statements which are true, and F next to those statements which are false.*

You will hear the piece twice.

1 Tin Pan Alley got its name from a kind of piano.

6 Publishers often changed their minds about songs.

2 It was the ambition of many good songwriters to work there.

7 Songwriters in Tin Pan Alley seldom had time off.

3 Many songwriters had offices in the Brill Building.

8 Songwriters in Tin Pan Alley became wealthy from songwriting.

4 Publishers often failed to promote songs adequately.

9 Songwriters liked each other to hear their ideas for songs.

5 Publishers liked songs that were similar to current hits.

10 Tin Pan Alley still existed after the birth of the film industry.

PART TWO

You will hear a report on fires in a National Park in the USA.
For questions 11–15, *choose the most appropriate answer, A, B, C, or D and write your choice in the box provided below each question.*

You will hear the piece twice.

11 Why did the firefighters stop fighting lightning fires?

   A They couldn't be controlled.
   B They happened outside the park.
   C They weren't doing much damage.
   D They were too dangerous.

Answer:

12 What happened concerning the park in 1988?

   A Some research into fires there was concluded.
   B The 'natural fire management policy' began there.
   C There was an enormous fire there.
   D Fires were caused by visitors to the park.

Answer:

13 What did research conclude about fires in the park?

   A None of the trees in one area survived the 1704 fire.
   B The number of fires has been increasing all the time.

   C The fire in the 1870s did little damage.
   D The first big fire happened in 1704.

Answer:

14 What does research indicate about trees in the park?

   A In one part the lodge pole pine has permanently disappeared.
   B Aspen survive fires better than other trees.
   C The lodge pole pine can adapt to the threat of fire.
   D Aspen grow back after fires more quickly than other trees.

Answer:

15 What is the report's conclusion?

   A The effect of forest fires has changed.
   B Fires can be beneficial to nature.
   C Trees grow bigger after fires.
   D Fires have no long-term effect on nature.

Answer:

PART THREE

You will hear an extract from a TV programme about Ocho Rios.
***For questions 16–23**, complete the notes.*

You will hear the piece twice.

Location:	**16** ....
Is now:	**17** ....
Was previously:	**18** ....
Unspoilt part:	**19** ....
Nearby attraction:	**20** ....
Major development:	**21** ....
In town centre:	**22** ....
	23 ....
	hotels

PART FOUR

*You will hear an interview with someone who started a business with her husband. **For questions 24–33**, write YES next to the feelings which she mentions they have or had, and NO next to the feelings which she does not mention.*

You will hear the piece twice.

24 envy of other people

25 acceptance that they might not be offered jobs by employers again

26 insecurity about their present position

27 admiration for people who start businesses

28 confidence in having greater abilities than others

29 interest in making money

30 unhappiness in their former jobs

31 nervousness when starting their business

32 boredom that is brought on very easily

33 desire to start a different business

Before you check your answers to this Paper, go on to page 60.

ATTITUDES, OPINIONS AND FEELINGS

Some of the pieces in the listening test require you to understand and identify the opinions, attitudes and feelings of the speakers, as well as the actual information stated. To answer questions of this type, you may need to tick boxes, for example to indicate whether a statement is true or false, or whether a particular view is expressed.

Listen again to Part 4 of the test on page 59 and tick the boxes next to those things that are stated in the interview. This will give you further practice in answering this type of question and enable you to check the answers that you gave in the test.

1 She would like to be in someone else's position from time to time. ☐

2 She would sometimes prefer to work for someone else again. ☐

3 She has acquired a high opinion of herself. ☐

4 Her attitude might not appeal to employers. ☐

5 She fears that her business might fail. ☐

6 Some people can't do anything other than work for themselves. ☐

7 Deciding to work for yourself takes courage. ☐

8 Not getting on with others at work makes people work for themselves. ☐

9 Not wanting to obey orders at work makes people want to work for themselves. ☐

10 Failing to get promotion can make you decide to work for yourself. ☐

11 Believing that others don't do work as well as you are capable of can lead you to

work for yourself. ☐

12 She doesn't care about money. ☐

13 They didn't enjoy their previous work. ☐

14 They enjoyed being in a large company. ☐

15 They sought advice on what kind of business to start. ☐

16 They were already familiar with how certain kinds of business were run. ☐

17 They knew the business would succeed when they started it. ☐

18 They like doing things that are not easy to do. ☐

19 They don't like to have a routine existence. ☐

20 They are losing interest in their current business. ☐

Now check your answers to the questions on these pages. When you have done so, decide whether you wish to change any of the answers you gave in Part 4 of the test on page 59.

Then check your answers to Part 4 of the test and then to Parts 1, 2, and 3 on pages 58–59.

PAPER 5 INTERVIEW

1 *Look at one or more of these photographs and answer the questions that follow them.*

What's happening in each picture?
Describe the people. What feelings do they appear to have?
What do you think is likely to happen?

How important are films/newspapers/television in your life?
If you could work in one of those fields, which would you choose and why?
Which one do you think is the most powerful means of communication?
Describe the media in your country. Which form is the most popular?

2 *Read one or more of these passages and then answer the questions that follow them.*

a I've always been very relaxed with journalists, and indeed was capable of mounting a rather stylish account of the fact that in a free society there would always be some friction between a free press and the government. I do think there are things the popular press do which are disgraceful, but I would have thought that whatever happened to me. My own experiences didn't change my mind; they re-inforced my point of view.

b I've got 35 CVs on my desk at the moment, all from people wanting me to get them a job. Many of them are doing media or communications courses at college, some are youngsters with a relation working in the media and others are just kids who have decided they should be making television programmes. This one reads: 'I want to get involved in the film industry ultimately as a camera person ...'

c The only time the evening news broadcasts do an overseas story is when it's so big they can't avoid covering it. It's just damn hard to get an international story onto the networks. I think they are underestimating both the appetite and the need for foreign news. I think they are pandering to one section of the public, which is insular. But it's not true to say that everyone is like that.

Who do you think is writing or speaking in each passage?
What opinions are they expressing?

3 *Do one or more of these tasks. If you are working with others, discuss them together.*

a Imagine that you could write a newspaper or magazine column regularly.
What sort of column would it be?
Why would you like to write such a column?
What kind of subjects would you write about?
What points of view would you express?

b Look at these headings from the contents of a daily newspaper:

- At home and abroad: Reporting the News
- Letters
- Political cartoons
- Leading Articles: Sharp Opinions on World Affairs
- Arts and Books: The Most Distinguished Critics
- Health: Our Doctor Writes
- Business and Finance: A Special Daily Section
- Fashion
- Provocative Columnists
- Sport: Live Action, Livelier Comment

In what order do or would you read them?
Which of these sections do or would you read?
What aspects of these sections interest you?
Which ones don't or wouldn't you read? Why not?
Describe a newspaper that you read regularly or one that is popular in your country.

c 'I've been thinking of getting rid of my television set to see if I can get my brain back.'

Would you get rid of your television? Why/Why not?
Could you live without a television? If you didn't have one, what would you do instead?
What damage do you think TV does?
What benefits come from television?
What do you like most on TV? Why?
What do you dislike on TV? Why?
Do you think you or other people watch too much TV? What results does this have?

TALKING ABOUT PASSAGES

In the interview you may be asked to identify the writer or speaker of a particular short passage or passages. There will be some evidence in each of the passages to lead you to a conclusion.

Look again at the three passages on page 62 and answer these questions, alone or with a partner.

1 Which of the three passages is **not** written by someone who works in the media?

2 What evidence in that passage supports your answer to 1?

3 What conclusions can you draw as to what kind of person the speaker or writer of that passage probably is? Give evidence.

4 Which of the three passages is critical of one aspect of the media?

5 What is the writer or speaker of that passage being critical of?

6 What do you think that person's job is? What is stated in the passage that makes you think that?

7 What seems to be the job of the writer or speaker of the passage you have not so far chosen? What in the passage leads you to that conclusion?

8 What problem is referred to in that passage?

9 What does the writer or speaker think are the causes of this problem?

Now check your answers to these questions.

TALKING ABOUT THE TOPIC

The three activities in question 3 of the interview on page 62 require you to discuss various aspects of the media. To talk about this topic, certain words and phrases may be essential.

Newspapers and magazines

1 All newspapers and magazines together are called ....

2 Critics write .... of books, plays, films, etc.

3 A magazine printed on shiny paper is called a .... magazine.

4 A person whose job it is to write regular reports for a newspaper on a particular subject, such as politics, economics, foreign news, etc is called a _____ .

5 A magazine that comes out every week is called a _____ . One that comes out every month is called a _____ .

6 The article giving a newspaper's opinion on something is called the _____ .

7 A _____ column is one in which the affairs of famous people are discussed.

8 A small newspaper, especially one containing short news stories and articles that are not very serious is called a _____ .

9 A large newspaper containing a lot of news, analysis and serious articles is called a _____ newspaper.

10 The business of writing and producing newspapers and magazines is called _____ .

Television

1 If something is shown _____ on TV, it is shown at the time when it happens.

2 The best parts of an event shown after it has taken place are called the _____ .

3 Advertisements on TV are also called _____ .

4 Each part of a TV series that tells a continuing story is called an _____ .

5 A programme in which famous people are interviewed is called a _____ .

6 A programme in which people play something and win prizes is called a _____ .

7 Programmes being shown for the second time are called _____ .

8 A series showing the everyday lives of a family or group is called a _____ .

9 A comedy series in which the same characters get into amusing situations is called a _____ .

10 A _____ is a factual programme dealing with a particular subject.

Now check your answers to these questions.

TEST THREE

PAPER 1   READING COMPREHENSION   1 hour

SECTION A

In this section you must choose the word or phrase which best completes each sentence. Indicate the letter A, B, C, or D against the number of each item 1 to 25 for the word or phrase you choose.

1 She took the course with a .... to improving her employment prospects.

   A regard   B view   C consideration   D relation

2 .... how little experience she has, she's doing very well at the job.

   A Allowing   B Considering   C Regarding   D Assuming

3 .... the expression on his face, I'd say he wasn't very pleased.

   A As for   B Provided   C Judging by   D Seeing as

4 Thank you for your invitation to stay with you and I'll .... you up on it soon.

   A get   B take   C turn   D put

5 In my opinion, they have all these special offers to .... people into buying things they don't really want.

   A persuade   B convince   C sway   D tempt

6 Something had obviously amused him because he was .... quietly to himself.

   A groaning   B chuckling   C grunting   D squealing

7 In the .... of any real evidence against them, the case had to be dropped.

   A scarcity   B lack   C absence   D want

8 Last year they had record sales and .... all their competitors.

   A excelled   B outdid   C outweighed   D overdid

9 If you wash that pullover in boiling water, it will ....

   A shrink   B crumple   C condense   D compress

10 Most of the shareholders were in .... at the Annual General Meeting.

   A company   B attendance   C presence   D appearance

11 When asking for our money back in a reasonable manner failed, we had to .... to threats.

   A resort   B employ   C apply   D adopt

12 He comes .... to the voters as a trustworthy politician.

   A along   B up   C off   D over

13 She couldn't concentrate because her personal problems were .... in her mind.

   A supreme   B principal   C uppermost   D superior

14 Despite having a low income, she manages to ....

  A get by   B keep up   C live on   D stand for

15 Their relationship has become so bad that it is too late to .... the situation.

  A remedy   B recover   C cure   D heal

16 Some of the company's working methods are .... on those used in the USA.

  A moulded   B modelled   C adapted   D shaped

17 She paints .... for pleasure, not because she wants to make any money out of it.

  A singly   B fully   C directly   D purely

18 I really .... for her at what must be a very difficult time for her.

  A commiserate   B feel   C sympathize   D pity

19 Jackie is a good student and has a .... future .

  A prospective   B potential   C promising   D thriving

20 Experts are .... into the causes of the accident.

  A inquiring   B seeking   C investigating   D exploring

21 It suddenly .... her mind that she had promised to meet a friend that night.

  A hit   B touched   C struck   D crossed

22 Although she .... confidently, she was in fact very nervous.

  A behaved   B posed   C acted   D pretended

23 She carried on talking, without even .... in my direction.

  A blinking   B squinting   C glancing   D glimpsing

24 She shows little .... for the feelings of others and does exactly what she wants to.

  A sensitivity   B regard   C awareness   D perception

25 Despite his .... as a player, he has had a successful career.

  A deficiencies   B shortages   C disabilities   D snags

Before you check your answers to this section of the test, go on to pages 67 and 68.

CONNECTING

A few of the questions in this part of the test require you to choose from words and phrases that are used for connecting sentences.

The numbers of the exercises below refer to questions 1–3 of Section A on page 65, which are questions of this type. In each exercise, choose which of the four options in the test best fits each gap. This may help you to identify the correct options in the test to which they refer.

1 | regard   view   consideration   relation |

   a On ...., I decided that the proposition did not suit me.

   b I contacted him with a .... to setting a date for a meeting.

   c I am writing with .... to our recent discussion.

   d I asked a number of questions in .... to the details of the scheme.

2 | Allowing   Considering   Regarding   Assuming |

   a .... for the time it will take to get through Customs, we should get there at

about 10.

   b .... that we don't run into any heavy traffic, we'll be there at about 8.

   c .... my travel arrangements; I shall be coming by car and arriving at about 6.

   d .... how far it was, the journey was remarkably quick.

3 | As for   Provided   Judging by   Seeing as |

   a .... he had been so badly treated, he had every right to be annoyed.

   b .... his accent, I'd say he's from the south of the USA.

   c .... Tom, he was even more furious than I was.

   d .... you don't go too far, I think you should say how annoyed you are.

PHRASAL VERBS

A few of the questions in this section of the test require you to choose or complete phrasal verbs. The options may be complete phrasal verbs, or parts of them.

This exercise refers to question 4 of Section A, in which you are required to select the correct verb part of a phrasal verb. It will give you practice on four verbs from which a large number of phrasal verbs are derived.

4 Put in the correct forms of **get**, **take**, **turn** or **put**.

a We had arranged to meet at 8, but he .... up half an hour late.

b It must be .... on for eight o'clock now.

c If you'd like to stay the night, we can .... you up in the spare room.

d He doesn't have much of a social life – his job .... up all his time.

e I'm not looking forward to going to the dentist's – I just want to .... it over with.

f She always .... to her parents when she's got a problem.

g Lately, he's .... to phoning us very late at night.

h They shouldn't .... away with charging such high prices.

i I'm simply not going to .... up with his rudeness any longer.

j Even though they offered him a better job, he .... them down.

k I decided to .... them up on their offer of a lift.

l That terrible experience has .... me off ever going there again.

Now check your answers to these exercises. When you have done so, decide whether you wish to change any of your answers to questions 1–4 in the test.
Then check your answers to the test.

SECTION B

*In this section you will find after each of the passages a number of questions or unfinished statements about the passage, each with four suggested answers or ways of finishing. You must choose the one which you think fits best. Indicate the letter A, B, C, or D against the number of each item 26–40 for the answer you choose. Give **one answer only** to each question. Read each passage right through before choosing your answers.*

FIRST PASSAGE

On the night of 10 May, Moni Hourt came home to Crawford from Chadron. Her house sits on a low knoll above the Chicago & North Western rail track; the White River's beyond that. When I got there, Moni poured me an iced tea – then she told me what happened that Friday night, when she tried to get home.

5 'I couldn't get here. Down where the barn is, it had flooded across the road, and there was a car stuck there already. I was coming to get my horses – it was hailing really bad, and they'd said there was flooding, and I could hear the river – but to be honest, at that point I wasn't too concerned, I just wanted the horses out. So I went back to town to get my husband Joe and the four-wheel drive and we got here.

10 'We walked down to the track and looked at the river – and it was fifty times as big as it had ever been, I'm not joking. Trees, trees as big as this table, were floating ...... no, not floating, there was no floating involved – they were snarling and snapping, they were just *shoving* down that river. It was this dirty brown river that I'd never seen before, it was so much wider, so much larger ...... Then my nineteen-year-old son said, 'Dad, what's that noise?'

15 'You could hear it like ...... like when the cattle move through the underbrush, snapping, echoing. We looked up the track and there was this great, muddy, chocolate-milk coloured wall of water coming straight down it right at us, about four feet tall. Joe said we'd better run. There were ditches five feet deep either side of the railroad tracks. We went down, and up – and the water *followed* us, it followed us – it was like it was trying to catch us, like it was a *thing*. It was coming
20 up the hill behind us, surging ...... I was fascinated. I kept stopping. I just could not believe this was happening, in a country that gets fifteen inches of rain. Water is precious here, you pray for it ......

'We got up to the yard and it hit the barns and the chicken houses, then it split around us. It filled the corrals, it got within five feet of the house, it went into Kenny's alfalfa field to the west of us, it filled the gully on the east side; we were surrounded. Joe said we had to get out of there. We
25 drove to the bottom of the drive, but it was four feet deep on the road there, we couldn't get out. So we cut the fence and went across the alfalfa field. The truck tried to die on us halfway, the water was getting up the doors by then – but we got across, higher up the hill to our neighbour's place.

'Even then, I still couldn't understand that it was dangerous. And you have to understand that in this country, you do not drive across your neighbour's alfalfa field, especially at this time of
30 year – *you do not do that*, it's not *courteous*. So I was standing there apologizing. I mean, the truck's dying, the hail's hailing, the river's flooding, the house is surrounded by water – and I'm saying, Kenny, I'm sorry we drove across your alfalfa field. Crazy.'

26 When Moni first got home, she thought that

    A there was going to be severe flooding.
    B the horses needed to be rescued.
    C the barn was likely to be flooded.
    D there was likely to be a bad storm.

27 What struck Moni about the river when she first saw it?

    A It was making a peculiar noise.
    B It was moving in a violent way.
    C It was threatening the trees.
    D It was getting bigger and wider.

28 When Moni saw the water coming towards them, she

    A felt that it was acting deliberately.
    B feared they would be swept into a ditch.

    C was too amazed at the sight to move.
    D tried to analyse the danger.

29 Why did they drive across the field?

    A The water could not reach it.
    B It was their only escape route.
    C The drive was blocked by water.
    D It led to a piece of higher ground.

30 What does Moni think was 'crazy'?

    A the whole incident that night
    B the drive across the field
    C local customs of politeness
    D her thoughts as they drove

SECOND PASSAGE

One of the purposes of my trip across my native country was to listen – to hear speech, accent rhythms, overtones and emphasis. For speech is so much more than words and sentences. I did listen everywhere. It seemed to me that regional speech is in the process of disappearing; not gone, but going. Decades of radio and television must have this impact. Communications must
5 destroy localness, by a slow, inevitable process. I can remember a time when I could almost pinpoint a man's place of origin by his speech. That is growing more difficult now and will in some foreseeable future become impossible. It is a rare house or building that is not rigged with the spiky combers of the air. Radio and television speech becomes standardized, perhaps better English than we have ever used. Just as our bread, mixed and baked, packaged and sold without
10 benefit of accident or human frailty, is uniformly good and uniformly tasteless, so will our speech become one speech.

I who love words and the endless possibility of words am saddened by this inevitability. For with local accent will disappear local tempo. The idioms, the figures of speech that make language rich and full of the poetry of place and time must go. And in their place will be a national speech,
15 wrapped and packaged, standard and tasteless. In the many years since I have listened to the land, the change is very great. Travelling west along the northern routes, I did not hear truly local speech until I reached Montana. That is one of the reasons I fell in love again with Montana. The West Coast went back to package English. The Southwest kept a grasp, but a slipping grasp on localness. Of course the deep south holds on to its regional expressions, just as it holds and
20 treasures some other anachronisms, but no region can hold out for long against the highway, the high-tension line and the national television. What I am mourning is perhaps not worth saving, but I regret its loss nevertheless.

Even while I protest the assembly-line production of our food, our songs, our language, and eventually our souls, I know that it was a rare home that baked good bread in the old days.
25 Mother's cooking was with rare exceptions poor, that good unpasteurized milk touched only by flies and bits of manure crawling with bacteria, the healthy old-time life was riddled with aches and sudden death from unknown causes and that sweet local speech I mourn was the child of illiteracy and ignorance. It is the nature of a man as he grows older, a small bridge in time, to protest against change, particularly change for the better. But it is true that we have exchanged
30 corpulence for starvation, and either one will kill us. We, or at least I, can have no conception of human life in a hundred years or fifty years. Perhaps my greatest wisdom is the knowledge that I do not know. The sad ones are those who waste their energy in trying to hold it back, for they can only feel bitterness in loss and no joy in gain.

31 What did the writer discover during his trip?

   A Television and radio had destroyed local speech.
   B He had forgotten what local accents were like.
   C Local accents were starting to sound different from before.
   D He found it hard to detect differences in speech.

32 What does the writer say about changes in bread and speech?

   A They have produced an improvement in both.
   B Both have become uniform throughout the whole country.
   C He has noticed them taking place gradually over a long period.
   D They have been caused by people's desire for progress.

33 According to the writer, the deep south is

   A the only region where everyone uses local speech.
   B changing in the same way as other regions.
   C similar in many ways to the Southwest.
   D a region that likes to remain old-fashioned.

34 What does the writer say about the past?

   A Life was harder for many people but it was also better in many ways.
   B Many aspects of the way of life in former times should have been preserved.
   C Older people tend to have a false impression of what life was like then.
   D The disappearance of that way of life has been beneficial in every way.

35 According to the writer, the people who react wrongly to change are

   A those who gain no benefit from it.
   B those who want to prevent it.
   C those who have correctly predicted it.
   D those who are critical of it.

THIRD PASSAGE

What is it that attracts so many people to diving? The reasons are as diverse as the available experiences.

Drift divers roll off their boats into strong tidal currents which shoot them rapidly down gullies and over reefs for a kilometre or more. Stopping is nigh impossible – like trying to stand in a
5 hurricane. With one hand firmly gripping your partner, it is just possible to steady yourself and steer with your free hand, dodging the rocks that emerge ghost-like from the fog. This is underwater motorway madness, a crazy freedom. In these fast currents, plankton feeders emerge for an easy meal and divers with quick reflexes can sometimes grab an unwary scallop.

Depth divers enjoy a different kind of trip. Ascending and descending is like night flying:
10 unable to see either surface or bottom, you depend on your depth gauge to measure progress. If there is a line to follow to the bottom, it will gradually disappear into eerie nothingness. This is the limbo of diving; weightless and apparently motionless, you see nothing but your fellow diver. When the bottom finally rises from the gloom to meet you, the surrounding world is completely blue-green, because the deeper you go the more the colours from the red end of the colour
15 spectrum are progressively absorbed by the water. Pressure squeezes your suit, your mask, your buoyancy regulator and your lungs, all of which have to be repeatedly inflated. You are in a dark, cold and totally alien environment.

Then there are wreck divers. Some, armed with navigation charts and comprehensive underwater toolkits strapped to their waists, become so weighed down with mementoes it is a
20 wonder they manage to surface at all. Most, however, are happy simply to swim along hulls that sometimes stand 15 metres or more from the sea floor, forming artificial reefs that attract a profusion of marine life. Most wrecks are just huge chunks of broken steel and many of the more intact or important ones are protected.

Wrecks offer plenty of enticing enclosed spaces, but only the foolhardy or the very experienced
25 venture deep inside them. Sounds of breathing are amplified by chambers of rusting steel, and bubbles run horizontally along the plates above, seeking a way to the surface. Lobsters and conger eels peer out from their crannies, grotesquely enlarged by their proximity and the magnifying effects of water.

For me, the ultimate thrill is night diving. All kinds of creatures, hidden during the day,
30 emerge at night to feed, mate and exercise. Because it is only possible to see what the torch beam picks out, colours are more defined and your attention becomes more focused. Switch off your torch and you are surrounded by the dull glow of phosphorescence, which gradually fades to total inky blackness.

36 According to the writer, what is the main attraction of drift diving?

A   the chance to catch sea creatures
B   the fact that it is done in pairs
C   the speed at which the diver moves
D   the distance that the diver travels

37 When describing depth diving, the writer emphasizes

A   the effect on the diver.
B   the colours that can be seen.
C   the reliability of the equipment.
D   the distance that has to be travelled.

38 According to the writer, the majority of wreck divers

A   bring back a large number of items from the wrecks.
B   are not looking for items of value in wrecks.
C   often cannot carry to the surface what they find.
D   are prevented from entering most wrecks.

39 The greatest problem with wrecks is that

A   they attract divers to dangerous places.
B   it is difficult to breathe in them.
C   dangerous creatures are found there.
D   it is hard to move around in them.

40 The writer likes night diving because

A   sea creatures cannot see the diver then.
B   the colours then are different from during the day.
C   more sea creatures can be seen then.
D   there is a lot of activity to be seen then.

Before you check your answers to this section of the test, go on to pages 72 and 73.

A DETAILED STUDY

The questions on these pages will help you to make sure that you have chosen the correct options for the questions on the third text, on page 71.

Question 36   *Look at the first paragraph of the text and answer these questions.*

1   Which verb refers to moving at speed?

2   Does the writer suggest that drift divers cover a greater distance than other divers?

3   In what way is a partner useful?

4   If you 'dodge' something, you
    a   fail to notice it
    b   move towards it
    c   avoid colliding with it

5   Which of the following does 'motorway madness' involve?
    a   driving very fast
    b   driving a long way
    c   driving on empty roads

6   Are drift divers able to catch sea creatures?

Question 37   *Look at the second paragraph and answer these questions.*

1   In what way is a depth gauge important to depth divers?

2   Which two adjectives describe what depth divers feel themselves to be as they descend?

3   What is remarkable concerning colour at the bottom?

4   What happens to the equipment when the diver reaches the bottom?

5   Which of these does the writer mention more than once? (you may choose more than one)
    a   what happens to the diver
    b   the colours seen by divers
    c   the equipment used by divers
    d   the distance to the bottom

Questions 38 and 39   *Look at the third and fourth paragraphs and answer these questions.*

1   Why are some divers 'weighed down'?

2   What are 'mementoes'?
    a   souvenirs
    b   pieces of equipment
    c   ancient items

3   What does 'wonder' mean in this context?
    a   surprise
    b   doubt
    c   joy

4 Why can't divers enter certain wrecks?

5 Are most wrecks in many pieces?

6 Which of these words is closest in meaning to 'enticing'?
  a tempting
  b dangerous
  c frightening

7 If you are 'foolhardy', you
  a act with great care
  b do something inadvisable
  c conquer your fear

8 Which three words refer to something being made bigger or greater?

9 If you 'peer out', you
  a rush out
  b float out
  c look out

10 Does the writer say that it is hard to move around in all parts of wrecks?

Question 40 *Look at the final paragraph and answer these questions.*

1 Does the writer state that sea creatures are very active at night?

2 Does the writer state that different sea creatures can be seen at night?

3 Does the writer describe various colours you can see at night?

4 Does the writer compare the number of sea creatures that can be seen during the day with the number that can be seen at night?

5 Does the writer state that divers are invisible to sea creatures at night?

Now check your answers to the questions on these pages. Then decide whether you wish to change any of the answers that you gave to the questions on the third text, on page 71.

Then check your answers to this section of the test.

PAPER 2   COMPOSITION   2 hours

*Write **two only** of the composition exercises. Your answers must follow exactly the instructions given. Write in pen, not pencil. You are allowed to make alterations, but make sure that your work is clear and easy to read.*

1   Describe someone who you particularly admire and explain your reasons for admiring that person. (About 350 words)

2   'People take sport too seriously.' Do you agree with this statement? (About 350 words)

3   Describe a trip that you would particularly like to take. (About 350 words)

4   You are going to receive a guest of the same age as you on an exchange visit from another country. Write a letter suggesting what you can do together during this visit. (About 300 words)

Before you write your compositions, go on to pages 75 and 76.

PLANNING A COMPOSITION

One of the questions in Paper 2 requires you to write a **narrative** or **story**. You may be required to use your imagination for this and write something fictional, or you may be asked to describe real events. Your story may take place in the past but this is not always the case.

Look at question 3 on page 74 and then answer the following. This will help you to plan your composition for that question. It is advisable to practise each of the types of composition.

1 Decide where your trip would be to.

....

2 Tick which of the following would be reasons why you would like to take this trip and add any others that apply.

☐ the risk/danger involved

☐ the luxury

☐ the weather

☐ the chance to learn about another culture

☐ the chance to see certain well-known places

☐ the exciting atmosphere of the place

☐ the people you might meet

....

....

....

....

....

....

3 Tick those of the following which a description of this trip would include and add any others you can think of.

☐ the countryside

☐ the local people

☐ the buildings

☐ the climate

☐ your means of transport

☐ famous attractions

☐ your accommodation

....

....

....

4 Tick those of the following that you would do on your trip and add any others you wish to.

☐ take it easy

☐ visit interesting places

☐ speak to the people in their own language

☐ be very active

☐ fulfil an ambition

☐ try to meet people

☐ experience new tastes, music, etc

....

....

....

Now use these ideas to write your composition. Remember that the question asks you to describe a trip, not just a place, and so your composition should describe a sequence of events and actions.

Then write one or more of the other compositions.

Now read through the following sample composition for question 3 on page 74. When you have done so, answer the questions that follow it.

Travelling is one of my biggest hobbies. In last 10 years I have visited many countries in Europe, Asia, North America and Africa. I have experienced many exiting adventures, have seen beautiful landscape and buildings and have met interesting people. I have enjoyed it all. However, one aspect of travelling has always bothered me; flying. Don't understand me wrong. I am not afraid of flying. On the contrary. I enjoyed flying a lot. I love looking down the earth, on mountains or sea, and I always admire the sunset from the window of the plane. If additionally food is good and the on-board cinema offers a good film, what could be more pleasurable? After ten or twelve hours of flight you reach your destination, and start your holiday in a exotic place.

After doing that I have always felt that something was missing. I have eventually realized that I enjoy the actual process of getting somewhere and would like to be able to follow the progress of my journey. For a long time now I wanted to have a holiday during which I could concentrate on the journey itself rather then on the destination. The ideal mean of transport for this purpose is a train. There are many famous railway journeys in the world, but my choice is the transsiberian crossing from Moscow to Beijing.

I would love to start my journey in London and go by train to Moscow. This trip should take around two days. I haven't been to Moscow and it will be lovely to see this famous city. From there I should take the second train to Beijng. This journey is much longer and definitely more interesting. First of all I would be crossing through three huge countries: Russia, Mongolia and China. I could sit by the window and watch the changing landscapes. The train would cross the Ural mountains, the dividing line between Europe and Asia. This itself should be very exiting. After another 24 hours the train should reach the Baikal lake – the deepest lake in the world. If only possible I would love to leave the train here and spend day or two visiting this area. After couple of days I should board the next train to Beijing. The journey to the capital of China should take another three days and I hope to see some beautiful scenery on the way. I should be able to complete this trip in two weeks and have another week or two to travel around China – by train of course.

1 Does the composition actually answer the question set or does it contain irrelevant parts, 'waffle' – writing that is simply intended to fill the space but does not really say anything – or 'padding' – writing that is repetitious in order to reach the required number of words?

2 Is the composition well-organized? Is it divided into paragraphs appropriately? Explain what each paragraph contains.

3 Are appropriate linking words and phrases used for connecting sentences and paragraphs. Give examples of some that are; if some are not, correct them.

4 Does it have a good range of appropriate vocabulary or is the vocabulary used mostly too simple? Give examples and correct any inappropriate or incorrect vocabulary.

5 Is there a good range of accurate structures forming sentences that are not very simple or are the structures used mostly too basic? Give examples and correct any incorrect structures or other mistakes.

6 Is the style appropriate for this type of composition?

Now check your assessment of and corrections to this sample composition.

PAPER 3   USE OF ENGLISH   2 hours

SECTION A

1   *Fill each of the numbered blanks in the passage with **one** suitable word.*

The first known mention of the Italian tomato in Italy dates back to the year 1544. It was then

(1) .... the herbalist Mattioli called it 'Pomodoro', (2) .... means 'Golden

Apple', (3) .... possibly to the golden colour of the original yellow vegetable known at

that time. Tomatoes were then cultivated into bright red varieties and (4)........................... to Matioli

were first eaten fried in oil with salt and pepper.

In 1811 the Italian cook Filippo Re discovered that if tomatoes (5) .... crushed,

cooked and (6) .... dried in the sun they turned (7) .... a dark red paste. This

was an ideal (8) .... of preserving the tomato throughout the year, allowing

(9) .... preparation of many dishes such as sauces and stews. Around the 1840s

(10) .... product started to be commercialized and sold in markets, (11) .... it

was cut into slices and served on fresh fig leaves.

(12) .... was recognized that the tomato was packed (13) .... of many

precious qualities such as vitamins (14) .... other substances contained in the seeds,

(15) .... with a low calorie count and a vast number of culinary uses. The initial

technology for preservation (16) .... the various forms that we now know was created,

(17) .... tomatoes to be used throughout the year and in the (18) 150

years the tomato has become second (19) .... to the potato (20) .... the most

popular vegetable in the world.

2   *Finish each of the following sentences in such a way that it is as similar as possible in meaning to the sentence printed before it.*

Example: She said that he was a brilliant musician.
Answer: She described *him as a brilliant musician.*

a   It was an impressive building but it wasn't to my taste.

Impressive ....

b   I am not willing to discuss this matter at the moment.

This matter is not ....

c He assumed incorrectly that I held the same opinions as he did.

He made ....

d It is more than likely that she will succeed as an actress.

She has ....

e He didn't try to conceal his dislike for me.

He made ....

f They gave me a place to stay and they didn't want any money in return.

Not only ....

g Such a ridiculous proposal isn't worth serious consideration.

There is ....

h As she hadn't been there before, America was a whole new experience for her.

Not ....

3 *Fill each of the blanks with a suitable word or phrase.*

Example: She had difficulty *making up her* mind which one to buy.

a John Walker will be playing in .... Keith Groves, who is injured.

b The accident blocked the road, with .... a long queue of traffic built up.

c This is a very difficult problem to solve, ... we approach it.

d You could try repairing it yourself but I think you'd .... taking it to a professional.

e No, it wasn't me who travelled around Africa in the summer – you .... of someone else, although I don't know who.

f My remark was meant to be a compliment but she took .... insult.

4   *For each of the sentences below, write a new sentence* **as similar as possible in meaning to the original sentence**, *but using the word given. This word* **must not be altered** *in any way.*

     Example: She paid no attention to his warning.
                notice
     Answer: *She took no notice of his warning*

a   It is highly unlikely that the meeting will end before 8.
    chances

    ....

b   The address that I sent the parcel to does not exist.
    such

    ....

c   She writes notes on everything that is said in the meetings.
    record

    ....

d   Have you had any experience of using this kind of computer?
    familiar

    ....

e   When I realized how much it was going to cost, I changed my mind.
    realization

    ....

f   I tried to make it clear to them that urgent action was required.
    impress

    ....

g   At the moment the company is reorganizing its departments.
    process

    ....

h   Tina has a habit of upsetting people unintentionally.
    inclined

    ....

Before you check your answers to this section of the test, go on to pages 80 and 81.

FILL IN THE MISSING WORD

Look again at question 1 of the test on page 77, and then decide which of the words below fit into each of the twenty gaps there. You may choose any of the words below only once. Some of the words do not fill any of the gaps. You may wish to change some of the answers you gave in the test after you have done this. However, if an answer that you gave there is not among the choices here, this does not necessarily mean that it is wrong.

according	into	then
allowing	is	there
along	it	this
and	of	to
as	only	way
but	plenty	were
following	referring	where
full	so	which
had	that	while
in	the	with

1 ....

2 ....

3 ....

4 ....

5 ....

6 ....

7 ....

8 ....

9 ....

10 ....

11 ....

12 ....

13 ....

14 ....

15 ....

16 ....

17 ....

18 ....

19 ....

20 ....

Now check your answers to these questions and to question 1 of the test on page 77. Then go on to page 81.

COMPLETE THE SENTENCES

Look again at question 2 of this test on page 77, and then decide which of the following choices for each question there could be the next word in each sentence. Sometimes only one of the choices could come next and sometimes more than one of them could come next. You may wish to change some of the answers you gave in the test when you have made your choice or choices. However, if the first word of the answer that you gave there is not included among the choices here, your answer is not necessarily incorrect.

a	1	that	**e**	1	not
	2	while		2	out
	3	though		3	no
	4	the		4	it
	5	as		5	clear
b	1	what	**f**	1	they
	2	something		2	gave
	3	it		3	did
	4	that		4	have
	5	a		5	a
c	1	the	**g**	1	such
	2	himself		2	not
	3	up		3	no
	4	incorrectly		4	so
	5	it		5	pointless
d	1	every	**h**	1	to
	2	good		2	going
	3	probably		3	gone
	4	possibilities		4	there
	5	a		5	having

Now check your answers to these questions and to question 2 of the test on page 77. Then check your answers to questions 3 and 4 of the test on pages 78 and 79.

SECTION B

Read the following passage, then answer the questions which follow it.

The Travel Bores

I don't want to travel. I don't know why, but when God was handing out the wanderlust, he forgot to give me any. I'm quite happy to watch the world go by through my living room window and I have no desire to go out there and see it, explore it, or eat any of it. The fact that other people have done so – and destroyed vast acres of its natural resources to regale the stay-at-homes with
5   their travelogues – just increases my resolve to stay put.

Why should I go back-packing in Outer Mongolia when friends, or friends of friends, have been there before me, photographed it from every possible angle and harangued me with long, unsolicited testimonials about it? And when all is said and done, the main preoccupation of the average traveller is not with the places they've seen or the people they've met, even if they do
10 feign an interest in the lost Amazonian tribe they ran into.

There's an unwritten motto among travellers: He travels faster who dresses appallingly. Travellers all wear the same uniform – open-toed sandals, bermuda shorts and beanie hat. The accessories are minimal and they make a virtue of the fact that they've traversed three continents with hardly anything in the sturdy rucksack.

15 I know all this because I have formed several enthusiastic airport welcome-home receptions for friends who have come back from their round-the-world stint. They all look the same and say exactly the same thing: 'Oh it was such fun, it's all so beautiful out there and the people are so friendly.' But if that's the case, why come back? If travelling is all so refreshing, why do they immediately demand a bath and a good rest? And if foreigners are such friendly, hospitable
20 people, why aren't they summoning the removal men instead of stuffing their faces in the airport canteen and chattering with the relish of a mute to whom the power of speech has just returned?

I suppose it's just that I'm not imbued with the spirit of imperialism: the burning desire to go to far-flung corners of the globe, trample a couple of blades of grass underfoot and claim them as my own. I prefer charter flights and package deals, a full complement of luggage and the fact that
25 my destination is likely to be a hotel with my name indelibly etched in its register. It's not that I've confined myself to this country but I like to know precisely what I'm going to get or the reason why I haven't got it. I just couldn't bear the unpredictability of being in foreign climes and not having a brochure to wave in anger at the hotel manager. And I can't face more excitement than whether or not the plane will leave on time. The casual attitude of the intrepid travellers is
30 anathema to me. I run my holidays with the precision of a military campaign.

Even then I find it all an uncomfortable business. Planes are invariably late and I've felt myself growing old in departure lounges. And this business about 'just hopping onto a plane' is rot. Even when you've got to the airport – usually a trek of no mean significance – there are at least three miles of walkways and several involuntary work-outs as you juggle suitcases on the way to the
35 check-in counter. I don't travel hopefully so much as doom-laden, envisaging my flight number with the words 'ill-fated' prefixed to it on the front page of the next morning's newspaper. And there's always the risk that as you jet off to Barcelona some idiot has labelled your luggage 'Bolivia'. What's more, if you do manage to get through the labyrinth of officialdom which is any airport in the world, there's always the inevitable child screaming in the seat behind.

40 Some people, I gather, enjoy the whole process – the business at the airport, the roar of the engines, not to mention the regulation, mass-produced cabin food – but for me it's a misery and I can't wait to get home.

a   What does the writer mean by 'stay put'? (line 5)

....

....

b   What are the 'unsolicited testimonials' that the writer refers to in line 8?

....

....

....

c   According to the writer, what do travellers say about the things they take with them?

....

....

....

d   What does the writer want to ask the travellers she describes when they return?

....

....

....

e   What do the travellers' demands at the airport suggest to the writer?

....

....

....

f   What does the writer imply about 'foreigners'? (line 19)

....

....

g   Why does the writer say that the travellers who have just returned are like people 'to whom the power of speech has suddenly returned'? (line 21)

....

....

....

h   In what way is travelling like imperialism, according to the writer?

....

....

....

i   In your own words, explain why the writer prefers charter flights and package deals.

....

....

....

....

j Explain the phrase 'is anathema to me'. (line 29– 30)

....

k In your own words, explain what the writer dislikes about airports.

....

....

....

....

l Why does the writer think that her flight will be described as 'ill-fated'? (line 36)

....

m What is meant by the phrase 'a labyrinth of officialdom'? (line 38)

....

....

n In your own words, explain what the writer dislikes about being on an aeroplane.

....

....

....

....

o In a paragraph of 70–90 words, summarize the writer's criticisms of the travellers she describes.

....

....

....

....

....

....

....

....

....

Before you check your answers to this section of the test, go on to pages 85 and 86.

For general guidance on the questions for this part of the test, see Answering the Questions –
General Notes on page 28.

A DETAILED STUDY

For general guidance on this type of question, see page 28.

Look at question c

1 How much do the travellers described take with them?

....

2 If you 'make a virtue of something', you
  a manage to survive without it.
  b try to improve it.
  c take advantage of it.
  d claim that it is good.

....

Look at questions d, e, f, and g

1 What do travellers usually say about their trips when they get back?

....

2 What do they say that they want?

....

3 What opinion do they express of foreigners?

....

4 What **two** things do they do at airports?

  A ....

  B ....

5 What does each of these suggest about their trips?

  A ....

  B ....

6 Why would someone be 'summoning the removal men'? (line 20)

....

Look at question i

Tick which of the following advantages of package deals the writer mentions in the article.

1   the amount of luggage you can take

2   the high quality of hotels

3   the company of other people

4   the fact that accommodation has been firmly booked

5   the certainty of what you are entitled to

6   the knowledge of what the weather will be like

7   the ability to complain if something isn't right

8   the reliability of flights

Look at question k

Tick which of the following disadvantages of airports the writer mentions in the article.

1   the delays of flights

2   the cost of getting to them

3   the difficulty of reaching them

4   the distance to them

5   the distance to be travelled within them

6   the difficulty of carrying luggage in them

7   the length of time at the check-in counter

8   the lack of directions from them

Look at question n

How many aspects of being on a plane does the writer say that she dislikes? ....

Now check your answers to these questions. When you have done so, decide whether you wish to change any of the answers you gave in the test. If you have phrased anything you wrote in the test differently from the choices given on these pages, this does not necessarily mean that you answered incorrectly in the test.

Then check your answers to questions a–n of the test on pages 82–84.

WRITING A SUMMARY

For general guidance on writing a summary for this part of the test, see Writing a Summary – General Notes, on page 29.

Read the summary below for this test and answer the questions that follow it.

o	She doesn't like travellers who roam all around the world and destroy it just in order to report on their journey to their friends. Travellers are not really interested in the places they visit and in the people they meet. Besides they are dressed in the same ugly way and travel with little luggage. When returning from their holiday they all have the same appearance and the same enthusiastic comment on it.

1 Is anything irrelevant included or anything relevant not included? If so, what?

2 Are there any language mistakes? Correct any that you think there are.

3 Has any of the passage simply been copied in the summary? If so, what? Is the summary too short, too long or the right length?

Now look again at your summary on page 84 and decide whether you wish to change anything.

Then check your marks for your summary and the assessment of this sample summary.

PAPER 4   LISTENING COMPREHENSION   about 30 mins

PART ONE

You will hear a series of advertisements on a radio station.
For questions 1–8, write in the box the first letter of the company whose advertisement matches each statment.

You will hear the piece twice.

> T   Trafficmaster
> E   Eurokitchen
> S   Southern Business Group
> M   Mobile Phone Warehouse
> C   Curtain Mill

1   We do certain work without charge.

2   We do not give things away with our goods.

3   Our prices are lower than those of any other firm offering similar goods.

4   We explain everything to you very carefully.

5   You can change your mind after making an agreement with us.

6   We are leaders in our field.

7   We do not favour particular brands.

8   You can use our goods without paying first.

PART TWO

You will hear an extract from a programme about coffee drinking in Britain.
For questions 9–18, write YES next to those views that are expressed in the discussion, and NO next to those views which are not expressed.

You will hear the piece twice.

9   A surprisingly large number of British people drink instant coffee.

10 It is wrong to think that instant coffee is easier to make than real coffee.

11 It is easier to make real coffee than to make tea.

12 It has been proved that coffee is not damaging to health.

13 Stories about the damage caused by drinking real coffee have been invented.

14 It is always possible to distinguish real coffee from instant coffee.

15 It is best to buy real coffee that has already been ground.

16 You should use water that has not quite boiled when making real coffee.

17 It is possible to buy good quality real coffee in a supermarket.

18 Only experts on coffee should buy coffee beans.

PART THREE

You will hear a report about a discovery in the Alps.
For questions 19–30, *complete the sentences below .*

You will hear the piece twice.

The discovery was made while two people were crossing **19** .... in the Alps.

The first thing found near the body was **20** ....

They used **21** ....to free the body from the ice.

The body was unusual because it was **22** ....before being frozen.

The knife suggested that the body was very old because it was **23** ....

They also found **24** ....and **25** ....close to the body.

At first they decided that the body was from the **26** ....period in Central Europe.

Other frozen bodies do not have **27** ....

The oldest frozen bodies previously discovered are **28** ....as the Iceman.

The discovery of the cape suggested that people at that time **29** ....

The body probably survived because it was **30** .... animals.

PART FOUR

You will hear an extract from a radio programme, about soap operas.
For questions 31–35, *choose the most appropriate answer, A, B, C, or D and write your choice in the box provided below each question.*

You will hear the piece twice.

31 According to Hilary, to be called a soap a programme must

   A be set somewhere that does not really exist.
   B leave you guessing what will happen next.
   C concern people with something in common.
   D run for a very long time on television.

   Answer: [   ]

32 Hilary thinks that soaps differ from other dramas in that

   A they show people faced with ordinary problems.
   B they have changed little since they started.
   C they have more female than male characters.
   D they are popular with housewives.

   Answer: [   ]

33 Which of the following is a typical situation regarding soaps?

   A Comments made by critics stop people watching them.
   B People are ashamed of the fact that they watch them.
   C People tend to believe that characters in them are real.
   D They destroy our interest in reading and the theatre.

   Answer: [   ]

34 What does Hilary state about the watching of soaps?

   A Women tend to watch them more consistently than men.
   B Their popularity with women is a regrettable matter.
   C They tend to have little appeal to the majority of men.
   D They enable women to occupy their minds with trivial things.

   Answer: [   ]

35 Which of the following is said by the presenter to be an attraction of soaps?

   A They show us people always solving their problems.
   B They are easier to follow than formal dramas.
   C They make us feel comfortable about life.
   D They have no connection with real life.

   Answer: [   ]

Before you check your answers to this part of the test, go on to pages 91 and 92.

ATTITUDES, OPINIONS, AND FEELINGS

Some of the pieces in the test focus on the views expressed by speakers, as well as the information given. Questions on pieces of this type may be of the multiple-choice type, in which you choose A, B, C, or D, or they may involve ticking boxes. They require you to identify and understand precisely what speakers say and to eliminate what is not stated.

Listen again to Part 4 of the test on page 90, and answer the following questions by ticking the appropriate boxes. You may need to tick more than one box in each question. This will give you further practice in answering questions on this type of piece and enable you to check the answers that you gave in the test. The numbers below refer to the questions in the test on page 90.

31 Which of the following are true of real soaps, according to Hilary?

A Each episode leaves something unresolved. ☐

B They are always set in fictional places. ☐

C They always involve families or colleagues. ☐

D Each episode continues the story. ☐

E They last for a number of years. ☐

F The characters in them seem to have lives beyond the programme. ☐

32 Which of the following does Hilary state about soaps and other dramas?

A The first soaps were about everyday life. ☐

B Soaps revolve around the female characters. ☐

C Other dramas focus on men. ☐

D Current soaps are about everyday life. ☐

E Soaps were initially aimed at housewives. ☐

F Housewives are less keen on other dramas. ☐

33 Which of the following does the presenter say about soaps?

A Some unfortunate people believe them to be real. ☐

B People pretend that they don't watch soaps. ☐

C Critics make people feel stupid for watching soaps. ☐

D We pretend that we do more sophisticated things than watching soaps. ☐

E Soaps distract us from our normal cultural habits. ☐

F Many people don't watch soaps because of what critics say. ☐

34 Which of the following does Hilary say about watching soaps?

A Like most programmes watched by women, they are often of low quality. ☐

B Soaps are watched by a considerable number of men. ☐

C Soaps focus entirely on unimportant matters. ☐

D Soaps require no mental activity from the viewer. ☐

E Her son disapproves of people watching soaps. ☐

F Her daughter watches more episodes of soaps than her son. ☐

35 Which of the following does the presenter say about the appeal of soaps?

A They have less complicated plots than formal dramas. ☐

B They show unlikely events. ☐

C The same kinds of thing keep happening in them. ☐

D They show people with problems. ☐

E They make our own lives seem better. ☐

F The problems in them are always resolved. ☐

Now check your answers to the questions on these pages. When you have done so, decide whether you wish to change any of the answers you gave in Part 4 of the test on page 90.

Then check your answers to Part 4 of the test and then to Parts 1, 2, and 3 on pages 88–89.

PAPER 5   INTERVIEW

1   *Look at one or more of these photographs and answer the questions that follow them.*

What's happening in each picture?
Describe the people. What feelings do they seem to have?
Where do you think each photo was taken?
When do you think each photo was taken?

Describe your journey to work/school/college.
Describe a typical day for you at work/school/college.
Would you like to change your occupation? If so, what would you prefer to do?
When are you most busy?

2 *Read one or more of these passages and then answer the questions that follow them.*

a   Commuting – the daily mass movement of office workers – was heralded by the first suburbanites in the Twenties as the perfect way to link home with workplace. Now, however, as more commuters are owning up to the horror of their journeys, travelling to work begins to seem more like a form of institutionalized madnesss. People get up extremely early in the morning and are totally stressed by the time they get to work. They arrive there exhausted by all the people and pollution and by the worry about whether they will get to work on time.

b   If you're going to progress, you'll have to take risks. This may mean taking the initiative when an urgent problem arises and your superior isn't there to make a decision. Some risks are worth taking but make sure that they're well calculated. Don't act without knowing all the facts and be prepared to account for, and live with, your mistakes. Even the best-laid plans can fail because of unforseeable problems. But few employers will forgive you for jumping in blindly.

c   Leaving a job is an experience whose reverberations extend beyond the outward signs, the farewell present and the gruff handshakes. It calls up questions about what one's life is *for*: the uses to which it is being put or has been put since the last time we stopped to question it. Have we been wasting time for years without noticing it? Have we been simply swapping our days and talents for money until we discover too late what we have lost? Have our youthful ambitions been sidetracked, derailed, buried under the everyday rubble of contingencies?

What is the purpose of each passage?
Who do you think wrote each one?
What point of view is expressed in each one?

3 *Do one or more of these tasks. If you are working with others, discuss them together.*

a   'Work and pleasure are the same thing.'
Can you think of a job of which this would be true for you?
What aspects of it would be the most enjoyable?
Is job satisfaction more important to you than money?
What kinds of people do you think find this to be the case?
What is the general attitude to the relationship between work and pleasure in your country?

b   Look through the following list of personal qualities required for various jobs:
- ability to deal with the public
- common sense
- initiative
- desire to be the best at what you do
- sense of humour
- willingness to take advice
- smart appearance
- persistence
- ability to take criticism
- managerial skills
- instinct

In your job, or any job you would like, which three are the most important? Why? In what ways? Choose three which you think you possess. Explain when and how they have been required in your life, at work or otherwise.

c   Would you like to work at home?
Why/Why not?
If you could do your job, or get a job, that allowed you to work at home, what would be the advantages/disadvantages of this for you? In what ways would it differ from going out to work?

TALKING ABOUT PICTURES

When you are talking about pictures you may need to **guess** or **deduce** what the situation is in the picture. Instead of simply saying 'I think', 'Probably' or 'Maybe', you can use a number of phrases for guessing and deducing.

Look again at each of the three pictures on page 93 and then try to use as many of the following phrases as possible to make guesses or deductions about them.

It looks (to me) as if ....

....

It looks (to me) as though ....

....

I'd say ....

....

He/She/They seem to (have) ....

....

He/She/They seem to be .... -ing

....

In my opinion ....

....

I reckon ....

....

I should think ....

....

He/She/They might/may/could (have)

....

He/She/They might/may/could be .... -ing

....

The way I see it ....

....

If you ask me ....

....

Judging by ....

It's (quite/very/more than) likely that

....

He/She is (quite/very/more than) likely to

....

In my view ....

As far as I can tell ....

....

My impression is ....

....

I get the impression that ....

....

The impression I get is that ....

....

I expect ....

He/She/They must (have) ....

....

He/She/They must be .... -ing

I assume ....

....

I suppose ....

It's hard to say, but ....

I've got a feeling that ....

....

I guess ....

I imagine ....

It would appear that ....

I suspect ....

Now check your answers to these questions.

TALKING ABOUT THE TOPIC

The three activities in Part 3 of the interview on page 94 require you to talk about jobs and work. To talk about this topic, certain words and phrases may be essential.

Employment

1 If you are given a job of higher rank in the same company, you ....

2 If you lose a job because you do it badly, you ....

3 If you lose a job because there is no longer a requirement for it and you receive a sum of money according to how long you worked there, you are ....

4 If you inform an employer in writing that you intend to leave a job, you ....

5 If you leave a job in protest or because you are dissatisfied, you ....

6 If you have no job, you are .... or .... work.

7 If you work independently for an employer or a number of employers, you are ....

8 If you depend on a job or type of work to survive financially, it is your ....

9 If you do a job that enables you to survive financially, you earn a ....

10 Jobs that require physical work, such as building, are .... jobs.

11 A job that requires practical work for which training is given, such as being a carpenter, is called a ....

12 A job such as being a doctor, lawyer, teacher, etc is called a ....

13 All the people in charge of a company are called the ....

14 The amount of work that you have to do is your ....

15 The time or date by which a piece of work must be finished is the .... for that work.

16 If you work for longer than your normal working hours, you do ....

17 If you have a lot of work that you haven't done yet but should have done by now, you have a .... of work.

18 When you stop working because you have reached a certain age, you ....

19 Sums of money taken off your salary, such as tax and national insurance, are called ....

20 All the people who work for a company or industry are called the ....

Now check your answers to these questions.

TEST FOUR

PAPER 1   READING COMPREHENSION   1 hour

SECTION A

In this section you must choose the word or phrase which best completes each sentence. Indicate the letter A, B, C, or D against the number of each item 1 to 25 for the word or phrase you choose.

1 I'm not .... your version of events but I think that you have interpreted them wrongly.

   A disputing   B disagreeing   C disapproving   D differing

2 He .... along the road, in no particular hurry to get there.

   A limped   B paced   C ambled   D stumbled

3 The real .... is not whether the scheme is possible or not but whether it's desirable or not.

   A question   B case   C factor   D topic

4 It isn't the funniest film I've ever seen but it is .... amusing.

   A softly   B modestly   C mildly   D barely

5 She was on her .... throughout the interview because she didn't want to say anything stupid.

   A defence   B lookout   C caution   D guard

6 When our original plan failed, we had to think of something to do ....

   A otherwise   B instead   C or else   D in place

7 Eventually he .... up the courage to ask for a pay rise.

   A plucked   B grabbed   C grasped   D snatched

8 All the arguments between the staff don't .... a good atmosphere in the office.

   A make for   B get at   C head for   D run into

9 It .... to be seen whether I've made the right decision or not.

   A remains   B continues   C stands   D keeps

10 I can't .... of any circumstances in which I would behave so dishonestly.

   A visualize   B dream   C picture   D conceive

11 We left early, in .... of traffic jams on the way there.

   A forethought   B foresight   C prospect   D anticipation

12 Before I agree to your suggestion, I'd like to know what I'm .... myself in for.

   A taking   B putting   C getting   D letting

13 It was such a funny sight that I couldn't keep a .... face.

   A plain   B smooth   C straight   D level

14 She's a good player and her chances of winning the tournament cannot be ....

    A discounted   B skipped   C ejected   D snubbed

15 Since they had stopped serving meals, we had to .... ourselves with sandwiches and coffee.

    A settle   B please   C reduce   D content

16 A committee was .... to get the project started.

    A composed   B formed   C associated   D compiled

17 .... that there is no perfect solution to the problem, I think that you've made the right decision.

    A To accept   B Truly   C Granted   D Taken

18 When she had made a number of bad decisions, people began to .... her judgement.

    A disbelieve   B suspect   C question   D wonder

19 .... there are no unforeseen delays, I'll see you at about 8.

    A In case   B Except for   C Presumed   D Supposing

20 What was it that .... you to change career so suddenly?

    A moved   B originated   C resulted   D drew

21 Occasionally serious crimes are committed there but they are .... incidents, not part of a widespread problem.

    A isolated   B solitary   C detached   D unique

22 With .... it's obvious that the policy was a mistake.

    A hindsight   B retrospect   C afterthought   D review

23 Here's my address, and if you're ever in my area, look me ....

    A out   B round   C on   D up

24 George .... to be an expert on the subject of international politics.

    A asserts   B alleges   C declares   D professes

25 The conversation ended .... when she got angry and put the phone down.

    A impulsively   B briefly   C shortly   D abruptly

Before you check your answers to this section of the test, go on to pages 99 and 100.

WORD SETS

The numbers of the exercises below refer to questions 1–4 of the test on page 97. In each exercise, choose from the list of words at the top which one best fits into each gap. All of the words are related in meaning.

1 | contradict   oppose   differ   disapprove   dispute   disagree   object |

   a My parents .... of me using bad language.

   b Though their views on politics ...., they get on well.

   c Players should not .... the referee's decisions.

   d The majority of local residents .... the plan.

   e I .... to her using my phone without asking me.

   f The versions of events given by the two witnesses .... each other completely.

   g It's his methods, not his aims, that I .... with.

2 | paced   crawled   stumbled   crept   limped   ambled   sprinted |

   a Following the injury to his leg, he .... for the rest of the game.

   b She .... on the steps but managed not to fall.

   c They .... around the park without a care in the world.

   d I .... for the bus but I wasn't quite quick enough.

   e He .... up and down the room, waiting anxiously for news.

   f We .... into the house as quietly as we could.

   g She .... across the floor on her hands and knees.

3 | question   point   theme   topic   aspect   case   factor |

   a The scandal is the main .... of conversation in the country at the moment.

   b In the .... of that incident, the circumstances were entirely different.

   c The money involved was a major .... in my decision to agree to the deal.

   d My main .... is that I don't think the idea will work.

   e The .... of whose fault it was never arose.

   f We discussed every .... of the problem thoroughly.

   g The way society has changed is a .... that runs through the whole novel.

4 | *weakly   narrowly   mildly   remotely   barely   softly   modestly* |

   a His income has improved .... in the last year.

   b She smiled .... but I could tell that she was still depressed.

   c I'm not .... interested in his personal problems.

   d They were .... defeated in an exciting game.

   e I'm not astonished but I am .... surprised.

   f It was a bad line and her voice was .... audible.

   g He's a shy, ... spoken man.

Now check your answers to these exercises. When you have done so, decide whether you wish to change any of your answers to questions 1–4 in the test.

Then check your answers to the test.

SECTION B

*In this section you will find after each of the passages a number of questions or unfinished statements about the passage, each with four suggested answers or ways of finishing. You must choose the one which you think fits best. Indicate the letter A, B, C, or D against the number of each item 26–40 for the answer you choose. Give **one answer only** to each question. Read each passage right through before choosing your answers.*

FIRST PASSAGE

In the early hours of the night it had rained and the iron gate that led to the gatekeepers' houses had rattled loose in the wind, and as it cringed and banged it disturbed Mrs O'Brien's spaniel where he lay on a mat in the dark, drafty hallway. Time and again he gave a muffled growl, padded about the hall, and scratched at the door. His uneasiness and the noise of the wind had
5   wakened Mrs O'Brien in the room above him, and she lay in bed wondering if she should go down and let him into the warm comfort of the kitchen. Beside her her husband was asleep, snoring loudly, unaware of her wakefulness or of the windows shaking in their heavy frames. The rain rattled like hailstones against the panes. How on earth anybody could sleep through that, she wondered – it was enough to waken the dead and there he was deep asleep as if it were a calm
10 summer night. What kind of a man was he! You'd think he'd be worrying about his journey to the Rock in the morning and his long six weeks away from her.
    The dog growled again, and throwing back the bedclothes she got up and groped on the table for the matchbox. She struck one match but it was a dead one, and she clicked her tongue in disapproval. She was never done telling Tom not to put his spent matches back into the box but he
15 never heeded her. It was tidy, he told her, but it was exasperating if she knew anything. She struck three before coming upon a good one, and in the spurt of flame she glanced at the alarm clock and saw that it was two hours after midnight. She slipped downstairs, lit the lamp and let the dog into the kitchen. She patted his head and he jumped on the sofa, thumped it loudly with his tail and curled up on a cushion.
20   On the floor, Tom's hampers lay ready for the morning, when the boatmen would come to row him out to the lighthouse to relieve young Frank Coady. She looked at the hampers with sharp calculation, wondering if she had packed everything he needed. She was always sure to forget something – boot polish or a pullover or a corkscrew or soap – and he was always sure to bring it up with her as soon as he stepped ashore for his two-weeks leave. She could never remember a
25 time when he arrived back without some complaint or other. But this time she was sure that she had forgotten nothing, for she had made a list and ticked each item off as she packed them into the cases. No, he wouldn't be able to launch any of his ill humour on her this time!

26 What did Mrs O'Brien notice when she woke up?

    A   The dog was at her door.
    B   The gate to the house collapsed.
    C   The dog was making a loud noise.
    D   The wind was blowing in strong gusts.

27 What did Mrs O'Brien think when she saw that her husband was still asleep?

    A   She was annoyed because she wanted him to attend to the dog.
    B   She envied his ability to sleep while she was disturbed.
    C   She felt that it reflected a lack of concern for her.
    D   She realized that he needed plenty of sleep that night.

28 What was the problem concerning matches?

    A   Tom unintentionally put spent matches back into the box.
    B   They disagreed about what to do with spent matches.
    C   Mrs O'Brien didn't know why Tom kept dead matches.
    D   They never had enough unused matches.

29 What was different about the trip that Tom was about to take?

    A   Everything he wanted had been packed for him.
    B   He wanted to take more with him than he usually took.
    C   He would be returning for two-weeks leave this time.
    D   His mood before leaving was better than usual.

30 Which of the following best sums up Mrs O'Brien and Tom's relationship?

    A   She was happier when he was away.
    B   He didn't want her to look after him.
    C   She found his moods unpredictable.
    D   He didn't show affection for her.

SECOND PASSAGE

Do you work with problem people? You know the type – the boss who is always moving the goal-posts, uncooperative colleagues, underlings who fail to do things as well as you do. If you are plagued by these or other problem types, perhaps you think the situation is beyond your control. If so, think again. A good starting point is to recognize that behaviour breeds behaviour, which is
5 one of those great truths that hasn't really dawned on a lot of people. Through your behaviour you may, quite unintentionally, be triggering a behaviour pattern in someone else that is for you a problem.

One of the commoner problem types is the authoritarian. Authoritarians talk too much and don't listen enough. They assume that people are basically lazy, can't be trusted and must not be
10 allowed to make their own decisions because they would get it wrong. Authoritarians expect unswerving obedience and for someone with ideas and initiative it can be very frustrating. Doing nothing is not a good idea – unless it suits you to have someone taking all the decisions and telling you what to do.

You can alter your perception of the problem by recognizing that authoritarian behaviour
15 indicates not strength but rather feelings of inadequacy. But there is little point in trying to persuade authoritarians to change, so try to modify the situation. Nobody is authoritarian all the time: sometimes they are extremely bossy, sometimes less so. The key lies in understanding what sort of situation triggers their authoritarian behaviour. It could be the risk of chaos, which authoritarians loathe. Or it might be a threat to or violation of a non-negotiable matter, or
20 insubordination by a junior. You will reduce the problem if you are compliant on the issues that are sacrosanct and non-negotiable, but otherwise assertive. A useful approach is to assume that it's all right to do things until told otherwise. This will give you some space for initiatives, and you can win their trust slowly – but make sure that any initiatives you take do not jeopardize the orderliness which the authoritarian holds so dear.

25 The defensive person is another problem type. Defensive people do not accept responsibility for their actions, and therefore never learn from their experience. Nothing is ever their fault; there is always a seemingly plausible explanation. The best way to tackle a defensive person is to choose a time when he has made a mistake and invite him to join you in analysing why it happened and what should be done to avoid it happening again. A softly-softly approach is essential to stop the
30 defensive barriers being raised. So start by asking for their advice, initially about what you should do differently, and then slowly turning it round to establish what they are going to do differently in future. This will provoke more defensiveness, but you must not let them off the hook. Just keep repeating your challenge and eventually they will accept responsibility for their part in the mistake. When they do, ease up on them. In this way they will learn that defensiveness doesn't pay.

31 What should people realize about 'problem people' in general?

   A Their behaviour results from personal ambition.
   B Their behaviour stems from a lack of clear purpose.
   C Their behaviour will get worse if it is not controlled.
   D Their behaviour is not necessarily a problem for others.

32 Which of the following is true of authoritarians, according to the writer?

   A They do their jobs less efficiently than they think they do.
   B They are a problem for everyone who has to work with them.
   C They are disguising their own lack of self-confidence.
   D They fear that other people are trying to get their jobs.

33 The writer advises that when dealing with authoritarians you should

   A try to make them realize that they are being unreasonable.
   B obey every order that they give to you without question.
   C try to discuss things with them when they are feeling tolerant.
   D challenge their attitude to people who show initiative.

34 When approaching defensive people, you should

   A express disbelief of the explanations they give.
   B suggest that you have made mistakes yourself.
   C accuse them of being to blame for something.
   D wait until they have made a particularly bad mistake.

35 The best way of solving the problem of defensive people is to

   A force them to admit that nobody else is to blame.
   B show them the advantages of admitting guilt.
   C prevent them from becoming defensive.
   D accept some of their denials of responsibility.

THIRD PASSAGE

I first met William Shawn thirty years ago. A telegram had summoned me – at the age of 23, a would-be writer – from my basement room in Greenwich village to the midtown Manhattan offices of the *New Yorker*. I had done some trial pieces for the magazine. Mr Shawn stood up to shake my hand as I entered his plainly furnished corner room. He was a small, rosy-cheeked man
5 in a dark three-piece suit. For 40 minutes, he quietly asked me about my upbringing, education and aspirations. Then he said: 'Well, Mr Bailey, I'm sorry' – and my heart sank; clearly the job wasn't to be mine. But he went on: 'I'm sorry, we don't have a spare office now on the 18th floor, where most of the reporters are. Would you mind one on the 16th?'

Over the years, Shawn's apologetic tone – his diffident, almost whisper of a voice – became
10 evident as camouflage for a man who had very firm notions of what he was doing and who was convinced that he alone could do it. He seemed hermetic; he never travelled far; he never flew in a plane. Even in summer, no air-conditioning on, he gave the impression of wearing a scarf. But behind this timidity lay an immensely determined curiosity about the world that his writers could put him in touch with. Unlike many editors, who often appear to compete with their staff, needing
15 to demonstrate greater knowledge and acquaintance, Shawn made a point of seeming almost ignorant. When I approached him on one occasion about making a journey the length of the Iron Curtain, he said: 'Yes – where exactly is the Iron Curtain, Mr Bailey?' He wanted to know all about it. And on the journey and while writing the piece, I had him in the back of my mind – my first, expectant reader.
20 Shawn was open to just about anything, yet had clear ideas about what the magazine would not do. His *New Yorker* was against the sensational, the sordid and the self-seeking. It eschewed topicality in favour of the oblique. It was 'writer-driven', at Shawn's behest. Writers, not editors, had the ideas. And – as in no other periodical in the world – writers were given the room to probe and worry out the depths of a subject, where truth may reside.
25 Shawn had a perfect sense of whether a writer was really excited about the project being proposed. If he sensed enthusiasm, even for an obscure subject, he would give the go-ahead. He had precise ideas about language – every comma, every semi-colon in the magazine was weighed by him, several times, before an issue went to press. Once in a rare while, in the margins, among Shawn's meticulous corrections and suggestions, all aimed at greater exactness, one would find a
30 word like 'wonderful' or 'beautiful'. I've never had such praise.

36 What surprised the writer when he had his interview with Shawn?

   A Shawn's apology to him.
   B The length of the questioning.
   C The fact that the job was on the 16th floor.
   D Shawn's physical appearance.

37 What was deceptive about Shawn?

   A He knew about subjects he pretended not to know about.
   B He tried to make people think he was less determined than he was.
   C He spoke in a way that disguised his strength of purpose.
   D He travelled little but knew about a great many places.

38 In what way did Shawn differ from other editors, according to the writer?

   A He was willing to accept that writers knew more than him.
   B He expected writers to produce articles that entertained him personally.

   C He lacked the knowledge that an editor ought to have.
   D He took a personal interest in what the writers were doing.

39 What was Shawn's attitude towards the *New Yorker*?

   A He had fixed ideas about what its content should be.
   B He thought it should contain only serious articles.
   C He thought that its writers should dictate its content.
   D He was determined that it should be up to date.

40 Which of the following opinions does the writer have of Shawn?

   A He was too fussy about grammar.
   B He didn't praise writers enough.
   C He was a good judge of writing.
   D He wasn't strict enough with writers.

Before you check your answers to this section of the test, go on to pages 105 and 106.

A DETAILED STUDY

The questions on these pages will help you to make sure that you have chosen the correct options for the questions on the second text, on page 103.

Question 31 *Look at the first paragraph of the text and answer these questions.*

1   In the context of the article, someone who keeps 'moving the goal-posts' is most likely to
    a   have no definite aims.
    b   cheat other people.
    c   change their instructions.

2   What is an 'underling'?
    a   an employee of a much lower rank
    b   a colleague who is incompetent
    c   a worker who wants promotion

3   What does the writer mean when he says 'think again'?
    a   You have not come to the right conclusion.
    b   You have not taken the situation seriously enough.
    c   You have not thought about the problem for long enough.

4   If you are 'triggering' something, you are
    a   making it worse.
    b   causing it.
    c   avoiding it.

Questions 32 and 33 *Look at the second and third paragraphs and answer these questions.*

1   Does the writer suggest that authoritarians are less competent than they think they are?

2   Which of the following is true of authoritarians, according to the writer?
    a   They are aware that there are rivals for their jobs.
    b   They have a low opinion of the efficiency of others.
    c   They disagree with the decisions of others.

3   What kind of people find authoritarians a problem?

4   If you have 'feelings of inadequacy', are these feelings about yourself or about other people?

5   If you say that there is 'little point' in doing something, you are suggesting that
    a   there is a possibility that it will work.
    b   it is not likely to work.

6   Are authoritarians more tolerant on some occasions than on others?

7   What is 'insubordination'?
    a   incompetence
    b   disobedience
    c   independence

8   If you are 'compliant', you
    a   reach a compromise.
    b   act obediently.
    c   question something.

9 Under what circumstances should you take initiatives, according to the writer?
 a when you have persuaded an authoritarian to trust you
 b when you can no longer tolerate an authoritarian's attitude
 c when no orders have been given about something

10 Which word in the paragraph means the opposite of 'chaos'?

Questions 34 and 35 *Look at the final paragraph and answer these questions.*

1 If something is 'plausible'
 a it sounds as if it might be true.
 b it is believed by people in general.
 c it cannot be disproved.

2 The writer says that you should talk to a defensive person when
 a you have just done something wrong.
 b a quiet moment is available.
 c they have just done something else wrong.

3 What should you tell a defensive person?
 a Their explanations for their mistakes are not good enough.
 b A mistake that they have made is completely their fault.
 c You have something in common with them.

4 In the context of the article, if you 'let them off the hook', you
 a let them reach their own conclusions.
 b stop putting pressure on them.
 c make them feel guilty.

5 If something 'doesn't pay', it
 a is of no benefit.
 b makes no difference.
 c is not believed.

Now check your answers to the questions on these pages. Then decide whether you wish to change any of the answers that you gave to the questions on the second text, on pages 102–103.

Then check your answers to this section of the test.

PAPER 2 COMPOSITION   2 hours

*Write **two only** of the composition exercises. Your answers must follow exactly the instructions given. Write in pen, not pencil. You are allowed to make alterations, but make sure that your work is clear and easy to read.*

1   Describe a celebration or festival that you have attended. (About 350 words)

2   'Travel broadens the mind.' Do you think this is true? (About 350 words)

3   'I couldn't believe my luck....' Write a story that begins or ends with these words. (About 350 words)

4   You have bought a piece of electrical equipment which is faulty. Write a letter of complaint to the shop from which you bought it. Your letter could cover the following points: (About 300 words)
    – the item, where and when you bought it and the cost
    – what the fault is
    – what action you have taken so far and the results of that
    – what you want the shop to do

Before you write your compositions, go on to pages 108 and 109.

PLANNING A COMPOSITION

One of the questions in Paper 2 requires you to do some **formal writing**. *You may be required to write a formal letter or a report, for example. You will normally be required to write a little less for this question than the others (300 instead of 350 words). However, to answer this question well, you will have to make sure that everything you include is relevant and that you use language appropriate for such formal writing.*

Look at question 4 on page 107 and then answer the following. This will help you to plan your composition for that question. It is advisable to practise each of the types of composition.

1 Decide which piece of electrical equipment your letter will concern.

....

2 Decide which fault or faults it has from the following. Add any others you prefer.

☐ it doesn't work at all

☐ it keeps breaking down

☐ it makes a terrible noise

☐ it makes a strange smell

☐ the instructions are impossible to understand

☐ it doesn't do something that it is supposed to do

☐ it isn't of the quality described in the advertisements or by the shop

....

....

....

....

....

....

3 Tick which of the following you have done so far. Add any others you wish.

☐ tried to repair it yourself

☐ written to the shop already

☐ checked the guarantee

☐ phoned the shop already

☐ checked the information given with it carefully

☐ visited the shop already

☐ used the item properly

....

....

4 Tick which of the following actions you would like the shop to take and add any others you wish.

☐ replace the item

☐ refund your money

☐ repair the item

☐ apologize

☐ collect the item

☐ explain why the problem has arisen

☐ explain how they will solve the problem

....

....

....

....

Now use this information to write your composition. Remember to make your points clearly and to follow the conventions of formal letter writing.

Then write one or more of the other compositions.

Now read through the following sample composition for question 4 on page 107.
When you have done so, answer the questions that follow it.

21, Forth Street
OXFORD OXD 1H3
30th June 1994

Sound and Stereo
20, Meadow Drive
Oxford OX2 1HP

Dear Sir,

I am writing to express my dissatisfaction with reference to the stereo I bought from your shop just a week ago. Indeed, I am afraid that the equipment was faulty on several counts, which I would really like to let you know.

Firstly, the turntable does not rotate as it should, so that I am totally unable to play my records on it. And considering that it was the main reason why I bought this particular stereo, I think that it is completely unacceptable.

On the other hand, the tape deck is functional. However, the play button on deck A came off, and in spite of the fact that it continues to work effectively, I am not willing to pay for shoddy workmanship.

I have already been to your shop to complain but I gained little satisfaction from your sale staff – besides they were not polite at all with me, which is a shame.

Consequently, I am writing this letter to you with the hope that you will be able to take necessary measures in either refunding my money or providing me with other equipment of the same or a different brand which, this time, would be fine.

If my desires are not fulfilled, I will be obliged to take further steps and even lead to court action, which I would really like to avoid.

I expect to hear from you concerning these matters and take my complaint very seriously.

I thank you in anticipation,

Yours faithfully,

JGSmith

1   Does the composition actually answer the question set or does it contain irrelevant parts, 'waffle' – writing that is simply intended to fill the space but does not really say anything – or 'padding' – writing that is repetitious in order to reach the required number of words?

2   Is the composition well-organized? Is it divided into paragraphs appropriately? Explain what each paragraph contains.

3   Are appropriate linking words and phrases used for connecting sentences and paragraphs? Give examples of some that are; if some are not, correct them.

4   Does it have a good range of appropriate vocabulary or is the vocabulary used mostly too simple? Give examples and correct any inappropriate or incorrect vocabulary.

5   Is there a good range of accurate structures forming sentences that are not very simple or are the structures used mostly too basic? Give examples and correct any incorrect structures or other mistakes.

6   Is the style appropriate for this type of composition?

Now check your assessment of and corrections to this sample composition.

PAPER 3   USE OF ENGLISH   2 hours

SECTION A

1 *Fill each of the numbered blanks in the passage with* **one** *suitable word.*

Although the great detective Sherlock Holmes is read in almost every language, his first appearance in print was a (1) .... than auspicious occasion. His creator, Conan Doyle, was a practising doctor when he wrote his first Sherlock Holmes story, *A Study in Scarlet*, (2) .... was rejected three times (3) .... a publisher agreed to pay the author £25 for the copyright. The story appeared in 1887 but neither (4).......................... nor its follow-up *The Sign of Four* (5) .... very much attention in the literary world.

Then, in 1891, Conan Doyle sent *A Scandal in Bohemia* to *The Strand* magazine. The story (6) .... in the July issue and Sherlock Holmes achieved fame at (7) .... This fame, (8) .... , grew to such an (9) .... that Doyle is reported to (10) .... said 'he takes my mind from better things', complaining that he would (11) .... spend his time writing more worthy historical novels. At one (12) .... he 'killed' Holmes but was forced by public outcry to restore him to life for a (13) .... series of adventures.

(14) .... it is over a century since the (15) .... enduring detective of all time first took (16) .... residence at 221b Baker Street, which never (17) .... existed, his fame lives (18) .... and many admirers of his ingenious (19) .... of deduction still write to him (20) .... that address.

2 *Finish each of the following sentences in such a way that it is as similar as possible in meaning to the sentence printed before it.*

Example: She said that he was a brilliant musician.
Answer: She described *him as a brilliant musician.*

a The audience were delighted by her performance.

She gave ....

b It is my impression that she's enjoying her new job a great deal.

She seems ....

c Just after solving one problem, I was faced with another.

Hardly ....

d According to the evidence, the crimes seemed to have been committed by the same person.

The evidence suggested ....

e Jack loses his temper easily.

It doesn't ....

f The defence contributed enormously to the team's success.

The defence made ....

g People at work gossip about him, which he doesn't like.

He doesn't like ....

h Although it was expected that he would stand for election, he decided not to.

Contrary ....

3 *Fill each of the blanks with a suitable word or phrase.*
Example: She had difficulty *making up her* mind which one to buy.

a The service .... we had paid was not provided.

b Boring .... to do it, it's a job that has to be done.

c He was given the job on .... he was the best candidate and not for

any other reason.

d I know you were irritated by him but you .... your feelings so

obvious!

e I knew my speech so well that I was able to give it .... look at my

notes at all.

f Since there was no other way of getting home, we had no .... walk.

4 *For each of the sentences below, write a new sentence* **as similar as possible in meaning to the original sentence**, *but using the word given. This word* **must not be altered** *in any way.*

Example: She paid no attention to his warning
            notice
Answer: *She took no notice of his warning.*

a Getting a specialized qualification will benefit you.
interests

....

b When they said that they wouldn't give me my money back I was furious.
refusal

....

c It's whether we'll be able to afford it or not that I'm not sure about.
what

....

d The latest sales figures are better than the previous ones.
improvement

....

e Everyone who comes to this city notices the beauty of its architecture.
fails

....

f Recent research has changed theories about the causes of the disease.
light

....

g I was reluctant to make a promise to buy more goods from the same company.
commit

....

h Payment will be made when the order is received.
receipt

....

Before you check your answers to this section of the test, go on to pages 113 and 114.

FILL IN THE MISSING PHRASE

Look again at question 3 of this test on page 111, and then decide which one of the four options given below for each question there correctly fills each gap. You may wish to change some of the answers you gave in the test as you do this. However, if an answer that you gave there is not among the choices here, this does not necessarily mean that it is wrong.

a **1** that
    2 for it
    3 which
    4 for which

b **1** is it
    2 though it is
    3 so it is
    4 it may be

c **1** the grounds that
    2 account of
    3 condition that
    4 the conclusion of

d **1** mustn't have made
    2 mustn't have let
    3 shouldn't have let
    4 shouldn't have made

e **1** so as not to
    2 without having to
    3 so that I didn't
    4 without needing

f **1** possibility than to
    2 way apart from
    3 choice but to
    4 option for

Now check your answers to these questions and to question 3 of the test on page 111.

Then go on to page 114.

RE-WRITE THE SENTENCES

Look again at question 4 of this test on page 112, and then decide which one of the four choices given below for each question there is correct and has the same meaning as the given sentences. You may wish to change some of the answers you gave in the test as you do so. However, if the answer that you gave there is not among the choices here, this does not necessarily mean that it is wrong.

a 1 Your interests are to get a specialized qualification.
   2 It interests you to get a specialized qualification.
   3 It is in your interests to get a specialized qualification.
   4 Your interests are getting a specialized qualification.

b 1 I was furious with their refusal to give me my money back.
   2 Their refusal to give me my money back made me furious.
   3 Their refusal of giving me my money back had me furious.
   4 I was furious at their refusal of giving me my money back.

c 1 What I'm not sure about it is whether we'll be able to afford it or not.
   2 Whether we'll be able to afford it or not it's what I'm not sure about.
   3 The thing what I'm not sure about is whether we'll be able to afford it or not.
   4 What I'm not sure about is whether we'll be able to afford it or not.

d 1 The latest sales figures are an improvement on the previous ones.
   2 There is improvement in the latest sales figures from the previous ones.
   3 The latest sales figures make an improvement to the previous ones.
   4 The improvement of the latest sales figures on the previous ones is there.

e 1 It is nobody who comes to this city who fails to notice the beauty of its architecture.
   2 Nobody fails to notice the beauty of its architecture who comes to this city.
   3 Nobody who comes to this city fails to notice the beauty of its architecture.
   4 There is nobody comes to this city and fails to notice the beauty of its architecture.

f 1 The light of recent research has changed theories about the causes of the disease.
   2 Recent research has put new light on the causes of the disease.
   3 Theories about the causes of the disease have changed in the light of recent research.
   4 Theories about the causes of the disease have changed with light from recent research.

g 1 I was reluctant to commit that I buy more goods from the company.
   2 I was reluctant to commit to buy more goods from the same company.
   3 I was reluctant to commit buying more goods from the same company.
   4 I was reluctant to commit myself to buying more goods from the same company.

h 1 With receipt of the order, payment will be made.
   2 Payment will be made at the order receipt.
   3 Payment will be made on receipt of the order.
   4 There will be payment once the receipt of the order.

Now check your answers to these questions and to question 4 of the test on page 112.

Then check your answers to questions 1 and 2 of the test on pages 110 and 111.

SECTION B

Read the following passage, then answer the questions which follow it.

The Money Game

I recently saw one of the world's most famous women tennis players reel with shock at a
linesman's call. She stopped play, walked over to her chair, gathered the five or six racquets that
are now required to play one game of tennis, tucked them under her arm and, as she walked off
the court, she poked a forefinger up at the umpire in what the spectators applauded as an obscene
5 gesture. She hadn't quit. She was just biding her time, and temper, till the officials came running,
or kneeling, begging her to return. Which, about three minutes later, she graciously consented to
do, as thousands of spectators came to their feet to pay tribute to an act of bravery in giving the
umpire his come-uppance. The umpire didn't fume or shout. He blushed. He cowered. He knew
he had behaved badly. He seemed truly sorry. And the crowd cheered their heroine again and
10 forgave him.
  Money has got to be the reason, a primary reason anyway, why the insulted umpire sent his
officials to beg the tennis star to return to the court and go on with the game. She earns a fortune.
The fans pay to subsidize that fortune. The fans come not merely to see a game superlatively
played, they have learned to expect high jinks and low jinks as part of the show. Any sports
15 promoter will tell you that a sports crowd spurned is a dangerous social animal. In other words,
the officials, who sometimes seem so cowed, must have in mind the maintenance of public order,
which has come to have little to do with public courtesy.
  I may seem to have been reacting so far in the old man's standard fashion to the disappearance
of amateurism in first-class sport. And, of course, it is true that much of the genteel air of sports
20 such as tennis in the old days has been drowned out by the roar of the cash register. But I must say
that that genteelism, with its pleasant manners, was due to the comfortable fact that most players
were upper-middle-class offspring who didn't have to work for a living. But plainly – it ought to
be plain today – it is not only absurd, it is unjust, to expect people who earn a living at a game to
have the same nonchalant code of behaviour as the loitering heirs of company directors who could
25 afford to travel to France or Britain or America to play a game, while professionals, footballers
being the worst example, were being paid at the going rate of plumbers' assistants. I applaud the
fact that games can now be a career, and a profitable one, and that the expert should be considered
like any other star entertainer and be paid accordingly.
  But there has to come a point where the impulse to take up a game is often the impulse to earn
30 a million dollars and, so far, in the rush of a whole generation to make the million, there has not
yet evolved a decent ethic that can discipline the game for the audience that has its mind more on
the game than the million. A million, I suggest, is some sort of turning point in the career, and too
often the character, of the very young. A twenty-year-old who earns a million dollars, or pounds,
is encouraged by the media to see himself or herself as a movie star entitled to adoration, the
35 pamperings of luxury and no questions asked about behaviour on or off the course, the rink, the
court or the field. I suppose the television satellite has a lot to do with it. The best players know
that, by virtue of world-wide exposure, the organizers will take in many millions, so they don't
pause for long before saying, 'Some of those millions should be mine.' And if the difference
between winning a hundred thousand and fifty thousand turns on a linesman's call, it takes
40 considerable character not to blow up. I heard a young fan say it would take a superman.
  Well, it doesn't take a superman. It takes simply a type of human being who was taught when
young the definition of a brat.

a What does the writer seem to think of the number of racquets the player had?

....

b What did the player expect when she left the court?

....

c Why is the writer's use of the word 'graciously' (line 6) ironical?

....

....

d Why did the crowd applaud the player when she returned?

....

....

e In your own words, explain how the umpire reacted when the player returned and why he reacted in this way.

....

....

f According to the writer, what do spectators at sports events want to see?

....

....

g Why don't sports officials treat badly-behaved players more severely, according to the writer?

....

h Why were players in the past better behaved than those of today?

....

....

i What is meant by 'the loitering heirs of company directors'? (line 24)

....

....

j What were footballers 'the worst example' of? (line 26)

....

k What does the writer mean by 'a decent ethic'? (line 31)

....

l How do the sports stars of today expect to be treated, according to the writer?

....

....

....

....

m How have the top players reacted to the arrival of satellite television?

....

....

....

n When is it difficult for a sports star 'not to blow up' (line 40) and why?

....

....

....

o In a paragraph of 70–90 words, summarize what the writer thinks is wrong with sport today.

....

....

....

....

....

....

....

....

....

....

Before you check your answers to this section of the test, go on to pages 118 and 119.

For general guidance on answering the questions for this part of the test, see Answering the Questions – General Notes on page 28.

A DETAILED STUDY

(see page 28 for guidance on this type of question)

Look at question a

What does the writer say about the number of racquets used by players?

....

....

Look at question b

Had the player decided to take no further part in the match?

....

Look at question d

If someone is given their 'come-uppance', they
a   receive forgiveness
b   are treated respectfully
c   deserve to suffer
d   are obeyed

....

Look at question g

What might happen if sports officials were more strict with players, according to the writer?

....

....

Look at question h

What **two** pieces of information about the players of the past does the writer give?

A...

....

B...

....

Look at question l

Tick which of the following today's sports stars want, according to the writer.

☐ 1   privacy in their private lives

☐ 2   worship from the public

☐ 3   freedom to be ill-mannered

☐ 4   enormous comfort in their personal lives

☐ 5   sympathy because of their youth

☐ 6   large sums of money for doing little

EXPLAIN THE MEANING

(see page 56 for guidance on this type of question)

Look at question c

If someone agrees to do something 'graciously', they agree to do it
a   pleasantly
b   elegantly
c   gratefully
d   sympathetically

....

Look at question i

What, in the context, is 'loitering' most likely to mean?
a   enjoying wealth
b   behaving pleasantly
c   living aimlessly
d   feeling superior

....

EXPLAIN THE REFERENCE

(see page 56 for guidance on this type of question)

Look at question j

> Which of the following is said to be true of footballers of the past?
> **a** They were dissatisfied.
> **b** They travelled a lot.
> **c** They were poorly paid.
> **d** They behaved badly.

Look at question n

> What is said to cause a player to 'blow up'?
> **a** losing a game
> **b** not being paid enough
> **c** officials' decisions
> **d** lack of respect

Now check your answers to these questions. When you have done so, decide whether you wish to change any of the answers you gave in the test. If you have phrased anything you wrote in the test differently from the choices given on these pages, this does not necessarily mean that you have answered incorrectly in the test. Then check your answers to questions a–n of the test on pages 115–117.

WRITING A SUMMARY

For general guidance, see Writing a Summary – General Notes on page 29.

Read this summary for this test and answer the questions that follow it.

> The author is very critical of the sports stars behaviour nowadays. He believes that large amounts of money involved in the game have spoilt them and make them convinced that they are entitled of adoration. He proposes a decent ethic in order to discipline the game. However, he points out that the main problem of the sports stars refers to their backgroung; they were not taught when young what a bad behaviour is.

1 Is anything irrelevant included or anything relevant not included? If so, what?

2 Are there any language mistakes? Correct any that you think there are.

3 Has any of the passage simply been copied in the summary? If so, what? Is the summary too short, too long or the right length?

Now look again at your summary on page 117 and decide whether you wish to change anything.

Then check your marks for your summary and the assessment of this sample summary.

PAPER 4   LISTENING COMPREHENSION   about 30 mins

PART ONE

You will hear an extract from a radio programme about Boots the Chemist, a chain of shops in Britain.
For questions 1–10, *answer each of the questions below.*

You will hear the piece twice.

What did Boots originally sell?   **1** ....

What did Jesse Boot start to sell when he took over?   **2** ....

What did he employ someone to do?   **3** ....

What did he have at the back of the shops?   **4** ....

What else did Boots sell at that time?   **5** ....

What were readers not supposed to do with some books?   **6** ....

What did books that might offend people have on them?   **7** ....

What were the two sides of the business?   **8** ....   **9** ....

What was John Boot's position?   **10** ....

PART TWO

You will hear an extract from a radio programme about memory.
For questions 11–20, *write YES in the boxes next to those views that are expressed in the discussion, and NO in the boxes next to those views which are not expressed.*

You will hear the piece twice.

11 Women and men remember different things about the same events.   ☐

12 Men remember things like birthdays as well as women do.   ☐

13 Women remember disagreements more clearly than men do.   ☐

14 It is possible to generalize about the kinds of things people are likely to remember.   ☐

15 The fact that women have stronger feelings than men affects their memories.   ☐

16 A good memory can spoil a relationship.   ☐

17 Differences of opinion about the past are a waste of time.   ☐

18 Disagreements about the past can change the way people remember things.   ☐

19 Techniques for improving memory only work well for remembering things that happen to you personally.   ☐

20 Few people attempt to remember all the details of what happens in their lives.   ☐

PART THREE

You will hear an extract from a programme about publicity for new films.
For questions 21–25, *choose the most appropriate answer, A, B, C, or D and write your choice in the box provided below each question.*

You will hear the piece twice.

21 What has the Director of Advertising and Publicity discovered?

   A He sometimes has to change the publicity he had prepared.
   B Films made for children are often more popular with adults.
   C Films can be more popular with children than he had expected.
   D Action movies are often more popular than he expected.

Answer:

22 What do film companies currently believe about spending money on publicity?

   A They get a lot of publicity without spending any money.
   B Spending money on publicity is likely to lead to good reviews.
   C Too much money is spent on giving publicity material away.
   D More money should be spent on publicity in the media.

Answer:

23 What is the attitude of film companies towards radio stations?

   A They believe they need incentives for mentioning films.
   B They think they demand too many free goods.
   C They expect them to review films in exchange for goods.
   D They think they are of little use in promoting films.

Answer:

24 When journalists are dealing with film companies, they

   A are told what they can ask in interviews with the stars.
   B treat all film publicists with great suspicion.
   C can choose not to write about the film at all.
   D are not allowed to accept presents from film publicists.

Answer:

25 Jon Anderson thinks that bad reviews of a film

   A can deter a significant number of people from seeing it.
   B may reflect the ignorance of the critics who write them.
   C may have no effect on the number of people who go to see it.
   D can sometimes be more useful than good reviews.

Answer:

PART FOUR

You will hear an interview about things that are named after real people.
For questions 26–35, write the first letter of the correct person's name or names in the space or spaces next to each question.

You will hear the piece twice.

G	Gusset
C	Coffin
K	Ketchup
T	Trowser
P	Pocket
W	Walkman

Which of the people mentioned:

invented something considered ridiculous at first? **26** ☐

27 ☐

claimed that their invention gave value for money? **28** ☐

invented something that was too big to succeed? **29** ☐

gave their name to something invented by someone else? **30** ☐

became rich as a result of their invention? **31** ☐

invented something that already existed in a different form? **32** ☐

33 ☐

had been unsuccessful at other things? **34** ☐

had an idea that could not be carried out at the time? **35** ☐

Before you check your answers to this Paper, go on to pages 123 and 124.

FACTS AND INFORMATION

Some of the pieces in the listening test require you to understand and identify particular facts and pieces of information. Questions on these may come in a variety of forms – you may be required to fill in missing details in notes, tables or incomplete sentences or phrases with a word or short phrase; you may be given multiple-choice questions; or you may be required to tick boxes, for example, to match information or to identify which picture shows something that is described.

Listen again to Part 4 of the test on page 122, and put a tick (✔) next to those things that are stated about each of the people. This will give you further practice in answering questions of this type, and enable you to check the answers that you gave in the test.

Gusset:

A She added something to existing clothing. ☐

B A whole item of clothing was named after her. ☐

C Her idea did not catch on at first. ☐

D She created a larger piece of clothing. ☐

E Her invention was attractive because it was cheap. ☐

Coffin:

A He originated burial in boxes. ☐

B His invention was commercially successful. ☐

C Others had already had his idea. ☐

D He created something in a different material from the usual one. ☐

E His invention did not become popular for some time. ☐

Ketchup:

A He had attempted other ventures in the past. ☐

B The product named after him became commercially successful. ☐

C He did not invent the product named after him. ☐

D He gave his name to a product that was already widely sold. ☐

E He had previously invented unsuccessful products. ☐

Trowser:

A His invention was longer than what people wore at the time. ☐

B People laughed at his invention at first. ☐

C His idea came from someone with a similar name. ☐

D He made a lot of money from his invention. ☐

E He drew attention to the financial advantages of his product. ☐

Pocket:

A People called him a fool for his idea. ☐

B He was not the first to have his idea. ☐

C His invention was initially considered too big. ☐

D He advertised his product successfully. ☐

E People realized that his invention was useful. ☐

Walkman:

A He improved on something that already existed. ☐

B His idea was too advanced at the time. ☐

C He had already invented other things. ☐

D His idea was laughed at at the time. ☐

E The product is now smaller than the one he invented. ☐

Now check your answers to the questions on these pages. When you have done so, decide whether you wish to change any of the answers you gave in Part 4 of the test on page 122.

Then check your answers to Part 4 of the test and then to Parts 1, 2, and 3 on pages 120–121.

PAPER 5　INTERVIEW

1　*Look at one or more of these photographs and answer the questions that follow them.*

What's happening in each picture?
Describe the people. What feelings do they appear to have?
Where do you think each picture was taken?

Which of the places would you prefer to be? Why? Why not the others?
What is the attraction of these places to people who go there?
What unattractive aspects do these places have?
Are these leisure activities popular in your country? Give details.

2 *Read one or more of these passages and then answer the questions that follow them.*

a Concerts – at least for the big stars – have also become far more complex. Computer and video technologies have been harnassed so that audiences can both see and hear what is happening on stage. Although the price of tickets for the big concerts often seems high, rising costs mean that it is difficult for artists to make money on tour. Most bands make their profits from the merchandising of souvenirs, such as T-shirts and posters, rather than from ticket sales.

b Every summer theme parks, those giant fun farms, open their doors to many thousands of thrill-and-spill seekers, who are variously bounced, dropped, swirled round and round and turned upside-down before being packed off home in their cars. Most of the big parks try to strike a balance between the heart-stopping and the heart-warming, from terror rides to multi-coloured water fountains.

c It was a magnificent game of football; it had everything, not just class and pace and action but persistent bloody-minded guts as well. And of course, a really cracking goal. Applause rang out round the whole of the magnificent arena, pure and wholly merited by both sides. In the centre circle, players from both sides shook hands, put arms round each other's shoulders, and exchanged congratulations on the game.

Where do you think each passage is taken from?
What is the purpose of each passage?
What views are expressed in each of them?

3 *Do one or more of these tasks. If you are working with others, discuss them together.*

a 'It's essential to be able to relax.'
Do you find it easy or difficult to relax?
What do you do to relax? How does it relax you?
In what ways does modern life make it easy/difficult for people to relax?
Do you think that people in your country find it easier/more difficult than people in other countries to relax? Explain.

b GET A HOBBY!

Do you do any of these? What do you find enjoyable about it?
Explain one of these hobbies to someone who knows nothing about it.
Do you have any other hobbies? Explain it to someone who knows nothing about it.
Is there a hobby you'd like to take up? What appeals to you about it? Why haven't you taken it up yet?

c *Look at the following list of leisure activities:*
* going to the theatre
* going to a rock concert
* reading a book
* visiting an art gallery or museum
* doing a sport
* going round a market
* going to an opera

Choose one or more of these that you have done and describe the experience/event.
Why did/didn't you enjoy it?
Put them into the order in which you prefer them. What kind of each one that you like do you prefer?
Are there any others not on the list that you like? Give details.
What opportunities do you have to do the things on the list where you live?

TALKING ABOUT PASSAGES

When you are talking about passages, you may be asked to say what you think they come from, what you think their purposes are and what opinions are given in them. There will be some evidence in each of the passages that will enable you to draw conclusions about these.

Look again at the three passages on page 126 and answer these questions about them, alone or with a partner.

1 Which of the three passages has probably been taken from a brochure?

2 What about the passage in general has led you to that conclusion?

3 What does the writer of that passage particularly emphasize? Give examples of words or phrases used to emphasize this.

4 Which of the three passages is entirely factual?

5 What is the main topic of that passage?

6 What results does the writer describe?

7 Where does the passage you have not so far chosen seem likely to have come from?

8 What is the writer of that passage trying to convey?

9 What opinions of the people described does the writer have? Give evidence from the passage.

Now check your answers to these questions.

TALKING ABOUT THE TOPIC

The three activities in Part 3 of the interview on page 126 require you to talk about entertainment and leisure. To talk about this topic, certain words and phrases may be essential.

Entertainment and leisure

1 The people who go to a concert, play or film are called the ...

2 The people who go to a sports event are called the ...

3 A pop or rock group is also called a ...

4 If a large group of people express praise for a performer or at a sports event by making a sound with their voices, they ...

5 If a large group of people express praise for a performer or at a sports event by hitting their hands together repeatedly, they ...

6 A large group of people playing classical music is called an ...

7 If a large group of people express disapproval of a performer or at a sports event by making a sound with their voices, they ...

8 The break in the middle of a play or film is called the ...

9 The story of a book is called the ...

10 Anything that can be seen at an exhibition or at a museum is called an ...

11 The fictional people in a novel, play or film are called the ...

12 A book that has been bought by an enormous number of people is called a ...

13 The place where you buy tickets for a film or play is called the ...

14 A play, film or record that is very successful is called a ...

15 If a film has a translation at the bottom of the screen, it has ...

16 If a book, film or play is supposed to take place somewhere, it is ... in that place.

17 The most important person in a play, book or film is called the ... character.

18 Each separate part of a film is called a ...

Now check your answers to these questions.

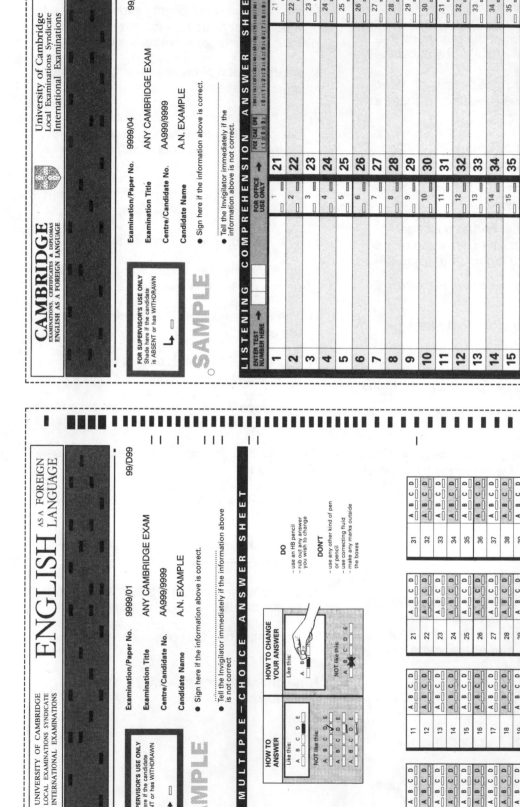

KEY AND EXPLANATION

TEST ONE

p 6–7 PAPER 1 SECTION A

Note that all explanations in this part refer to the meaning or use of each option most closely related to the question, not necessarily to the only meaning or use of these options.

One mark per question (Total: 25)

*For questions 1–4, see also the questions in **Further Practice and Guidance** on pages 8–9.*

1 **B** *LOOK OUT!* In this type of question, all the choices are similar or related in meaning but only one can be used to form the collocation required (the others cannot be used after *power*).

2 **D** *LOOK OUT!* Again, all the choices are similar or related in meaning but only one fits the structure of the sentence (only *unsuited* can be followed by *to-ing*).

3 **C** *LOOK OUT!* The choices are all related to one thing (money) but only one is suitable in the context **and** fits grammatically (*refunds* would be possible – *refund* is not an uncountable noun, whereas *compensation* is).

4 **C** *LOOK OUT!* Again, the choices are all related to one thing (making negative statements) but only one fits the context and is grammatically correct (*reject* could fit the meaning but it is followed by an object, not an infinitive).

5 **B**: If you **grow in confidence**, your confidence increases.
A: If your *confidence rises*, it increases.
C: If you *advance in* knowledge or ability, you increase it.
D: If *something lifts* you, it makes you feel happier when you are feeling unhappy.

6 **B**: If you **envisage doing** something, you imagine or predict that you will do it or that it will happen.
A/C: You can *predict/forecast something* or *predict/forecast that* something will happen, but *predict* and *forecast* are not followed by *-ing*.
D: You can *suppose that* something will happen, but *suppose* is not followed by *-ing*.

7 **D**: **Ample** is more than enough of something.
A: A *spacious room/flat*, etc is one that is large inside.
B: A *lavish party/place*, etc is one on which a lot of money has been spent.
C: An *extensive period of time* is a long one.

8 **B**: The **symptoms** of an illness are the signs that you have it.
A: The *traces* of something are the things left behind that show that it

was there or happened there (*the traces of an ancient civilization*).
C: *Emblems* are objects or designs that symbolize something such as an organization (*the club emblem*).
D: *Tokens* are objects or actions that are meant to indicate feelings (*give a present as a token of thanks*).

9 **A**: If you **cease to do** something, you stop doing it.
B: If you *discontinue something*, you stop doing it (*discontinue a bus service*).
C: If you *terminate something*, you make it end (*terminate a conversation abruptly*).
D: If something *halts something*, it causes it to stop (*strikes halting production*).

10 **D**: If you **shed tears**, you cry.
A: If you *pour a liquid*, you transfer it from one container to another (*pour wine into a glass*).
B: If *a liquid leaks*, small amounts of it come through or out of something because there is a hole in it (*the roof leaks*).
C: If you *spill a liquid*, you accidentally cause it to come out of its container (*spill a drink by knocking it with your elbow*).

11 **D**: If you are **intent on doing** something, you are very determined to do it.
A: If you are *willing to do* something, you don't mind doing it (*be willing to work hard*).
B: If you are *desperate to do* something, you want or need to do it very much (*be desperate to find a job*).
C: If you are *eager to do* something, you would very much like to do it (*be eager to impress*).

12 **A**: **Beyond doing** something = in addition to doing it, as a further action.
B: *Further to something/doing something* = as the next action following in addition to it (*Further to our recent meeting, I am writing ...*).
C: *Over and above something* = in addition to it (*expenses over and above the usual ones*).
D: *Beside* = next to. *Besides* = in addition to (*Besides working all day, she also has a job in the evening*).

13 **B**: **While** = although it is true that ... in this context.
A/C: *Even so/Nevertheless* = in spite of that (*I was ill but I went even so/nevertheless*).
D: *Whereas* = although when contrasting two facts (*You're tolerant, whereas I'm impatient*).

14 **B**: If something **gives rise to** something, it causes or produces it.
A: If there are *grounds for* something, there are good reasons for it (*grounds for suspicion*).
C: If one thing is *the cause of* another, it is the reason for it (*the causes of an accident*).

D: If one thing *happens as a consequence of* another, it happens as a result of it (*sales falling as a consequence of prices rising*).

15 **D**: **As to** = with regard to.
A: *As for* = in the case of (*As for me, I couldn't care less what happens*).
B: *As with* = in the same way as (*As with all such cases, there is no easy solution*).
C: *As of* = from the date of (*I will be in Italy as of the 13th*).

16 **A**: If you **splash** something, you make it wet by hitting it with separate drops of liquid.
B: If you *scatter* solid things, you put them in different places in an area (*scatter cushions around a room*).
C: If you *squirt* something, you cause it to come quickly out of its container by squeezing the container (*squirt toothpaste out of a tube*).
D: If you *sprinkle* something, you cause small amounts of it to go over an area (*sprinkle herbs over vegetables*).

17 **C**: If something has little **relevance to** something, it doesn't have much connection with it.
A: If you have little *concern for* something, you don't care about it much (*show little concern for the feelings of others*).
B: If something is *in accordance with* something, it follows or conforms to it (*act in accordance with the rules*).
D: If you have little *involvement in* something, you don't take much part in it (*have little involvement in a decision*).

18 **C**: If something **distracts you from doing** something, it makes it impossible for you to concentrate on it.
A: If something *disrupts something*, it causes it to stop functioning or proceeding properly (*An accident has disrupted train services*).
B: If someone *disturbs someone*, they make it impossible for them to continue doing something (*Don't disturb him while he's asleep*).
D: If someone *disperses* people, they make them move away in different directions (*Police dispersed the demonstrators*).

19 **A**: If something **puts you off something/doing something,** it makes you not want to do it or repeat it.
B: If *something puts you out*, it is inconvenient for you (*Don't put yourself out to help me*).
C: If you *put something away*, you put it into the place where it is usually kept (*put your clothes away*).
D: If you put *someone through something*, you cause them to suffer an unpleasant experience (*put your parents through a lot of worry*).

20 **D**: If you **take something out on someone**, you make them suffer because you feel angry or upset about something.

A: If you *let something out*, you reveal something secret or private (*let out an embarrassing secret*).

B: If you *put something out*, you publish a book or magazine, or you release a record or film.

C: If you *get something out* of a place, you remove it from that place (*get some money out of your pocket*).

21 A: If you **set an example** to someone, you behave in a way that they should follow because it is the right way to behave.

B: If you *give someone an example of something*, you tell them something that illustrates it (*Give me an example of how this word is used*).

C: If you *make an example of someone*, you punish them in order to discourage others from doing the same bad thing they did (*The judge decided to make an example of him and gave him a long sentence*).

D: If you *lay the blame for something on someone*, you say that they are responsible for it (*lay the blame for an accident on the driver*).

22 C: **Crumbs** are very small pieces of bread, cake or biscuit.

A: *Grains* are small pieces of wheat, rice, sand, salt, etc.

B: *Drops* are small amounts of liquid (*drops of rain*).

D: *Shreds* are small pieces of something that has been torn or cut (*tear a piece of paper into shreds*).

23 C: A **firm** agreement, arrangement, etc is one that has been definitely fixed.

A: A *hard rule* is one to which there are or can be no exceptions.

B: If something is *stable*, it is firmly established and unlikely to change suddenly (*a stable relationship/ income/ government*).

D: If something is *settled*, it is unlikely to keep changing (*have a settled life after years of moving from place to place*).

24 C: If you **welcome** something, you react to it with pleasure because it is something you want.

A: If you *greet something with something*, you react to it in that way (*greet a suggestion with enthusiasm*).

B: If you *rejoice*, you show how pleased you are by something and celebrate it (*crowds rejoicing after their team's victory*).

D: If you *cheer*, you react to something by making a noise that expresses pleasure or approval (*The audience cheered when she came on stage*).

25 A: If you **get round to doing** something, you eventually find the time to do it.

B: If you *come round to something*, you are finally persuaded to agree with or accept it (*come round to a view*).

C: If you *go round to a place*, you visit a place that is not far away (*go round to a friend's house*).

D: If you *turn round*, you move so that you are facing the opposite direction.

FURTHER PRACTICE AND GUIDANCE

p 8–9 PAPER 1 SECTION A

1 **a strife**: A period of *strife* is one when there is considerable conflict between people.

b row: If a *row* breaks out, people start to argue with each other angrily.

c competition: If people are in *competition for* something, they are all trying to get it but not all of them can have it.

d rivalry: If there is *rivalry* between people, they compete against each other, with each wanting to do better than the other.

e struggle: A *struggle for* power, control, supremacy, etc is a situation in which people are fighting against each other (not necessarily physically) in an attempt to gain power, etc for themselves.

f confrontation: A *confrontation* is a situation in which people who are in disagreement face and oppose each other.

g controversy: If something *causes controversy*, it causes argument among a group of people.

2 **a unfit**: If something is *unfit for* a purpose, it is of such poor quality that it cannot serve that purpose without causing harm.

b inapt: If a remark or action is *inapt*, it is inappropriate in the circumstances.

c incongruous: If something looks *incongruous*, its appearance does not fit in with the rest of what is there.

d inconvenient: If something is *inconvenient for* someone, it is at a time or in a place that doesn't suit them because it causes them problems.

e wrong: If something is *wrong for* someone, it does not suit their personality.

f unsuited: If something is *unsuited to* something, it is not of the right type for it.

g incompatible: If one thing is *incompatible with* another, it cannot exist together with it because it is so different.

3 **a proceeds**: The *proceeds of* an event or collection are the amount of money raised by it, usually for a certain purpose.

b refunds: A *refund* is money given back to someone because they didn't receive something they paid for, or because what they paid for was not acceptable.

c rewards: A *reward* is money offered or paid to someone who helps to solve a crime.

d compensation: *Compensation* is money paid to someone because something they suffered was another person's fault.

e bonuses: A *bonus* is extra money paid to an employee because they have done particularly well.

f receipts: *Receipts* are the amount of money received by an organization, particularly from the public paying for entrance.

g subsidies: A *subsidy* is money paid by a government to support something, or enable it to continue.

4 **a declined**: If you *decline to do* something, you politely refuse to do it.

b disowned: If you *disown* something, you say that you don't wish to be associated with it.

c denied: If you *deny doing* something, you say that you did not do it when accused of doing it.

d rejected: If you *reject* something, you say that you don't accept or agree with it at all.

e dissented: If you *dissent from* something, you say that you don't agree with it, even though others do.

f defied: If you *defy* someone, you refuse to obey them.

g retracted: If you *retract* something you have said, you say that you now believe that it was wrong and you were wrong to say it.

p 10–14 PAPER 1 SECTION B

Two marks per question (Total: 30)

First Passage

26 C: They were *likely to swoop at any time* (line 4) so employees never knew when they would appear and they could dismiss people for one small offence (line 4–6).

A: *hollow laughter* (line 3-4) is false laughter.

B: *There might be a plain-clothes inspector* (line 7-8) suggests that not all of them were in ordinary clothes, some were in uniform.

D: They might dismiss someone *with twenty years' service* (line 4–5), but there is no suggestion that they were particularly suspicious of older employees (they seem to have been suspicious of all employees).

27 D: He couldn't collect any fares (line 9) because it was so *jammed* (crowded) (line 13) in the bus that his feet *weren't touching the floor* (line 13).

A: He had difficulty reaching the *bell-push* (electric bell button) to signal to the driver to close the doors and drive off (line 12–15) because there were so many people in the bus, not because of his height.

B: The buses went very slowly in the traffic, *crawling nose to tail* (line 11).

C: He couldn't collect fares because he couldn't move, not because people tried to avoid paying.

28 C: The lady's head was stuck in the door, her body was outside the bus (line 22–24) and the bus had *surged forward* (suddenly begun to move) (line 20), so it must have pulled her along.

A: It is possible that her mind had been *temporarily dislocated* (that she couldn't think normally for a time) (line 27-28) but there is nothing to suggest that she was physically injured.

B: The woman dropped to the road (line 26-27) because the driver stopped and opened the doors, not because she lost consciousness.

D: Her head was trapped in the door and perhaps she couldn't think normally afterwards but she didn't actually hit her head on anything.

29 B: If they had dismissed a student, it would have made *headlines* (sensational articles in the newspaper) and they gave him the opportunity to *leave quietly*, so clearly they didn't want his dismissal to appear in the papers (line 29–31).

A: He had made his decision (to resign) when the lady hit the ground, not before the incident (line 32–33).

C: They told him he could *leave quietly* (without any fuss) but he was not given any opportunity to stay on.

D: He expected to be able to leave the job without being told to (he decided to resign the moment the lady fell to the ground). However, he was not given the chance to resign - the inspectors told him he could *leave quietly* first (line 30–32).

30 D: In the second paragraph, he explains how difficult it was to do the job well because of conditions on the buses, and then states that *In the circumstances I was scarcely to blame* (line 18). This refers to the incident with the lady, which he then describes, and which he thinks was not his fault.

A: He feels that he was not to blame for the incident.

B: He does not seem to feel that the inspectors were unfair to him – they gave him the opportunity to *leave quietly* rather than dismissing him unpleasantly, and the incident made him want to leave anyway (line 32–33).

C: He couldn't do the job properly but he doesn't think that was his fault.

Second Passage

*For the questions on this passage, see also the questions in **Further Practice and Guidance** on pages 15–16, and the answers to them below.*

31 B: The advertisement would only be read by passengers on aircraft who had nothing else to do but waste time reading inflight magazines. These people are therefore not too busy to read books, as the headline says (line 2–4).

A: The headline asks whether the reader is too busy to read books, it doesn't suggest that there is no point in reading them.

C: Since the people reading the advertisement are not too busy to read books (they have nothing else to do but read inflight magazines, according to the writer) such a headline is unlikely to appeal to them, he thinks. He believes that the advertisement asks its question *a little perilously* (it is taking a risk in asking such a question) (line 3) because the question is unlikely to apply to those reading it.

D: He doesn't suggest that the

phrasing of the question is strange but that it is a risky question to ask of people who are not at all busy.

32 C: People who were *still relying on reading* are described as cultural dinosaurs (line 11). *Dinosaurs* is used figuratively here to mean people whose attitudes or methods are completely out of date and belong in the past.

A: The advertisement refers to a *status hardback* (line 6) and the *bulky book connected with your profession* (line 8) that a businessman is likely to have but not to have read; there is no reference to what businessmen do read.

B: The service advertised will enable businessmen to *plausibly* (believably) *discuss* books they have not read (line 10–11); this implies that they do not already do that.

D: Books about their profession are described as *bulky* (large and heavy) (line 8), but this does not necessarily mean that they are too long.

33 C: The second magazine provided brief summaries of arts reviews so that the reader did not have to read the review itself. This was for people *too harrassed* (too busy, under too much pressure) (line 15) to read the whole review. The advertisement was for businessmen too busy to read professional books.

A: The second magazine is not for business people, it is for anyone too busy to read complete reviews.

B: They are both aimed at people who are too busy to read and do not refer to people who find reading boring.

D: The advertisement would enable people to discuss books they hadn't read but the magazine doesn't refer to discussing books, it refers to reading summaries of reviews, for example, of a travel book, and finding out the gist of what the review said (line 15–17).

34 B: The book argued that people could no longer *assimilate* (understand and learn) facts from television news and newspapers. Televison news was now 24-hour (on all the time) and newspapers had *added sections like a field adds new rabbits* (increased the number of its sections greatly and very quickly, just as rabbits reproduce). People were as a result now *battered by facts* (attacked or hit over and over again by them), so they could no longer assimilate them (line 25–27).

A: The book refers to people *with wide general interests* suffering as a result of television and newspaper expansion (line 24-26) but not to any change in people's interests.

C: The book does not suggest that people have trouble retaining information in general, but that people have trouble retaining information from television and newspapers because there is so much of it.

D: The book argues that television and newspapers give too many facts, not that the facts contradict each other.

35 D: The researcher offered him a summary of a book he hadn't read, which she had boiled down (reduced)

to two A4 sheets (line 32). This would enable him to discuss the book *on a programme the following day* (line 29) and would therefore be useful to him. This was the same as the service advertised in the first magazine – a summary of a book that would enable businessmen to discuss it without reading it.

A: The service in the second magazine was to provide summaries of *reviews*, not of books, and the researcher offered him a summary of a book. Furthermore, the service in the second magazine was not specifically aimed at enabling people to *discuss* books they hadn't read.

B/C: The television researcher didn't tell the writer anything about what was in *Information Anxiety* in their conversation, only that she could give him a summary of it. In addition, *Information Anxiety* seems to have described a problem but not talked about services to solve it (B). Although *Information Anxiety* describes a problem that is considered to affect a lot of people, this is not something the writer learned from his conversation with the researcher.

36 A: The writer sees the *summary culture* (the kind of services offered in the magazines) as another of *the time-saving devices available in the modern world* (line 19). This summary culture fits in with developments in the modern world which provide things that save time. *Information Anxiety* describes a problem caused by modern developments in the media and the services in the magazines are logical as a problem-solving response to these developments (line 32–34).

B: The writer does not suggest in the passage that there is anything wrong with the *summary culture*, only that it is a logical development.

C: The writer thinks that it is logical that the *summary culture* has appeared, which suggests that he agrees with the author of *Information Anxiety* that a lot of people have trouble assimilating the amount of information they get from the media. Therefore the *summary culture* is likely to affect a lot of people, who may well use the services provided.

D: The author does not suggest that people have become too lazy to read, and does not argue with the idea in both the advertisement and the second magazine that a lot of people are too busy to read. His own problem about discussing the book was not due to laziness but to lack of time to read it.

Third Passage

37 B: People passing it would not realize from its external appearance, which is *formal and inexpressive*, what is inside (line 1–2).

A: The writer refers to anyone *who has ventured inside* (been into a place not previously visited) (line 3) but does not suggest that it is difficult to do so.

C: The writer talks about looking *at random* (looking without any system or for anything in particular) through one of its catalogues (line 4–5), but this does not mean that the Society's system is badly organized.

D: The outside of the building does not indicate to people passing what kind of organization is inside it but it's quite possible that a lot of people know where it is.

38 C: At that time only *eccentrics* (people considered a little strange) were collecting American *artefacts and ephemera* (objects connected with a society or civilization, and things that were briefly fashionable)(line 10–11).

A: It had to move seven times *to keep pace with its acquisitions* (line 12) as it grew, which means that it received so many objects that it had to keep moving to bigger and bigger buildings.

B: In 1804, when the Society was founded, New York was a *provincial town* (not a major city) (line 11).

D: The Society was the *self-appointed annotator* of New York's history (line 11–12), which means that it decided itself (it wasn't asked) to keep items and record information relating to the city.

39 C: The city had *awakened to its own history* (become aware of and interested in it) (line 14), and *dozens of volumes* (many books) (line 15) had been published about its *progress* (line 16) and its *growth* (line 17).

A: The history of New York, not of America in general, was being analysed.

B: People hurried to *document* (to keep a record of) *a way of life that was disappearing* (line 19), but there is no suggestion that people were sorry it was disappearing.

D: People wanted to *take stock* (to stop and consider what had happened so far) (line 19), and they wanted a record of the way of life that was disappearing but they felt *civic pride* (they were proud of their city) (line 20), which means they were not worried about the way it was changing.

40 A: Most of the collection is of *the everyday and the commonplace* (line 25) – objects that were ordinary in the past and so not of much interest then.

B: Architects, moviemakers and fashion designers get some of their ideas from the past (line 22–24) but the writer does not suggest that they actually get them from the Historical Society.

C: Writers and scholars regard the collection as *truly priceless* (of great value) (line 28), but this is as a *collective memory bank* (a source of information enabling everyone to remember the past) (line 27–28) not because the objects are financially valuable.

D: Things in the collection have acquired *star status* (are now very famous) (line 25), but that does not mean they are associated with famous people.

PAPER 1: SECTION A   25 marks
           SECTION B   30 marks

TOTAL   55 marks

To be converted into a score out of 40 marks.

FURTHER PRACTICE AND GUIDANCE

p 15–16 PAPER 1 SECTION B

*For explanations to the answers, see the **Second Passage** above.*

Question 31
1 passengers on planes
2 no   3 busy businessmen

Question 32
1 no   2 yes   3 yes   4 no   5 a

Question 33
1 c   2 no, only the advert   3 no

Question 34
1 no   2 the amount
3 information from particular sources

Question 35
1 a book   2 the advertisement
3 discuss a book he had not read
4 nothing

Question 36
1 yes   2 no   3 no   4 no

FURTHER PRACTICE AND GUIDANCE

p 19 PAPER 2

Assessment of sample composition

1 **Content**
The whole composition is relevant to the subject of the question – which job the candidate would like and why – with no padding or waffle.

2 **Organization**
The composition is very well organized. The first paragraph provides an effective introduction that makes a point which is more than simply which job the candidate has chosen. The second paragraph gets to the point, explaining which job and giving general reasons why it has been chosen; the third paragraph deals with what skills and qualities of personality the chosen job requires; the fourth paragraph gives further information about what the job requires; the final paragraph provides an effective conclusion, giving further general points that are not just a repetition of the introduction or something already stated previously.

3 **Linking**
There is some good linking, for example, *but for* and *so that* (second paragraph); *To choose ... requires* (third paragraph); *since* (twice), *where*, and *although* (fourth paragraph). The majority of the linking is otherwise simple but accurate.

4 **Use of vocabulary**
There is some good vocabulary appropriately used, for example: *strictly, a wide range* (para 1); *structural* (para 2); *joints, gain*

experience, meticulous (very careful in paying attention to every detail) (para 3); *an environmentalist, diminishing resources, teak, provider of, well-being* (para 4). There are one or two vocabulary mistakes: *work* (para 3) should be *piece of work* or *job* because *work* is an uncountable noun and can therefore not be preceded by *a*; *the risk to our well-being* (para 4) should be *the danger to our well-being* (something that threatens something or could harm it is *a danger to* it); *the risk of something* refers to what could happen as a result of doing something dangerous (*the risk of disease caused by smoking*); *next generations* (last para) should be *future generations*. There are also two spelling mistakes: *anchestors* (para 1 and 2) should be *ancestors* and *threathened* (para 4) should be *threatened*.

5 **Use of grammar**
The composition is mostly correct grammatically and in particular uses the passive consistently well, for example, *can only be gained* (para 3), *can only be obtained, is cut down, are often planted* (para 4). In addition, the sentences are not all simple and short. There are, however, a few errors: *the trees* (para 2) should be *trees* because it refers to trees in general, not particular ones or kinds; *the most of materials* (para 2) should be *most materials* because *the most of* is never a correct phrase and *the* is incorrect since the reference is to materials in general; *the only way to make it well is being* (para 3) should be *the only way to make it well is **by** being* (by doing something explains how something is done); *Each measurement have to be correct* (para 3) should be *Each measurement has to be correct* (*each* is followed by a singular verb); *the nature's* (para 4) should be *nature's* because in this meaning *nature* is an uncountable concept which cannot be preceded by an article.

6 **Style**
The style of the composition is entirely appropriate – it is natural, flows well and shows control of language. It is fairly simple without being basic and does not try unsuccessfully to be very complicated.

This composition is good and very competent, with some errors. It would be given a score of approximately 12–15 marks out of 20.

p 20 PAPER 3 SECTION A QUESTION 1

*See also the questions in **Further Practice and Guidance** on page 23 and the corresponding answers.*

One mark per question (Total: 20)

1 **early**: *As early as* = as long ago as; the writer is emphasizing that taxis were popular a long time ago.

2 **robbed/deprived**: If you *rob/deprive*

someone of something, you take from them something that belongs to them or something that they need or want.

3 **under**: If something *comes under a law/rule/regulation*, it is controlled by that law, rule or regulation.

4 **drawn/pulled**: Carriages, carts, etc are *drawn/pulled by horses*.

5 **and**: The sentence talks about the development of taxis, first of all the cabriolet, then the Hansom Cab. *And* links the two and means *and then*. (*And then* could link the sentence but only one word can be used. *Then* cannot be used because it would have to start a new sentence).

6 **of**: *of choice* = chosen or preferred by people in general.

7 **on**: If you *improve on something*, you do or produce something that is better than it.

8 **it**: *it was Harry N. Allen who was ...* = Harry N. Allen was ... but adds emphasis.

9 **For**: He imported the taxi-mètre *for* his New York vehicles – to be used in them.

10 **could**: *could* = was able to.

11 **or**: *or* = which were/are also called.

12 **Just**: *Just as* = In the same way as. The men who made Hollywood were dreamers and entrepreneurs (adventurous business people) and the men who made taxis were also dreamers and entrepreneurs.

13 **were**: *so were the men who made the taxis in America run* = the men who made the taxis in America run were dreamers and entrepreneurs too.

14 **Among**: *Among them was John Hertz* = John Hertz was one of them.

15 **into**: If you *get into a business*, you become involved in it.

16 **most**: He chose the colour yellow because it was *most easily spotted* – more easily noticed than any other colour.

17 **responsible/famous/(well-)known**: If someone is *responsible for something*, it happens or exists because of them or something that they do. If someone is *famous/well-known/known for something*, they are famous, etc because of it.

18 **made**: *he made it affordable* = he caused it to be affordable.

19 **been**: If something *is for someone*, it is intended that they should have it or it is directed at them. Taxis had previously *been for rich folk* because only rich people could afford them.

20 **like**: *like* = for example/of the type of, in this context.

p 20 PAPER 3 SECTION A QUESTION 2

See also the questions in **Further Practice and Guidance** *on page 24 and the corresponding answers and explanations .*

One mark per underlined word or phrase (Total: 13)

a is currently being installed/is being installed currently at our head office. (1 mark)
The verb has to be put into the present continuous passive; the adverb

currently can be put in several positions.

b until some time later(1) that I realized the full implications of what had happened(1)or until some time later (1) that the full implications of what had happened occurred to/dawned on me.(1) (2 marks)
If something *occurs to/dawns on you*, you realize it or become aware of it.

c a limit to/on the number of people(1) (that) we can invite(1)or only a limited number of people (1)(that) we can invite.(1) (2 marks)
In the second acceptable answer, *limited* is used as an adjective, *number* is singular and together *a limited number of people* is the subject of the sentence.

d anyone could do/could have done/did(1) would/could have prevented the problem from arising(1). (2 marks)
This is a hypothetical situation – no past action would have made/would have been able to make any difference but no past action was taken. *Could have done* can be transformed into *could do/could have done/did; to prevent* has to be transformed into *would/could have prevented* to correctly complete the past conditional.

e (a) high intelligence(1) doesn't mean that you have common sense.(1) (2 marks)
It is possible to use *intelligence* and other nouns describing people's qualities or feelings in the singular; such nouns are not usually used in the plural.

f the point/verge of phoning her office when she finally arrived. (1 mark)
If you are *on the point/verge of doing something*, you are just about to do it.

g responsible for re-organizing/for the re-organization of the department (1 mark)
The noun phrase can be used here – *the re-organization of something* = the act or process of re-organizing it.

h herself (how) to play the piece(1) by listening to a recording of it.(1) (2 marks)
You can teach *yourself/someone to do* or *how to do something; by + -ing* explains the method for doing something.

p 21 PAPER 3 SECTION A QUESTION 3

One mark per underlined word or phrase (Total: 9)

a a result/consequence of (1) *as a result of/as a consequence of something happening* = because something happened. In this sentence, the shop closed because of the large decrease in its sales.

b could/would have(1) given you (some)(1) (2 marks). The speaker does not understand why he/she wasn't asked to help because he/she was able to help. This is a kind of conditional – *If you had asked me, I could/would have given you some advice. I could have* = I

would have been able to do it; *I would have* = I would have done it. You *give someone advice. Advice* is an uncountable noun, so you *give advice* or *give some advice*, not *an advice*.

c be bothered to do/with or face (doing) (1) The speaker wants to sit down and take it easy and is therefore too tired or lazy to do the washing up. *I can't be bothered to do/with it* = I'm too tired/ lazy/lacking in energy to do it or It's too much trouble/effort for me to do it. As in many phrases connected with tasks (*do the shopping/do homework/do exercise/do housework*), you *do the washing up*. If you *can't face something* or *can't face doing something*, you don't want to do it because it's unpleasant for you or requires too much effort.

d as well (1) If you *might as well do something*, it is quite a good idea to do it because there is no better alternative or because you prefer it and it will do no harm.

e as if/as though/like(1) they would/were going to/were bound to/were sure to/were certain to lose (1)(2 marks). If something *looks as if/as though/like something will/is going to/is bound, sure* or *certain to happen*, it is likely or certain that it will happen.

f I obliged/forced/supposed/meant(1) to pay the full (1)(2 marks). If you *are obliged or forced to do something*, you have to do it because you are told to or made to do it because it is a rule or an order. If you *are supposed or meant to do something*, you should do it because it is expected. If you pay *the full amount*, you pay the whole of the amount of money, not just some of it.

p 22 PAPER 3 SECTION A QUESTION 4

One mark per underlined word or phrase (Total: 12)

a It was discovered that the building had been deliberately/had deliberately been(1) set on fire.(1)orIt was discovered that someone/somebody had deliberately(1) set the building on fire/set fire to the building.(1) (2 marks)
(Note: *deliberately* can also be placed at the end of the sentence). If *someone sets something on fire* or *sets fire to something*, they cause it to burn. The adverb *deliberately* can be placed in several positions.

b The letter found its way to me even though it was wrongly addressed. or Even though it/the letter was wrongly addressed, the letter/it found its way to me. (1 mark)
If something *finds its way to someone/a place*, it reaches that person or place after taking an indirect route or getting lost.

c She resigned of her own accord. or She wasn't forced to resign, she did it of her own accord. (1 mark)
If you do something *of your own accord*, you make your own decision to do it,

you are not forced to do it.

d There is no comparison(1)between my/your situation and yours/mine(1).or My/Your situation bears no comparison (1) with yours/mine.(1) (2 marks)
If *there is no comparison between one thing and another* or if *one thing bears no comparison with another*, they are completely different, and therefore cannot be compared.

e I lost interest in the film half-way through. (1 mark)
If you *lose interest in something*, you stop being interested in it.

f He said that he wasn't worthy of such a high honour. (1 mark)
If you are *not worthy of something*, you do not deserve something good.

g I wasn't in the mood(1) for doing/for/to do(1) anything energetic. (2 marks)
If you are *not in the mood for/for doing/to do something*, you don't feel like doing it.

h She must have taken exception(1) to something I said.(1) (2 marks)
If someone *takes exception to something*, they are offended by it.

SECTION A:
QUESTION 1	20 marks
QUESTION 2	13 marks
QUESTION 3	9 marks
QUESTION 4	12 marks
TOTAL	54 marks

FURTHER PRACTICE AND GUIDANCE

p 23 PAPER 3 SECTION A QUESTION 1

For explanations, see **Section A question 1** *above.*

1	C	6	D	11	A	16	A
2	D	7	B	12	B	17	A
3	B	8	B	13	A	18	C
4	A	9	A	14	A	19	A
5	A	10	C	15	B	20	B

FURTHER PRACTICE AND GUIDANCE

P 24 PAPER 3 SECTION A QUESTION 2

For all the acceptable answers to question 2 of the test and further explanations, see **Section A question 2** *above.*

a 1: The verb in the original sentence is in the present continuous and the answer requires you to transfer it to the present continuous passive. *Currently* is in the original sentence and this can be (although does not have to be) put between the two parts of the verb.
In 2, the verb tense is incorrect; *currently* can, however, follow the verb.
In 3, the verb tense and word order

are incorrect – the place should come after the verb.
In 4, there is the same word order problem; *currently* is correctly positioned but the place should come after the verb.

b 4: The original sentence means 'I didn't realize the full implications of what had happened until some time later.' To rewrite the sentence beginning with *It wasn't*, the structure *It wasn't until ... that ...* must be used.
In 1, *then* is incorrect, it should be *that*.
In 2, the order of the sentence is incorrect – *until some time later* should come before *that I realized*.
In 3, the structure used is not possible. The original sentence could be rewritten as *The realization of the full implications of what had happened didn't occur to/dawn on me until some time later*, but this does not begin with *It wasn't*.

c 3: The sentence means that the number of people has to be restricted. If *there is a limit to something*, there is a maximum that cannot be exceeded.
1 is not possible; *limitation* is the act of limiting something (*arms limitation*).
2: *number* is singular and so *a limited number* would be correct; without *a* the sentence is incorrect.
4: It is not possible to say that there is a *limit for something* (it should be a *limit to/on something*); otherwise the sentence is correct.

d 3: The sentence has to be transferred into a kind of conditional – it means 'There was no possible action by anybody that would have prevented the problem from arising.' The whole situation is in the past. *Nobody* has to be transformed into *anybody* (= any person); *could have done* = was able to do but didn't do in the past; *would have prevented* = the result part of a conditional sentence referring to the past.
In 1, the first part is correct, but *had prevented* is not possible for the result part of a past conditional.
In 2, *nobody* is a double negative and therefore incorrect – it should be *anybody*.
In 4, the word order is wrong – *anybody could do* forms part of the subject of the sentence and should come first after *Nothing that*.

e 1: The adjective *intelligent* has to be changed into the noun *intelligence*; if one thing does not automatically lead to another, the first thing *doesn't mean that* the other is the case.
In 2, the adverb *highly* and the adjective *intelligent* are incorrect after *Having* in this sentence. *Being highly intelligent is nothing to do with having common sense* would be a correct sentence, but the question begins with *Having* not *Being*.
3: If you *mean to do something*, you intend to do it (*I didn't mean to offend you*); if one thing *means that* another is a case, the second thing is true as a result of the first one (*She's lost her job, which means that she'll have to*

look for another one).
4: The sentence would be correct if *doesn't mean that you have* replaced *doesn't mean*.

f 2: If you are *on the point of doing something*, you are going to do it almost immediately.
1: If you are *on your way to a place*, you are moving or travelling in that direction (*I got lost on my way to their house*).
3: If you are *on the verge of doing something*, you are likely to do it almost immediately (*I was on the verge of giving up when I finally got a job*), *on the verge to do* is not possible.
4: If you do something *the moment that something happens*, you do it immediately (*The moment I realized my mistake, I apologized*).

g 4: If you are *made responsible for something*, you are chosen to be the person who is in charge of it.
1: *Responsible* cannot be used as a noun to refer to someone who is responsible for something (*He/She is the responsible* is not possible).
2: *He is the one who has been made responsible* is possible here but this doesn't begin with *He has been made*.
3: If a person is *made into something*, they become something different (*an average player made into a great one by good coaching*). This has no connection with being in charge of something.

h 1: If you *teach yourself how to do something*, you learn how to do it without any help or guidance.
2: *Herself* should come before *from a recording*; otherwise this sentence is possible.
3: Again, *herself* should come first; otherwise the sentence is correct.
4: *By* instead of *with* would make this sentence correct. *By doing something* explains how something is done.

p 25–27 PAPER 3 SECTION B

Answers similar to or covering the same points as those given here are acceptable providing they are phrased accurately.

See also the questions in **Further Practice and Guidance** *on pages 28–29 and the corresponding answers.*

a **He was unhappy** (1) **because he realized that his colour blindess had made him unable to do something well again** (1). **(2 marks)**
If you *groan*, you make a sound expressing pain or unhappiness about something (line 5); if you are *handicapped by something* (line 5–6), it makes you unable to do something well or at all. In this case, he had painted the cake the wrong colour.

b **He kept changing the colours of the lines** (1), **which made the graph useless** (1). **(2 marks)**
If you *make a hash of something* (line 9), you do it very badly. If the lines kept changing colour, the graph was impossible to interpret.

c Because he doesn't think it is an accurate name./Because he thinks defective colour vision is a more accurate name. (1 mark)

d They think it is simply the inability to give the correct names to colours (1) but it is also the inability to distinguish between certain colours (1). (2 marks)
It is not just a matter of misnaming colours (line 16) means that it does involve giving the wrong names to colours but it also involves *problems distinguishing between colours* in the *red to green part of the spectrum* (line 15–16).

e The questions make no sense to him (1) so he either indicates that he doesn't know (1) or answers in a nervous, hesitant manner (1).(3 marks)
The questions are *meaningless*, he can only *shrug* (indicate by raising the shoulders that he doesn't know) and *stammer* (talk hesitantly and nervously)(line 18).

f I look at them for a long time (1) and select them without having any idea what I am doing (1). (2 marks)
If you *stare at something* (line 22), you look at it without moving your eyes for a long time; if *you pick at something* (line 22), you keep touching it and then withdrawing your hand. If you do something *helplessly* (line 22), you do it without having control over it.

g If I am given no help./If I make my own decisions. (1 mark)

h His evidence in court might involve identifying the colour of something (1) and a lawyer could easily prove that he was unable to do this (1). (2 marks)
The writer imagines a lawyer pointing to jackets and asking which one is the same colour as the one the policeman saw. The implication is that the policeman would be unable to answer this question correctly and his evidence would therefore be useless.

i He would not know which light on an oncoming ship was the port light and which one was the starboard light (1) so he might not take the right action to avoid a possible collision (1). (2 marks)
The writer suggests that you would not be happy to travel at night on a ship with a colour-defective captain because there would be an increased risk of a collision with another boat or ship (line 28–29).

j The inability to match things in the environment with coloured cards. (1 mark)
Although the writer would react differently today if asked to do this, he would still be unable to do it (line 32–33).

k If he was told to match things of the same colour (1), he would make jokes and pretend to be able to do it (1), whereas a young child would simply be confused and unable to react (1). (3 marks)
He says that if he was asked to *do that* (to match things in the environment to coloured cards) he would joke and *con*

my way through (deal with the situation by pretending to be able to do it and making people believe that he can do it). A six-year-old child would, however, be *bewildered* (confused, unable to understand and respond), as he was at that age (line 32–33).

l Not being able to distinguish between colours but knowing that those colours must be different. (1 mark)
The fact that the child *knows* the colours must be different *adds to his annoyance* (line 36–37).

m That it is relatively high/significant (1) and that teachers should therefore be aware of the problem (1).(2 marks)
He asks teachers to be aware of the problem because one in ten children is colour-defective (line 40–42).

n That they should talk to them (1) and let them know that it is not their fault they are unable to do certain classroom activities (1). (2 marks)
He says that it would help colour-defective children if their teachers talked to them and told them that *their frustration* (at not being able to do things involving distinguishing colours, as described in line 30–37), is caused by something real (having colour-defective vision) and is therefore not their fault (line 42–43).

Questions a – n: Total: 26 marks

p 27 PAPER 3 SECTION B – SUMMARY

o *One mark each for inclusion of the following points or points similar to them:*
- you do things involving colours badly – he couldn't paint properly at school (first paragraph) and did the job at the steelworks badly (second paragraph, see question b).
- people ask you questions about colours and you can't answer them (third paragraph, see questions d and e).
- you can't choose the right clothes to wear together and dress in clothes with colours that look strange together (line 17–18), see question f; without help he dresses in *bizarre* (strange and ridiculous) *shirt-tie combinations* (line 23).
- there are some jobs you can't get because being colour-defective makes you unable to do them well (line 25–29, see questions h and i).
- children can't do classroom activities involving matching or distinguishing between colours (line 30–33, see questions j and k).
- children in class get annoyed because they know colours are different but they can't see the difference (line 35–37, see question l).
- teachers aren't aware of the problem and don't explain it to children (line 40–43, see questions m and n).

Total: 7 marks

Plus maximum of 3 marks for general impression, based on the following criteria:
- *relevance*
- *general level of fluency*
- *accuracy of language*
- *absence of copying from passage*
- *length*

SUMMARY: TOTAL 10 marks

SECTION B TOTAL: 36 marks

PAPER 3   SECTION A: 54 marks
          SECTION B: 36 marks
          TOTAL   90 marks

To be converted into a score out of 40 marks.

FURTHER PRACTICE AND GUIDANCE

p 28 PAPER 3 SECTION B

For explanations, see the explanations for the answers to Paper 3 Section B above.

Question a: 1b
2 that he was colour blind/that he had a problem/that being colour blind was a problem for him/that there were things he couldn't do because he was colour blind
Question b: a number of different-coloured lines relating to production
Question d: 1 no 2 no
Question i: which light is the port (left) one and which one is the starboard (right) one
Questions j and k: b
Question l: to emphasize that colour blind children are aware of their problem

FURTHER PRACTICE AND GUIDANCE

p 29 PAPER 3 SECTION B SUMMARY

Tick 2, 6, 7, 9, 12, 13, 14, 15

Numbers 1, 3, 4, 10 and 11 are all stated but they are particular examples illustrating the problems the writer describes, not the problems themselves.
Numbers 5, 8 and 16 are facts but they are not problems caused by the condition.

For explanations of the correct choices, see Paper 3 Section B - Summary above.

p 30 PAPER 4 PART ONE

The line references are to the tape transcripts on pages 167-168.

One mark per question (Total: 10)

1 lane closures: line 11–12
2 junction 2 (is) (still) closed: line 15–17
3 roadworks: line 24–25; *tailbacks* (long

queues of traffic) have been caused by the roadworks and the question concerns causes, not results.

4 **faulty traffic lights**: line 27–28
5 **(a) fire**: line 30–31; this has caused *congestion* (traffic moving slowly or not at all).
6 **sunny**: line 38–42; it's not going to stay that way but it is like that now. (brilliantly = very in this context). There is a *breeze* (a light wind)(line 36) so it is not very windy.
7 **cloud**: line 42–43; there will be a *build-up* of cloud (an increase in it over a period).
8/9 **(fairly) cool/(very) windy (in any order)**: line 48–54; there is *an outside chance* (a very small possibility) of a *localized shower* (a short burst of rain in a small part of the area) but *there is little likelihood of this* (it is very unlikely). Therefore *rainy* is not a possible answer – rain is unlikely to happen anywhere and certainly will not happen everywhere. It will be *fairly cool* and there will be a *blustery wind* (one that blows in strong bursts). It will not *become* cloudy in the afternoon, because the cloud will build up in the morning; it will not *become* sunny because it is already sunny, and sunshine will continue *at times*.
10 **warmer**: line 55–59; today it will be warmer (three degrees higher) than it was yesterday but it will be the same amount (three degrees) lower than the *seasonal average* (than the average temperature at this time of year).

p 30 PAPER 4 PART TWO

One mark per question (Total: 8)

11 **false**: line 7–15; the presenter says that there are some films which have many excellent qualities and show terrible things – he does not say that there are some films with excellent qualities and then there are other films which have violence. He is not comparing types of film, he is talking only about films showing violence.
12 **false**: line 19–26; the director says that dramatists *throughout history* have based their stories and plays on real life and real life includes nice things, conflict and evil, which existed long before cinema and television were invented.
13 **true**: line 26–33; it was *far less safe to walk the streets of America in the nineteenth century than it is today* because, for example, in one park people got murdered and people carried *cudgels* (thick, heavy sticks that could be used as weapons) to *stave off* (resist) attack.
14 **true**: line 34–37; this view is expressed by the presenter. He says that as well as violence, there were also fatal diseases in the past that are not fatal now because successful efforts were made to *stamp* them *out* (to destroy or eliminate them) and that therefore the fact that violence existed in the past is no reason for *not trying to stamp it* (violence) *out*. It should therefore also

be considered important to eliminate violence in films and on television. The director disagrees with this view, describing it as *pathetic*(stupid) (line 38), but the view is stated.
15 **false**: line 39–51; the director says that violence in the past was not caused by television or films because they didn't exist and equally, it is not caused by them today, because if you took violent programmes off the television or didn't make violent films, the behaviour of violent people would not change. They would not decide to stop being violent and *mugging* people (violently robbing people in the street). However, she expresses no view regarding what the cause of their violent behaviour is, only that it is not caused by television or films.
16 **true**: line 58–64; the presenter says that film-makers impose intellectual reasons on the violence they show in films when in fact what they really want to do is to show *man's worst excesses* (people's worst and most extreme behaviour). They pretend that they do this for intellectual reasons but these are not the real reasons.
17 **false**: line 65–83; the director says that radio and TV stations and newspapers cannot be expected to stop reporting violence because you should not hide the truth from people, and that a government report came to the conclusion that there was no connection between violence on the screen or on television and violence in people. She therefore does not say that reporting violence makes people violent and an official report has concluded that watching violence does not make people violent.
18 **true**: line 83–88; the director says that most people are capable of knowing the difference between good and bad characters in films and they don't *knock anybody about* (attack anyone violently) after watching a violent film, they go for dinner.

p 31 PAPER 4 PART THREE

One mark per question (Total: 5)

19 **B**: line 12–25; the *main thing* he's interested in is the part of the *social revolution* that has taken place over the last hundred years that is connected with shopping. He therefore collects packs, advertisements and promotions, etc because of their part in this social revolution.
A: He collects things from both the past and the present day and there is no suggestion that he finds changes over the period his collection covers regrettable.
C: It is very likely that advertising fascinates him but he doesn't only collect adverts, he also collects packs, so this is not his main reason for collecting what he collects.
D: He collects the things that people buy when they go shopping but there is no suggestion that he is interested in

what particular kinds of people buy, or why, or how often they buy them.
20 **D**: He gets disappointed if there's a product he wants to buy and he has *already got the packaging* because when this is the case he has to *wait till the next change comes along* (until the packaging changes) before buying this product (line 45–49).
A: He implies that he doesn't buy something if he suddenly finds that he is *running out of money*, but that is because he has already bought other things and has little money left, not because the product is itself expensive (line 35–36).
B: He is interested in changes in design and looks for *what new designs have come along*, but he does not say that he only buys designs he likes (line 40–42).
C: His first priority when shopping is what he needs for the collection, not what he wants to consume. He implies therefore that he buys things he doesn't want to consume because they are new or have a new design (line 37–42).
21 **D**: He decided to start the collection when he realized that *something is always happening and changing in it*. If this is the case, there will always be new products, designs, advertisements, etc to collect (line 71–72).
A: He wanted to collect something that other children did not collect (line 61–62) but he decided on *this* collection because it was of something that was constantly changing, not because other children collected things.
B: His mother told him what the stone he found was (line 55–57) but she played no part in his later decision to start this collection.
C: He doesn't say why he stopped collecting stones, only that he went on to collect stamps and coins (line 58–60). He then tried to find something else to collect because he realized that other people would have better stamp and coin collections than him and because everyone else collected such things (line 61–67). There is no link between his decision to stop collecting stones and his decision to start this collection.
22 **B**: He is *driven by this commitment* that he is *saving the nation's heritage* (motivated by the feeling that he is saving something connected with the country's culture and life from past generations) (line 80–81), and believes that he is saving *something that I think should be saved* (line 85–87). He therefore feels that he is collecting things on behalf of and for the benefit of the country.
A: He implies that he agrees that other people might think his collection ridiculous and say that he is collecting *rubbish* that *is not really someone's heritage* (line 83–84) but he disagrees with that view because he thinks such things *should be saved*.
C: He compares himself with people who train for long periods each day for the Olympics (line 87–94) but he doesn't say that they are doing

something that is more important than his collection.

D: He believes that he is *probably dedicated* in the same kind of way that people training for the Olympics are and therefore thinks that his dedication is similar to theirs (line 92–94).

23 A: He says that the *big disadvantage* is that he will have to *add endlessly, endlessly, endlessly* to the collection because there will always be new things to collect (line 103–106).

B: It does take up *a certain number of hours every day* (line 84–85) but he doesn't suggest that he views this as a problem.

C: A lot of people *think that the rubbish aspect is not really saving the nation's heritage* (that he is saving rubbish that does not have the use he thinks it does) (line 82–84), but this doesn't seem to worry him.

D: He would find it difficult to give it up because *it's in the blood* (it's part of his nature) but he doesn't say that he regrets this and does say that *it's terrific fun* (extremely enjoyable) (line 98–99).

p 31 PAPER 4 PART FOUR

*See also the questions in **Further Practice and Guidance** on page 32 and the corresponding answers.*

One mark per question (Total: 10)

24 freelance news photographer: line 12–17; someone who is *freelance* or is *a freelance* works independently for different organizations and is paid separately for each piece of work they do.

25 the Picture Desk: line 21; at a newspaper or a radio or TV station, a *desk* is a department responsible for a particular subject; an editor is usually the person in charge of that department; the photographer states that it is the desk (someone in the department) that contacts him and that he is then given a *brief* (instructions regarding what he is expected to do) by the Picture Editor.(line 28–30)

26 the composition of the picture/picture composition: line 41–47; he says that a photographer gets so familiar with the equipment that *you hardly have to think about* the technical things (you don't have to think about them much) because you *really have to concentrate your whole mind on the composition of the picture.*

27 publicity photos (for a restaurant): line 51–54; at school he learnt basic printing and photography(line 49–51); after the restaurant he worked for local papers for a year(line 60–61).

28 processing and printing: line 74–80; he processes the negatives himself and prints them himself, although he *can also ask the printers to do it* – this suggests that he does the printing himself sometimes and on other occasions gets the printers to do it.

29 none (in particular): line 84–87; he has

a school qualification but *there aren't any in particular* = there are no particular formal qualifications for being a professional photographer.

30 press photography: line 88–90; courses in this are available at Linford College in Manchester.

31/32the Press Directory/the Press Guide (in any order): line 92–93; the addresses of local and regional papers can be found there; the Bureau of Freelance Photographers gives help and advice(line 93–95).

33 motivation/determination: line 96–101; *you have to be motivated, you have to want to do it* and *you have to push yourself.* The requirements mentioned do not relate to personality.

PAPER 4	PART ONE	10 marks
	PART TWO	8 marks
	PART THREE	5 marks
	PART FOUR	10 marks
	TOTAL	33 marks

To be converted into a score out of 20 marks.

FURTHER PRACTICE AND GUIDANCE

p 32 PAPER 4 PART FOUR

*For explanations, see **Part Four** above.*

1 no
2 news pictures
3 *The Independent*
4 The Picture Desk
5 The Picture Editor
6 the technical things/the equipment
7 basic printing and photography
8 in a restaurant
9 publicity photos
10 local papers
11 a picture agency
12 process the negatives
13 the printing
14 a qualification in photography
15 courses in press photography
16 A in the Press Directory
   B in the Press Guide
17 the Bureau of Freelance Photographers
18 A technical knowledge of photography
   B a good visual sense   C luck

FURTHER PRACTICE AND GUIDANCE

p 35–36 PAPER 5

Talking About Pictures

Picture one
1 on the left; on the left-hand side...on/to the right;on the right-hand side
2 in the top right-hand corner
3 In the background...behind
4 at the bottom
5 in the bottom right-hand corner
6 At the top...to/on the right; on the right-hand side (answers in either order)
7 between
8 in front of

Picture two
1 in the middle
2 behind
3 on/to the left; on the left-hand side
4 At the top...to/on the right; on the right-hand side(answers in either order)
5 In the foreground
6 In the top left-hand corner
7 between
8 At the bottom...to/on the left; on the left-hand side(answers in either order)

Picture three
1 on/to the right;on the right-hand side
2 In the foreground
3 next to/beside
4 in front of
5 between
6 in the bottom left-hand corner
7 on/to the left; on the left-hand side
8 In the background

TEST TWO

p 37–38 PAPER 1 SECTION A

Note that all explanations in this part refer to the meaning or use of each option most closely related to the question, not necessarily to the only meaning or use of these options.

One mark per question (Total: 25)

*For questions 1-6, see also the questions in **Further Practice and Guidance** on p39 and the corresponding answers.*

1 **A:** If something is **loosely** based on or connected with something, it is based on or connected with it but only to a small extent.
   B: If you say something *casually*, you say it in a relaxed way without giving it much emphasis.
   C: If you can *faintly* remember something, you can just remember it but not clearly or in detail.
   D: If you touch someone *lightly*, you touch them very gently.
   LOOK OUT! This is the type of question in which all the choices are related in meaning but only one can form the collocation required.

2 **C:** If you **omit to do** something, you fail or forget to do something that you should do.
   A: If you *ignore something*, you pay no attention to it.
   B: If you *disregard something*, you take no notice of it.
   D: If you *miss out something* or *miss something out*, you don't include it.
   LOOK OUT! This is the type of question where all the choices are related in meaning (in this case they are all connected with not including or paying attention to something), but only one fits the structure of the sentence (*omit* is the only one that can be followed by an infinitive).

3 A: Deep is often used with nouns describing feelings of sadness, with the meaning *very great* (*deep regret/sympathy/depression/despair*).
B: *Full* is used with nouns describing agreement, with the meaning *complete* (*full agreement/acceptance/permission*).
C: A *keen interest* is an intense or very great interest.
D: A *passionate commitment/desire/wish* is one that involves very strong emotion and caring a lot.
LOOK OUT! In this type of question, all the choices can be used in related ways – in this case, to describe feelings – but only one can form the collocation required.

4 B: If you **exaggerate** something, you add to the true nature or facts of it when talking about it.
A: If something is *overrated*, people say that it is better or of higher quality than it really is.
C: If something *multiplies*, it increases in number because more and more of the same things come into existence.
D: If a feeling is *heightened*, it is made more intense.
LOOK OUT! In this type of question, all the choices are related to one idea (here, increasing in some way) but only one has the precise meaning that the context requires.

5 A: If you do something **in expectation of something/something happening**, you expect that the second thing will happen when you do the first one.
B: If you do something *in the belief that* something is the case, you think that something is true when you do it.
C: If you say something *with certainty*, you are sure that it is true or correct.
D: *The likelihood of something/something happening* is the probability or chance that it will happen.
LOOK OUT! In this type of question, all the choices can be used to form phrases with similar or the same meaning but only one can be used to form the phrase in the question.

6 A: A **full** account is one that includes all the details, with nothing missing (*the full story; a full confession; a full report*).
B: *Total* can be used with some nouns describing feelings, to mean *complete* (*total confusion/relaxation/pleasure/fear*).
C: *The whole* is used with a singular noun, to mean *all of (the)*. (*the whole day/holiday/class*)
D: *Sheer* is used with uncountable nouns to mean *complete and nothing other than* (*sheer bad manners/hard work/nonsense*).
LOOK OUT! In this type of question, all the choices have the same meaning – complete – but only one can form the collocation in the question.

7 C: If you **set out to do** something, you have a particular intention when you start doing it.
A: If you *set up* something such as an organization, you establish or create it (*set up a company/committee*).
B: If something unpleasant *sets in*, it starts happening and seems likely to continue for some time (*the wet weather set in*).
D: If you *set about doing* something, you start dealing with a difficult task (*Tomorrow I'm going to set about replying to all these letters*).

8 C: If something is true **in terms of** something, it is true in connection with that thing.
A: If something is true *in the sense that* something else is the case, it is true in that way (*It was a useful experience in the sense that I learnt from it*).
B: If you do or think something *in the light of* another thing, you do or think it after considering that other thing (*In the light of recent developments, I have changed my mind*).
D: If something is true *as regards* something, it is true concerning it (*As regards salary, it's not a fantastic job*).

9 A: People **bow** when they are reacting to applause from an audience before, during or after a performance by bending the head or top half of the body forwards.
B: If you *duck*, you lower your head or the top part of your body in order to move under something or to avoid being hit by something (*duck to avoid hitting your head on the ceiling*).
C: If you *crouch*, you lower your body so that you are almost sitting on the floor (*crouch behind a table to avoid being seen*).
D: If you *stoop*, you bend your back and shoulders forward and down (*stoop to pick something up off the floor*).

10 B: If you do something **at random**, you do it without any particular system.
A: If something is *in a muddle*, it is disorganized or untidy (*files all in a muddle on the desk*).
C: A *fluke* is something lucky that happens or is done accidentally and not as a result of skill (*The second goal was just a fluke*).
D: If something is *in disarray*, it is very untidy and disorganized (*Clothes were in disarray all over the floor*).

11 A: If you **allay someone's fears**, you cause them to stop being afraid or to be less afraid.
B: If you *deter someone (from doing something)*, you discourage them from doing it by making them realize the bad consequences for them if they do it (*have guard dogs to deter burglars from breaking in*).
C: If something *soothes someone*, it makes them feel calmer or more relaxed (*music that soothes you*).
D: If you *placate someone*, you reduce their anger by saying pleasant things or doing what they want (*placate angry customers by offering to give them their money back*).

12 A: If something **proves to be** something, it is shown later to be that thing.
B: If *a situation/problem/subject, etc arises*, it occurs or appears.
C: If something *turns out to be* something, it is shown later that it is that thing (*turn out to be = prove to be*).
D: If something *develops into* something, it changes over a period into that thing (*a small problem that developed into a major one*).

13 C: Unduly = to an extent that is greater than necessary or appropriate in the circumstances (*be unduly critical/depressed/confident*).
A: *Additionally* = as well as/in addition to what has already been stated (*there will additonally be a charge for service*).
B: If something is *abundantly clear*, it is very obvious (*it is abundantly clear that she won't change her mind*).
D: If something happens *worthlessly*, it achieves nothing (*thousands of lives worthlessly sacrificed in war*).

14 A: If employees are **laid off**, they lose their jobs, perhaps temporarily, because there is no work for them.
B: If you *take something away*, you remove it (*take rubbish away*).
C: If something is *set apart for something*, it is made distinct or separate from the rest for a particular purpose (*rooms set apart for the use of guests only*).
D: If you *lose out (on something)*, you are the one who loses in a situation or you are unable to have or take advantage of something (*It was a bad deal and I lost out./I don't want to lose out on such a wonderful opportunity*).

15 B: If you **resent doing** something, you feel annoyed because you think that it is unfair that you have to do it.
A: If something/someone *exasperates someone*, they make them angry, impatient or frustrated (*His refusal to listen to common sense really exasperates me*).
C: If something *enrages someone*, it makes them extremely angry (*I was enraged by his appalling comments about me*).
D: If something *embitters someone*, it makes them feel bitter, angry and resentful for a long time after it happens (*Years of failure to succeed in her career have embittered her*).

16 B: If you are **resigned to doing** something, you do not want to do it but you accept that you have to do it.
A: If something is *acceptable to* you, it is satisfactory or suitable for you (*The arrangement was acceptable to me*).
C: If you *compromise with* someone, you reach an agreement in which you get something that you want and agree not to get something that you want (*You'll have to compromise with him because you won't get everything you're demanding*).
D: If you are *content with* something, you are satisfied or happy with it (*She's content with the way her life is going at the moment*).

17 A: If you **make a fuss**, you create an unnecessary problem by reacting too strongly.
B: If something *causes a sensation*, it shocks or surprises a group of people or the public in general (*News of his unexpected promotion caused a sensation in the office*).
C: If you *cause trouble*, you create a problem. *Trouble* is an uncountable or plural noun, so *a trouble* is not possible

(*His arguments about the way the company is run have caused a lot of trouble*).
D: If someone/something *causes a stir*, it creates shock, excitement or controversy (*The film caused quite a stir when it first came out because it had some very violent scenes*).

18 C: The way that you **go about something/doing something** is the way that you approach a task or start dealing with it.
A: If something *comes about*, it happens as a result of something else (*His problems came about because he was so poor at financial matters*).
B: If something *brings something about*, it causes it to happen (*Public opinion brought about a change in government policy*).
D: If you *see about something/doing something*, you consider it carefully because you are not sure about whether you want to do it or can do it ('*Can you come to a meeting next Wednesday?*' '*I'll have to see about that. I might be busy that day*').

19 C: If something is **deceptive**, it is not as it appears to be and so gives the wrong impression.
A: If someone/something is *cunning*, they/it deliberately deceive(s) people in a clever way in order to achieve something (*a cunning businessman/plan/plot*).
B: If someone is *deceitful*, they say things that are not true to make someone believe them or they hide the truth from someone (*It was deceitful of you to say that you were ill when really you didn't want to go*).
D: If someone/something is *insincere*, they are pleasant or what they say is pleasant but they don't really mean it (*an insincere person/insincere compliments*).

20 A: **In fairness to** someone = Being fair to them/To be fair to them.
B: *To do justice to someone* = to treat or talk about someone in a way that is fair to them (*To do justice to him, he tried his best and it's not his fault that he failed*).
C: If someone is given something *in recognition of* something, they are given it as a reward for something people know or can see that they have done, or for a particular good quality they have (*She was given a pay increase in recognition of her value to the company*).
D: If you are or do something *in sympathy with* someone else, you feel the same as them or do something because you sympathize with them (*I'm in sympathy with him because I think he has a right to be annoyed/strike in sympathy with other workers*).

21 A: If you aren't **averse to something/doing something**, you aren't against it or unwilling to do it (*He isn't averse to hard work/working hard*).
B: If you aren't *unwilling to do* something, you don't mind doing it (*I'm not unwilling to discuss the matter*).
C: If you are *reluctant to do* something, you don't want to do something even though you might have to do it (*She*

was reluctant to tell him the awful truth).
D: If someone is *contrary*, they behave in opposition to others in order to annoy them (*He refused to agree with everyone else simply to be contrary*).

22 B: A **course of action** is an action or series of actions taken in order to deal with or achieve something.
A: A *measure* is an action taken to deal with or achieve something (*a measure* = a course of action). (*What measures are you taking to improve food quality?*)
C: A *process* is the way or system by which something is done in stages over a period (*a legal/scientific process; the process of learning a foreign language; the process of elimination*).
D: A *policy* is an attitude to or way of dealing with something that has been decided or agreed and is then followed (*It is my policy not to make sudden decisions; the government's economic/foreign policy*).

23 B: If someone **dispenses with** something, they get rid of it because they no longer want it.
A: If you *discard something*, you get rid of it because it is not useful to or wanted by you (*He discarded his sweater because he was hot*).
C: If a building is *disused*, it is no longer used.
D: If you *dismiss someone* from a job, you sack them because they have done something wrong or because they are not good enough at the job (*If you are regularly late for work, you will be dismissed*).

24 D: If you are **apt to do** something, you tend to do something undesirable regularly (*be apt to worry too much/be apt to annoy other people*).
A: If something is *habitual*, someone does it regularly and often they have no control over it (*a habitual liar/drug user*).
B: If someone is *subject to something*, they regularly suffer from something unpleasant (*be subject to periods of severe depression*).
D: If someone is *susceptible to something*, they are easily influenced or harmed by it because they have no defence against it (*be susceptible to criticism/flattery*).

25 B: If you **avert something** unpleasant, you prevent it from happening by taking action.
A: If someone/something *hinders someone/something*, they/it make it difficult for someone to do something or for something to happen by being an obstacle (*problems that hinder progress/You're not helping me with all your useless advice, you're hindering me*).
C: If someone/something *impedes someone/something*, they stop them from making progress by getting in the way (*impede an opponent/Arguments between the parties have impeded the achievement of a political solution*).
D: If someone *swerves*, they move physically to one side in order to avoid something that is in their way or coming towards them (*swerve to avoid an oncoming vehicle*).

FURTHER PRACTICE AND GUIDANCE

P 39 PAPER 1 SECTION A

For questions 1–3 and explanations of questions 4–6, see ***Paper 1 Section A*** *above.*

4 a heightened   b exaggerated
   c overrated   d multiplied
5 a likelihood   b certainty
   c expectation   d belief
6 a full   b sheer   c whole   d total

p 40–42 PAPER 1 SECTION B

Two marks per question (Total: 30)

For the questions on this passage, see also the questions in ***Further Practice and Guidance*** *on page 43–44 and the corresponding answers .*

First Passage

26 B: In conversation with other travellers about bad hotels, he is usually able to *secure the decision* (win the contest) (line 6) because he can remember a hotel more awful than the ones described by the others. When he remembers – *on the recollection of –* (line 6) *an incontestably terrible place* (a place that others cannot argue about in terms of how terrible it is) (line 6) he wins the discussion. He can do this because he is *familiar with more wretched and abominable hotels than any other contender* (has experience of more terrible hotels than anyone else can claim to have) (line 3-4).
A: He has travelled extensively. He has moved *a great deal from place to place* (line 1) and he has done *five and a half circuits of the globe* (been round the world five and a half times) (line 3), but he doesn't claim to have travelled more than others.
C: A *hotel snob* (line 2) is someone who only likes to stay or talk about having stayed in the best hotels and is therefore particular about the hotels they stay in. The writer, however, is *a hotel snob in a perverse way* (line 2-3) (he likes to feel that he has stayed in the worst hotels).
D: He remembers more bad hotels he has stayed in than anyone else but he doesn't say he remembers more about any other aspect of his trips than anyone else.

27 C: He and his party were in the hotel because *a sudden whim struck the controllers of our magazine* (because the people they worked for had made a sudden decision to send them there). If this had not happened, they wouldn't have been there and *there would have been nobody at all* in the hotel (line 10-11).
A: Darjeeling was *a place of solitude and desolation* (a place that makes someone feel lonely and depressed) (line 7), but he had not chosen to go there, his employers had sent him there.
B: The hotel was big and empty so

that any sound echoed – it was *an echoing cavernous place* (line 8), but he was not staying there by choice and we are not told that it was the biggest hotel in the place.
D: Nobody had recommended the hotel, his employers had sent him there.

28 A: The lounge *resounded bleakly to every footstep* (echoed in a way that was depressing when people walked into it) (line 13-14), and the place was *abandoned* (people no longer stayed there) (line 13), making it a lonely place.
B: It was big – the lounge was *vast* and it had *vast lengths* of corridor (line 14), but he does not say that this surprised him.
C: It was very cold inside the hotel. The corridors were *freezing* (line 14) and they left their thick coats in the hallway so they could put them on rather than take them off when they came back inside because it was so cold in the hotel (line 16-17). However, although he found the cold uncomfortable, he does not state that it annoyed him. In fact he states *I bear no grudge against* the hotel, which means that he doesn't have angry feelings about it now (line 12).
D: He does not refer to the service at all. He says that the bar had an *untended chill* (was cold and unwelcoming because it wasn't well looked after) (line 14), and he says that it was a very cold hotel but he does not blame the staff for this.

29 C: The writer states that *it is customary to disparage the better known and generally praised aspects of famous beauty* (it is common for people to say that they are not as good as they are said to be) (line 21–22), and *to profess a sense of disappointment when confronted at last* by places famous for their beauty (to claim, perhaps untruly, to be disappointed when you finally see them(line 22–23).
A: He says that this is what people often say but he doesn't say that he agrees with that view.
B: He says that people are often disappointed by what are said to be the beautiful aspects of famous places, but he doesn't say that they find other things to appreciate.
D: He says that it is possible that *too much renown* (the fact that they are too well-known or familiar to people) (line 23–24) spoils them, but he does not say that too many people visit them.

30 D: The view *nearly bounced me out of bed* (nearly caused him to get suddenly and involuntarily out of bed) (line 19), and it *surpassed anything I had foreseen* (was better than anything he had been expecting) (line 25).
A: He couldn't see the world's highest mountain because the second-highest mountain in the world was in front of it but this did not spoil the view for him, because he describes it as *sensational* (wonderful) (line 19).
B: He was *trembling with cold* (shaking because he was very cold)(line 25) but this did not spoil his enjoyment of the

view, which he describes as *sensational*.
C: At first only the view of the world's highest mountain was *invisible* (impossible to see) (line 20), and what he could see was *sensational*. Later, clouds *engulfed* (covered completely) (line 26-27) the mountains, but by that time he had already seen a *sensational* view.

Second Passage

31 C: The writer states that the sports pages of every newspaper are *given over to describing just that (winning or losing a game)* (dedicated to or full of it) (line 7–8). She implies that it is not *so childish* (very childish) to care about this, but it is an example of *most of the things we do as adults* that contain *elements of childishness* (are childish to an extent) (line 3–7).
A: The writer refers to reports about sports, not to competing in them.
B: The writer says that people of many ages are likely to be told not to behave childishly and refers to adults reading the sports pages of newspapers, but does not compare what adults and children are interested in.
D: The reference to reading sports pages illustrates the fact that *most of the things we do as adults contain elements of childishness* (line 6–7), not the importance of being childish.

32 A: The writer states that she lives *in a culture that prizes self-restraint* (puts great value on controlling your feelings) (line 9), and that people are critical of *exuberance* (natural enthusiasm) and *unselfconscious self-expression* (expressing yourself freely without worrying, or being too shy to do so) (line 10–11).
B: Being *unselfconscious* (confident, not shy) does not necessarily mean being selfish and *self-restraint* is self-control.
C: The writer says that too much self-restraint *can be bad for you* (harmful to you as a person) (line 11-12). However, self-restraint is likely to stop you from being unpleasant to others when you would like to be.
D: Her culture disapproves of *being ruled by moods and emotions* (line 9–10) (which is what it views childishness as being) but the writer suggests that this stops people from being childish, not that it makes them want to be. She says that people are afraid of *letting go* (behaving freely and naturally) and this *prevents most of us from indulging in the luxury of being childish* (stops us from allowing ourselves to be childish and enjoy it) (line 14-15).

33 D: Playing with his plastic helicopter *gets my brain working again* (enables him to think and use his mind again when work is going badly) (line 23).
A: It is true that people *feel guilty about being childish* (line 13) and being childish stops her friend from worrying about his work (line 23) but he doesn't feel guilty about that because it gets his brain working again.
B: He may well enjoy playing with his

helicopter but the example is not intended to emphasize the enjoyment of being childish but the useful effect it can have on a person.
C: An adult playing with a plastic helicopter could be viewed by some people as strange but the writer thinks it's a good thing.

34 D: Playing is *good for you*, according to the writer (line 25) and the people *who enjoy old age* are those who *allowed themselves time off from the responsibilities of adulthood when they were younger* (were childish and played when younger) (line 26-29).
A: Those who enjoy old age took *time off from their responsibilities* (forgot about them for a while), so clearly they had responsibilities and there is no suggestion that they didn't have many responsibilities.
B: The writer says that people who enjoy old age were childish from time to time when younger; she does not say that they behave childishly when old.
C: The writer refers to the responsibilities people who enjoy old age had when younger; she does not say that they don't have any responsibilities when old.

35 C: She says that too much self-restraint *can be bad for you* (line 11-12) and that being childish is something that *everyone needs* (line 31). The last sentence of the article tells readers that if they feel too much pressure in their lives they should act childishly by showing annoyance (*stamp your foot, slam a door*), laughing in a childish way (*giggle*) or making silly facial expressions (*pull some silly faces*).
A: In lines 1–2, she says that she gives in to the desire (*succumb to the urge*) to behave childishly sometimes but the article is not mainly about her, it is about the advantages of behaving childishly sometimes and the fact that people feel that they can't do so.
B: She does refer to the *responsibilities of adulthood* (line 27) and to the pressures of adult life (line 31–33). She states that we want to stop being *responsible, capable* (line 34) sometimes and that we *crave a breather from 'grown-upness'* (desperately want to have a break from what is involved in being adult) (line 33). However, the main point of the article is not that it is terrible to have the pressures of adulthood but that being childish sometimes is good for you.
D: She does state that her culture prevents people from behaving childishly and that this is a bad thing (line 9-12) but the majority of the article is about childish behaviour being good for you, not her culture.

Third Passage

36 A: The things children watch on video, television and film *do nothing to build up reading skills* (line 9–10) and are replacing the work that *turns halting mechanical reading into the real thing* (enables children to progress from hesitant reading without really understanding what they are reading to 'real' reading, in which there is full understanding of what is being read) (line 10-11). The 'video wave' is largely responsible for *the declining interest in reading among the young* (line 1–2) and *the population would be better educated* if children did more reading (line 11–12).

B: The writer doesn't say that the stories on video, etc are not good stories or that not enough of them are good – she doesn't comment on the quality of them, only the effect on children of watching them and not reading.

C: Traditional stories (*mythologies and folk stories*) are simply examples of the kind of stories that satisfy our need for stories (line 4–7). They are therefore kinds of story that video is replacing but the fact that they are being replaced is not her main objection. Her main objection is that the reading of stories in general is being replaced by video, etc.

D: She describes many of the things shown on video, etc as *harmless in themselves* (the actual stories don't harm children) (line 9). It is the fact that they are replacing the reading of stories that she objects to.

37 D: The ideas in a written story are *sketched* (presented in a way that does not include every detail), and the reader's mind *creates the rest* (line 15). Watching stories *is a totally passive pastime* (an activity that requires nothing from the person doing it because everything in it has been decided by the people who made it and so there is nothing for the reader to imagine) (line 13).

A: Watching dramatized fiction *is easier for children whose reading is hesitant* because it is harder for them to *identify and enjoy the plot* (line 16-17) when reading fiction, but this does not mean that the stories in dramatized fiction are simpler.

B: Children who cannot read fluently can't understand and follow the stories they read, but this does not mean that there is less action and more description of character in written stories.

C: The writer states that all the details are provided for you in dramatized fiction, whereas you have to imagine some of them in written fiction, but she does not compare the amount of detail in each (line 13-15).

38 B: The writer talks about children who *read very slowly* (line 18-19) and says that they have books of only 100 words with them for a fortnight (can't read them in less than two weeks) and can only *decode a page or two* (work out the words on only a page or two) in class or for homework (line 20). For this reason, she says, it is *hardly surprising* (not at all surprising) that they *find reading boring and prefer to watch television* (line 21–22).

A: The problem is that they have to decode the words (work out what they mean). Their difficulty *is not reading the words – it is interpreting them*

(they can read the words easily enough, understanding them is the problem) (line 22–23).

C: They do read for homework and they do this *conscientiously* (with great care and attention) (line 20). Having to do it for homework is not what makes them dislike reading – the length of time it takes them to read a little is what discourages them.

D: They don't get bored because of the stories themselves but because of the length of time it takes them to read them.

39 C: She used to think that filmed stories were a *spur* (an encouragement) (line 27) to reading but she has now changed her mind and thinks that they *can spoil your reading for ever* (line 28-29).

A: She states that children need to practise daily (line 24) to become good readers. However, it is not stated that she now thinks differently about the importance of reading for children.

B: She says that parents ought to encourage children to read rather than watch television but this is not something she has changed her mind about.

D: The visual images of filmed stories *drown the imagination* (provide so much detail that the imagination cannot be used) (line 28), but she does not say that she now thinks children have less or more imagination than she previously thought they had.

40 C: Her main point is that it is a bad thing that video, television and film are replacing reading among children and that steps should be taken to change this situation. She says that parents should encourage children to read more and that children should practise reading (line 24–26) because reading involves the imagination and filmed stories do not.

A: She does analyse the differences between dramatized fiction and written fiction (3rd, 4th, last paragraph) but the purpose of her article is to express a view about the decline in reading among children and its replacement by video, etc.

B: She says that parents should encourage children to read and watch less television (line 25–26) but she does not blame them in particular for the fact that children don't read much – the fact that many of them read slowly and therefore find it boring is a major cause of the decline in reading.

D: The article is not aimed at children – it talks about them but does not address them directly.

PAPER 1: SECTION A   25 marks
          SECTION B   30 marks
          TOTAL   55 marks

To be converted into a score out of 40 marks.

p 43–44 PAPER 1 SECTION B

*For explanations to the answers see the **First Passage** above.*

Question 26
1 a great deal/five and a half circuits of the globe
2 c
3 b
4 the terrible hotels he has stayed in
5 which one of them has stayed in a worse hotel than anyone else

Question 27
1 c
2 cavernous
3 b

Question 28
1 b
2 vast
3 a
4 no
5 because it was colder inside the hotel than outside and they wanted to put them on when they came in

Question 29/30
1 the view outside his window
2 no   3 yes   4 b   5 yes   6 a
7 yes   8 yes

p 47 PAPER 2

Assessment of sample composition

1 **Content**
   This is a very good composition that directly addresses the topic at all times and contains no irrelevance.

2 **Organization**
   The composition is very well-organized, with paragraphing that is entirely appropriate. The first paragraph introduces the points of view expressed by the candidate (that there are good and bad aspects to modern technology) and acts as an effective beginning, providing background to the points to be made and a well-expressed and appropriate example (communications). The second paragraph deals with an example of the disadvantages; the third and fourth paragraphs give firstly an advantage and then a disadvantage, both concerning the same thing (medicine), and the final paragraph provides an effective conclusion that does not simply repeat or summarize what came before but moves on from it.

3 **Linking**
   In general, the linking of sentences and paragraphs is appropriate and accurate, for example, *on the one hand ... on the other hand* (first paragraph); *Or* (third paragraph); *But, as a matter of fact* (fourth paragraph). It is acceptable to begin a sentence with *but*. The use of *pros* (advantages, positive aspects) and *cons*

(disadvantages, negative aspects) in the third and fourth paragraph is highly effective for linking contrasting points. However, the first and second sentences are not correctly linked – the second sentence should begin *This progress, on the one hand* or *This progress can, on the one hand*. In the fourth paragraph *In a few words* would be better expressed as *In short*.

4 Use of vocabulary

There is a good range of more than simple vocabulary, for example, *made great strides* (made great progress) (first paragraph), *ethical, live ... in peace, get rid of, clubs, machine guns* (second paragraph), *eradicate, life expectancy* (third paragraph), *the abuse of* (fourth paragraph). None of the vocabulary is incorrect or inappropriate.

5 Use of grammar

The sentences are not all simple and although many are short, these are mostly accurately phrased. Some examples of good and accurate structures: *could have imagined that ... would be able to* and *convinced that ...* (first paragraph); *It is incredible how much time, spent on -ing* and *waste time -ing* (second paragraph), *because of which* (third paragraph); *instead of born* where the past participle is correctly used to continue the passive structure begun with *will be created* (fourth paragraph). There are a few mistakes. First paragraph: *Progresses* – progress is an uncountable noun and the plural is therefore incorrect, *lifes* should be *lives* and *realy* should be *really*. Second paragraph: The verb *proceed*, used twice, should be *progress*; since the paragraph refers to past causes of present situations, the past simple is inappropriate and the present perfect or perhaps a present tense should be used instead – *didn't proceed* (twice) should be *hasn't progressed* or *isn't progressing* (the present continuous is appropriate here because it refers to a current situation) and *couldn't get rid of* should be *haven't been able to get rid of* or *can't get rid of* ; *struggeling* should be *struggling*. Third paragraph: *an other* (twice) should be *another*; *implant* cannot be followed by a person and can only have as its object the thing that is implanted – this should be *implant another one*; *lifes* should be *lives*. Fourth paragraph: *prolongue* should be *prolong*; *like* should be *as*, meaning *in the way that*. Final paragraph: *made* should be *has made* or *makes*, (the past simple is inappropriate for the same reason as in the second paragraph); *breath* should be *breathe* and *the technological progress* should be *technological progress* because it refers to technological progress in general, not a specific example or aspect of it.

6 Style

The style is appropriate – fairly formal but with a conversational feel. The use of the question in the fourth paragraph is particularly effective in expressing a point of view. Points are clearly made and the composition flows well.

This composition is very good, with few serious mistakes and would be given a score of approximately 14–17 marks out of 20.

p 48 PAPER 3 SECTION A QUESTION 1

One mark per question (Total: 20)

1 **all**: *all over* a place = throughout a place.
2 **This/Such**: = the success/so much success and refers back to the success mentioned in the first sentence.
3 **demonstration/indication/example/ instance**: the company's success shows or is an example of how powerful news is.
4 **made**: if someone *makes their fortune by doing something*, they become rich as a result of doing it.
5 **by**: *by doing something* explains how someone does something or someone's method.
6 **to**: if you *use something to do something*, you use it to perform that function; *to forward* = to send (formal use).
7 **there/then**: *there* = in that place; *then* = at that time.
8 **By**: *by + a point in time* = before and at that time.
9 **establishing/setting**: if someone *establishes/sets a standard for doing something*, they do it in a good way that others follow.
10 **out**: if someone *sets out to do something*, they start with the intention of doing something.
11 **speed**: *speed* = being quick, in this context. If someone is *first with something*, they do it before anyone else and *speed* here refers to reporting the news quickly and before anyone else.
12 **away/out**: if something *fades away/out*, it gradually disappears.
13 **might/may/could**: if something *might/ may/could have happened*, it was possible that it would happen but it didn't happen.
14 **instead/actually**: this introduces what really happened (*it made a new start*) and was different from what was possible or expected – that Reuters would also fade.
15 **itself**: this indicates that Reuters changed on its own and that someone/ something else didn't change it.
16 **in**: if there is a *revolution in something*, there is an enormous change in the nature of it or the way in which it is done.
17 **made**: if something is *made possible*, something causes it to be possible or to happen. Here *made possible* = that/ which was made possible.
18 **the**: *the* + singular noun can be used to refer to something in general; *the microchip* here = microchips in general.
19 **now/currently**: this part of the sentence refers to Reuters' present operations.
20 **on**: *on screen* = shown on computer/television/cinema screens.

p 48 PAPER 3 SECTION A QUESTION 2

One mark per underlined word or phrase (Total: 15)

a <u>little enthusiasm</u>(1) <u>for the idea</u> (1) (2 marks)
If someone *has/shows enthusiasm for something*, they are enthusiastic about it; *little* = not much.
b <u>prefer playing golf</u> (1)<u>to watching it</u> (1) *or* <u>prefer to play golf</u> (1) <u>than to watch it</u> (1)(2 marks)
You can *prefer doing one thing to doing another*, or *prefer to do one thing than to do another*.
c <u>for the fact that I owed him a favour,</u>(1) <u>I wouldn't have agreed to help him.</u>(1)(2 marks)
But for = except for; *but for the fact that* = if it hadn't been the case that, if it hadn't been for the fact that; *but for the fact that* is used for giving the only reason why something happens or is done and forms part of a conditional sentence; the rest of the sentence is in the conditional form and explains what would have happened if that reason hadn't existed.
d <u>such wonderful news</u> that we decided to have a celebration (1 mark)
News is an uncountable noun and is therefore not preceded by *a*; however, any verb of which it is the subject is in the singular form; *so* is followed by an adjective, *such* is followed by an adjective and a noun.
e <u>great relief</u>(1) <u>that I heard (that)</u>(1) her condition was not serious (2 marks)
The adverb *greatly* has to be changed to the adjective *great*; the adjective *relieved* has to be changed to the noun *relief*; *with* is often used before nouns describing feelings to say that someone reacted to something with that feeling; *that* links sentences of this kind that begin with *it*.
f <u>her for not doing</u>(1) <u>her work carefully enough</u>(1)*or* <u>her for doing</u>(1) <u>her work carelessly</u> (1)(2 marks)
You *criticize someone for doing/not doing something*.
g <u>mind</u>(1) <u>being able to have</u>(1) as much time off work as he does.(2 marks)
If you *wouldn't mind doing something*, you would like to do it, although you don't have a strong desire to do it.
h <u>strong opponent/critic</u>(1) <u>of government policy</u>(1) for many years (2 marks)
Someone who opposes something is *an opponent/a critic of* it. The adverb *strongly* has to be changed to the adjective *strong*.

p 49 PAPER 3 SECTION A QUESTION 3

*See also the questions in **Further Practice and Guidance** on page 51 and the corresponding answers and explanations.*

One mark per underlined word or phrase (Total: 6)

a <u>in time to</u> (1) If you are *in time to do* something, you are not too late to do it.

b <u>save me (from)</u> (1) If something *saves someone (from) doing something*, it makes it unnecessary for them to do something that they don't want to do or that requires effort from them.

c <u>view of the fact that</u> (1) = because; *in view of* is followed by an object (*in view of the cost*); *in view of the fact that* is followed by subject, verb, etc.

d <u>a way of/a means of</u> (1) If you do something *as a way/means of doing something else*, that is how you do the second thing, that is your method for achieving it.

e <u>I supposed to put/write</u> or <u>I to put/write</u> (1) *am I supposed to do* = should I do because it is expected, it is a rule, it is what I have been told to do, etc; *am I to do* = am I required to do because it is an instruction; if you sign something, you *put/write your signature* on it.

f <u>couldn't (possibly) have been</u> (1) *couldn't have been more helpful* = was extremely helpful, was as helpful as possible; *couldn't have been* + comparative = was extremely ... , was as ...as possible (*the weather couldn't have been worse/better*).

p 50 PAPER 3 SECTION A QUESTION 4

One mark per underlined word or phrase (Total: 12)

*See also the questions in **Further Practice and Guidance** on page 52 and the corresponding answers.*

a <u>The course places/puts</u> (1)<u>(its) emphasis on practical skills</u>(1)*or*<u>The emphasis of the course is</u>(1) <u>on practical skills.</u>(1) (2 marks)
Someone/something *places emphasis on something* (gives most importance to); the emphasis of something *is on something*.

b <u>The meeting was rearranged at short notice/without much notice/with very little notice.</u> (1 mark)
If someone does something *at short notice, without much notice* or *with very little notice*, they do it only a short time in advance, without giving the other people involved much warning or time to prepare.

c <u>She'll never/will never/won't ever/can't forgive him</u>(1) <u>for letting her down.</u>(1) (2 marks)
If you *forgive someone for doing something*, you stop being angry with them because of something bad they have done to you personally; *will always* has to be transformed into *will never/won't ever*, etc to make it negative.

d <u>I agreed to do the work on the understanding that I would be paid for it.</u>or <u>It was my understanding when I agreed to do the work that I would be paid for it.</u>or <u>My understanding when I agreed to do the work was that I would be paid for it.</u> (1 mark)
If you do something *on the understanding that* something else will

happen, you do it because you have been told or believe you have been told that the second thing will happen; *someone's understanding* is what they have been told or believe they have been told is the case.

e <u>Her attitude is putting her job at risk.</u>or <u>She is putting her job at risk because of her attitude.</u>or <u>Her job is at risk because of her attitude.</u> (1 mark)
If someone/something *is putting something at risk*, they are doing something which is a danger to it and which might cause it to be lost or damaged; if something *is at risk*, it is in danger of being lost or damaged.

f (I think) <u>you should make allowances for other people's weaknesses.</u> (1 mark)
If you *make allowances for someone/something*, you are sympathetic or tolerant towards someone because they have a particular problem.

g <u>They are highly unlikely</u>(1) <u>to win the game.</u>(1)*or* <u>It is highly unlikely (that)</u> (1)<u>they will win the game.</u>(1) (2 marks)
If something is *highly unlikely to* happen or if someone is *highly unlikely to do* something, it is almost certain that it won't happen or that they won't do it.

h <u>I don't wish</u>(1) <u>to make you feel</u>(1) any worse about this.or <u>It is not my wish</u>(1) <u>to make you feel</u>(1) any worse about this. (2 marks)
If you *wish to do something*, you want or intend to do it; if *it is your wish to do something*, it is your desire or intention to do it.

SECTION A:
QUESTION 1	20 marks
QUESTION 2	15 marks
QUESTION 3	6 marks
QUESTION 4	12 marks
TOTAL	53 marks

FURTHER PRACTICE AND GUIDANCE

p 51 PAPER 3 SECTION A QUESTION 3

a 1: *I thought I was going to be late but* = I expected to be late but I wasn't (2 and 4); *just* indicates that I got there a short time before the start of the film (3).

b 4: *pick me up* = collect me in the car; if you do this, it will not be necessary for me to queue for a taxi (1, 2 and 3).

c 4: *hardly any tickets were sold* = very few tickets were sold; this is why the event was cancelled; there is nothing to suggest that this is a conditional sentence – there are no modal verbs (1 and 3); there is no suggestion that the event was cancelled a short time afer the tickets became available, only that not many tickets were sold (2).

d 1: Listening to music is how I relax, it makes it possible for me to relax; there is no suggestion that I am already relaxed when I do this (2) and no reference to coming home (3) or to my taste in music (4).

e 4: On a form, there is usually a place

where you should sign; you are unlikely to ask about the possibility of signing (1 and 2) or about which of a number of places is the best to choose (3).

f 2: The receptionist *gave me all the information I asked for* and was therefore very helpful (1, 3 and 4).

FURTHER PRACTICE AND GUIDANCE

p 52 PAPER 3 SECTION A QUESTION 4

*For explanations, see **Section A question 4** above.*

a 2, 3, 4
b 2
c 2, 3
d 2, 3, 5
e 2, 5
f 2
g 2, 4
h 2, 3

p 53–55 PAPER 3 SECTION B

Answers similar to or covering the same points as those given here are acceptable providing they are phrased accurately.

*See also the questions in **Further Practice and Guidance** on pages 56–57 and the corresponding answers.*

a **She was too shocked to speak (1) because she hadn't been expecting the portrait (1) and it was horrible/awful, etc (1). (3 marks)**
If something *renders someone speechless* (line 2), it surprises them so much that they are unable to speak; if something happens *out of the blue* (line 2), it is completely unexpected; *horrendous* (line 3) = very awful/terrible, etc.

b **That she spoke/reacted in an exaggerated way (1) with praise/compliments (1) that she didn't mean (1). (3 marks)**
If someone *goes over the top*, they act or react in a way that is more extreme than necessary; *flattery* = pleasant remarks made to someone about them or something they have done to please them or make them feel that they are good in some way; *vacuous* = empty, without meaning.

c **Her flatmate thought that the artist really hated her (1) and other people found it funny/thought it wasn't meant to be serious (1). (2 marks)**
Must is used for describing what her flatmate believed to be the case, based on the evidence she had (the painting); if someone *feels/does something with a vengeance*, they do it with enormous force; if you think that something *is a joke*, you find it funny or you think that it is not seriously intended (line 9–10).

d **the way/how the writer looked when the photograph was taken/the writer's appearance in the photograph (1)**
She had *looked like that* (line 12) only at the moment when the photograph had been taken and it was *in that form* that

the artist had captured her.

e **in a way but not exactly** (1 mark)
Sort of is often used when people are saying that something is not exactly the case.

f **She had attempted to show the writer's true personality (1), not to show her as she really looked** (1). (2 marks)
The artist was trying *to portray the essence of my personality, or some characteristic of my inner soul* (what the real nature of the writer's personality was or something that was deep within the writer's nature) (line 14–15), and *not trying for a literal likeness* (not trying to produce something that was exactly like the way the writer really looked) (line 13-14).

g **Because she had said how much she loved it (1)and because the fact that it wasn't displayed might prevent the artist from getting other commissions which she really needed** (1).(2 marks)
She was worried about its absence from her walls (the fact that it wasn't on one of her walls) after *declaring dishonestly* (after lying about) how much she loved it; her friend was unlikely to *attract new commissions* (be paid by other people to paint pictures for them) because of this, and she *desperately needed* (needed very much) these commissions (line 17–20).

h **That she liked it so much (1) that she had put it in the attic for others to find in the future** (1). (2 marks)
If you are *attached to something*, it has great importance or significance in your life and you don't want to lose it; an *attic* is the room or space at the top of a house, under the roof; *future generations* are people that will be born in the future (line 20–21).

i **that she had put the painting in the attic** (1 mark)
That lie refers back to the lie the writer was considering in the sentence *How could I say ...?* (line 20–21); the sentences beginning *Or should I* and *Supposing* refer to an alternative to and a consequence of that lie (line 21).

j **She thought that she should support and encourage her friend in her new career because that is what good friends do for each other**(1), **and it soved the problem of what to buy her mother for her birthday**(1).(2 marks)
She thought that it was her *duty to support and encourage* her friend; (*as good friends do*) = in the way that good friends act towards each other (line 23-24); she was *stuck for a present* for her mother's birthday =she couldn't think of anything to buy for her mother. (line 24–26).

k **Because it was where her mother lived and it was where she had had a wonderful childhood.** (1 mark)
The painting was *too personal* (related to her own life and feelings) because *it was my mother's home* and she *had spent an idyllic childhood there*; *idyllic* = perfect, in the sense of being extremely peaceful and pleasant.(line 31–33).

l **avoided giving an answer until she could think of one/tried to delay giving an answer** (1 mark)
If you *play for time*, you avoid or delay doing something that someone wants you to do until you are forced to do it or able to do it.

m **complicated lies (1) of the kind she told the first artist** (1). (2 marks)
If you get *tied up in knots*, you get involved in something complicated that confuses you; *deceit* is behaviour or speech that is intended to make someone believe something that isn't true; the writer says that she was determined to be honest *this time* and she is therefore contrasting what she says to the second artist with what she said to the first artist.

n **had been put in the most visible/noticeable/prominent place** (1 mark)
If something *has pride of place*, someone particularly likes it or is proud of it and has put it in a place, for example, in a room, where everyone who goes into the place will notice it.

o **She got annoyed and refused to speak to the writer** (1), **releasing a lot of feelings about what a bad friend the writer was** (1) **that she had been holding back for a long time** (1). (3 marks)
If someone *is sulking* or *is in a sulk* (line 39), they are angry and refusing to speak; if something powerful or violent is *unleashed* (line 39), it is released; *a string of* (line 39) = a lot of; if a feeling is *pent-up* (line 39), it is strongly felt but kept under control and not expressed.

Questions a–o: Total 27 marks

p 55 PAPER 3 SECTION B SUMMARY

p One mark each for inclusion of the following points or points similar to them.

First painting
– **it made her look ugly** (it was a *monstrous caricature* – it distorted and exaggerated her features in a horrible way) (line 7)
–**it showed her in a way she had only looked for a second, not how she really looked** (line 12)
–**she couldn't recognize any part of her personality in it** (line 15 -16)

Second painting
–**it didn't capture the character of the place** (line 26–27)
–**it didn't capture the peaceful atmosphere of the place** (line 29–30)
–**the colours weren't right and didn't go together** (line 30–31)

Total: 6 marks

Plus a maximum of 4 marks for general impression, based on the following criteria:
– relevance
– general level of fluency
– accuracy of language
– absence of copying from passage
– length

SUMMARY: Total: 10 marks

SECTION B TOTAL: 37 marks

PAPER 3   SECTION A: 53 marks
         SECTION B: 37 marks
         TOTAL   90 marks

To be converted into a score out of 40 marks.

FURTHER PRACTICE AND GUIDANCE

p 56–57 PAPER 3 SECTION B

For explanations, see the explanations for the answers for Paper 3 Section B above.

Question b	1b 2d
Question l	b
Question n	a
Question d	a
Question i	c
Question m	b

FURTHER PRACTICE AND GUIDANCE

p 57 PAPER 3 SECTION B SUMMARY

First Painting: tick 2, 4, 5
Second Painting: tick 2, 3, 4, 5

All the other choices are true but they are not relevant to the summary because they are not aspects of the paintings that she disliked.

For explanations of the correct choices, see Paper 3 Section B – Summary above.

p 58 PAPER 4 PART ONE

The line references are to the tape transcripts on pages 169 -170.

One mark per question (Total: 10 marks)

1 **false**: It got its name from a reporter's description of the sound of a lot of pianos being played at the same time and heard in the street through open windows; he said that they sounded like tin pans and the street subsequently became known as Tin Pan Alley (line 9–26).
2 **false**: Although many great songwriters worked there, they didn't consciously decide to do that, *they wound up there* (they found themselves there as a result of other events and circumstances) (line 27-33).
3 **false**: Publishers, not songwriters, had offices there – it was a place where a songwriter could demonstrate a song to a large number of publishers, all in the same place (line 39-46).
4 **true**: Many wonderful songs were published but failed to be hits because *they were not properly exploited* (not enough or not the right kind of effort was made to promote them) (line 55-60).
5 **false**: It was not a good idea to follow

what was popular at the time in order to write a song that a publisher would accept because if you did that publishers would consider that the song wasn't *individual enough to stand out from* (to be easily distinguished from) *other songs* (line 64 -70).

6 **false**: Publishers didn't really know what they were looking for, they simply hoped that something that appealed to their idea of what would become popular would be brought to them (line 47-52); it was worth taking your song to other publishers if one rejected it, because they didn't all have the same ideas and you might find one who liked it (line 61-65, 73-78). However, there is no suggestion that they would make a decision to publish a song or not and later change that decision.

7 **true**: There was *no big social life* and writing was the *entire life of the songwriter*. On most occasions when songwriters met, it was to write (line 89-94).

8 **false**: Songwriting provided them with their income but there is no mention of songwriters becoming rich, and the fact that a songwriter *tried to keep his family going* with this income suggests that it was not high and that it was therefore difficult for them to manage (line 94-97).

9 **true**: When one songwriter met another, they would always talk about new ideas they had had or one would hum his latest song to the other to find out what the other's opinion was (line 99-104).

10 **true**: It could be said to have *started to decline* when TV and radio started, but it moved to California because musical films were being made there and that was *where the action was* (where the most important activity in the music business was happening). It therefore continued to exist in a different place and although New York became *secondary* (of less importance in the music business) at that time, it clearly continued to exist in a less important form in New York also (line 105-115).

p 58 PAPER 4 PART TWO

One mark per question (Total: 5 marks)

11 **C**: The policy of not fighting lightning fires started when it was discovered that they *burnt themselves out* (stopped naturally, not because of any action taken to stop them) *in a fairly small area of land*. The *bulk* (the majority) of the park *remained untouched* (was not affected by the fires) (line 1–14).
A: There is no suggestion that attempts to fight the fires failed.
B: The fires referred to were in the park itself, but only affected small areas within it.
D: They watched them burn because they knew they would stop without any action being required, not because the fires were too dangerous to fight.

12 **A**: In 1988 the policy was *suspended*

(ended) because there were a number of fires that were not fought and this *enraged* the public (made them very angry) (line15 20). The *year when the policy ended* (1988) was also the year when *a study of the history of fires in the park ended.* (line 25–28).
B: This policy was the one that involved not fighting the fires and is the policy that was ended in that year – lightning fires were then fought rather than left to stop naturally (line 18–20).
C: *A series* (a number) *of unfought fires engulfed* (completely covered large areas of) the park, not one single fire (line 17-18).
D: The fires made the public very angry because they were not fought (line 16-18), but there is no suggestion that they were started by members of the public.

13 **A**: It was discovered that there was a huge area in the park where all the trees had started to grow in 1704, and it was concluded that this was because there was an enormous fire in that year that *destroyed all those trees' predecessors* (destroyed every one of the trees that had been there before the ones that replaced them and are now there) (line 34-40).
B: The research found that there had been a number of fires in the park in the past and the *fires a few years ago* gave them the opportunity to test their theories about fires in the park (line 55-57), but there is no suggestion that there has been an increase in the number of fires.
C: The researchers found that *some trees survived* the fire in the 1870s, which means that a lot did not, and that therefore there was a great deal of damage. Those that did survive *still bear the scars* (still have visible signs of damage) (line 42–44).
D: There was a big fire there in 1704 but the researchers found evidence of *periodic fires* (fires happening from time to time) *dating back over* (having happened during a period covering) *a thousand years* (line 45-47).

14 **C**: In one part of the park where there was a fire recently, only *one or two* lodge pole pines are growing back, whereas in other parts where there were recent fires, *it's thick with saplings* (a lot of young trees are growing) (line 61-67). This is believed to be because in the first part – where hardly any trees are growing – the cones (the reproductive parts of the pine tree) of the trees were open before the fire and so they burned easily, whereas in the other parts – where a lot of trees are growing – the cones were *closed up tight and able to withstand fire* (defend themselves against fire) (line 67-73). The researcher believes that this difference is because the places where a lot of trees are growing burnt in the 1870 fire, whereas the place where hardly any trees are growing last had a fire 150 years before that (line 73-78). He concludes that the trees in the

places where many are growing adapted to the threat of fire by closing their cones tightly because they had experienced fire more recently than the trees in the areas where hardly any are growing. His research therefore suggests that the lodge pole pine is capable of adapting so that it can be *prepared* for fire – those that had adapted were able to defend themselves better against the recent fires than those that had not adapted (line 78-80).
A: The lodge pole pine *is having a tough time* (is having difficulty) *fighting back* in one part of the park, but *one or two* are growing there, so it has not disappeared completely there (line 61-65).
B: Aspen have appeared in an area where there were none before the last fires. They therefore did not *survive* the fires, because they weren't there when the fires occurred. (line 84-87).
D: They don't know how the aspen appeared in that place but are sure that this wouldn't have happened if the fires hadn't been so big (line 87-91). There is, however, no reference to the speed at which aspen grow back and they are not growing back in that particular area because they weren't there before the fire.

15 **B**: The presenter concludes that *all that destruction is actually preserving nature* (line 93-101) because *fire creates opportunities and differences* in that the same things grow back again or new things grow in places affected by fire (line 94–96).
A: The presenter concludes that forest fires are a *cornerstone* (a fundamental part) of the *diversity* of (the range of different things to be found in) the park because they have caused changes in what grows in certain parts (line 99-100). The research described in the programme has made discoveries about the effects of the fires over the years. However, there is no suggestion that these effects have changed; instead there is a description of what those effects have been.
C: Although in one place the pines may *grow straight back* (grow back immediately after a fire), there is no suggestion that they grow bigger after one (line 94-96). The research described in the programme has drawn conclusions about how and where trees grow after fires but makes no reference to the size of these trees.
D: Although the programme concludes that fire does not damage nature in the long-term because some things grow back or new things grow after them, the fact that new things grow in places where there were fires means that there is a long-term result of those fires.

p 59 PAPER 4 PART THREE

One mark per question (Total: 8 marks)

16 **(on the) north coast of Jamaica**:

line 5–6

17 (a) tourist resort: line 9–10

18 (a) quiet fishing village: line 10-11

19 Fisherman's Beach: line 21–23; This is *the one part that has changed very little* – if a place is *unspoiled*, it has not been affected by modern developments.

20 Downs River Falls/a waterfall: line 31–35; It is *just down the coast* – not far down the coast.

21 (a) new pier: line 37–39

22/23 (the) craft market/(a) (new) shopping centre (in any order): line 43–44; line 63-66 – the cinema has been *torn down* and replaced by a new shopping centre.

p 59 PAPER 4 PART FOUR

*See also the questions in **Further Practice and Guidance** on page 60 and the corresponding answers.*

One mark per question (Total: 10 marks)

24 yes: Although she doesn't glance backwards – look back to when she worked for an employer (line19 and 21-22) – with any desire to do so (line 22-24), she does admit to *occasionally a glance sideways* (occasionally she looks at what other people are doing) and thinking *I wish I was over there* (I wish I was in their position) (line 20–21).

25 yes: She says that if you work for yourself you become arrogant and that therefore it's possible that they are not *employable any more* (she is not sure that an employer would want to give them jobs.) (line 24-28).

26 no: She says that a few of the businesses featured in her book have failed and that this is sad, but she doesn't mention having any fear that this will happen to their business (line 33-38).

27 no: She says that the people whose businesses failed have started others because the desire to work for yourself is *like a drug*. It is an addiction, something that you cannot stop yourself from doing because *once you're on it* (addicted to it) you probably can't *get off it* (give up the addiction) (line 38-43). It is therefore not something to be admired because it requires courage or any other admirable quality, it is something that those who do it cannot stop themselves from doing.

28 yes: She says that you are motivated to work for yourself if you don't fit in at work(don't get on with others there), don't like being told what to do (don't want to obey orders), and feel *that you could do it* (the work or a piece of work) *better yourself*, presumably better than the person who does or did it (line 48-54). Since she decided to work for herself, these must have been her reasons too and she must have believed that her abilities were superior to those of certain other people.

29 yes: She says that she is *not saying no to the money* (not refusing it) and therefore she does want to have it. For her *independence is the key thing* (the

main motive) but money is also *attractive* (line 57-61).

30 yes: They decided that they were not *going to be happy carrying on doing what we were doing* – working for large companies – and that therefore they should start their own business, since this would put them in a position where they were *interested and enjoying what we were doing* (line 71-80).

31 yes: Although they chose a kind of business in which they, particularly her husband, *had some sort of experience* (line 95-99 and 108–115), she says that there was a *sense of danger* and a *sense of fear* when they first started (line 118-121).

32 yes: They have a *low boredom threshold* (they get bored easily) (line 132-134) and change their lives completely if life is *going along in a humdrum way* (continuing in a dull way, with everything always the same) (line 126-128).

33 no: Although they get bored easily and like to completely rearrange their lives when they get bored (line 126-132), there is no suggestion that they are bored with the business they have now or are planning to make changes.

PAPER 4	PART ONE	10 marks
	PART TWO	5 marks
	PART THREE	8 marks
	PART FOUR	10 marks
	TOTAL	33 marks

To be converted into a score out of 20 marks.

FURTHER PRACTICE AND GUIDANCE

p 60 PAPER 4 PART FOUR

Tick 1, 3, 4, 6, 8, 9, 11, 13, 16, 18, 19. See the explanations to the questions for Part Four above.

FURTHER PRACTICE AND GUIDANCE

p 63–64 PAPER 5

Talking About Passages

1 a

2 He/She talks about being *relaxed with journalists*, gives an opinion about *the popular press* and refers to *my own experiences* with them, all of which indicates that he/she is not one of them.

3 He/She is likely to be a politician about whom journalists wrote unfavourable stories. He/She previously felt that *friction* (tension and disagreement) between the press and the government was an acceptable part of *a free society*, which indicates that he/she was a member of the government. He/She would have thought that some of the things the popular press do are *disgraceful* (terrible, unacceptable) *whatever happened to me*, which indicates that the press did something that could be regarded as disgraceful

to him/her.

4 c

5 The fact that TV or radio stations do not feature much foreign/overseas/international news. He/She says that they underestimate the public's interest in this and are *pandering to* (desperately trying to please) only one section of the public, who are *insular* (only concerned with what happens in their own country), but that *not everyone is like that*.

6 He/She probably works in the news department of a TV or radio station because he/she says that it is *damn hard to get an international story on the networks* (it is very difficult to have an international story broadcast on one of the national stations). This indicates that the person is involved in doing this and has tried and sometimes failed to make sure that an international story they think should be covered has been covered.

7 In b the writer/speaker seems to be someone whose job it is to employ others in some form of the media. He/She refers to having CVs (personal histories that accompany a job application) *on my desk* and to the backgrounds and aims of the people that contact him/her trying to get jobs in the media.

8 The large number of young people trying to get jobs in the media. This is implied in the first sentence.

9 The fact that a lot of young people take media courses at colleges, want to follow relatives into the media, or simply want to work in the media because they think it's a good idea for them.

Talking About The Topic

1 the Press/the press
2 reviews
3 glossy
4 correspondent
5 weekly; monthly
6 editorial
7 gossip
8 tabloid
9 quality/broadsheet
10 journalism

1 live
2 highlights
3 commercials
4 episode
5 chat show
6 game/quiz show
7 repeats
8 soap (opera)
9 situation comedy/sitcom
10 documentary

TEST THREE

p 65 - 66 PAPER 1 SECTION A

Note that all explanations in this part refer to the meaning or use of each option most closely related to the question, not necessarily to the only meaning or use of these options.

*For questions 1–3, see also the questions in **Further Practice and Guidance** on pages 67–68 and the corresponding answers.*

One mark per question (Total: 25)

1 B: If you do something **with a view to doing** something else; you do it with that purpose in your mind.
A: *With regard to* = on the subject of/regarding.
C: *On consideration* = having thought about it again/having thought carefully about it.
D: *In relation to* = with reference to/regarding.
LOOK OUT! In this type of question, all the choices fit the meaning of the sentence but only one completes the phrase required.

2 B: **Considering** = when you take something into consideration/when you consider.
A: *Allowing for* = taking into consideration.
C: *Regarding* = on the subject of.
D: *Assuming* = based on the belief that something is the case.
LOOK OUT! In this type of question, all the choices have the same function in sentences – they all link parts of them – but only one makes sense as a link for the parts of the sentence given, and is grammatically correct. (*Allowing for* would also be correct, but *for* is not supplied in the question.)

3 C: **Judging by** = basing my opinion on.
A: *As for* = in the case of.
B: *Provided* = as long as/on condition that/if.
D: *Seeing as* = since it is true/the case that.
LOOK OUT! Again, all the choices link parts of sentences but only one fits the meaning of this sentence.

4 B: (*see the explanations in Further Practice and Guidance question 4 below*).

5 D: If something/someone **tempts someone into doing** something, they succeed in persuading that person to do something they should not do by attracting them to it.
A: If someone *persuades someone to do* something, they cause them to agree to do it by giving them reasons or putting pressure on them (*He persuaded me to lend him some money*).
B: If someone *convinces someone that* something is the case, they make them believe that it is the true situation by giving them evidence or insisting (*He convinced her that he was telling the truth*).
C: If something *sways someone*, it causes them to make one decision rather than another or to do one thing rather than another (*I wasn't sure which job to take but it was the salary offered by the first that finally swayed me*).

6 B: If you **chuckle**, you laugh quietly.
A: If you *groan*, you make an involuntary sound that shows you are in pain, annoyed or bored (*groan with pain*).
C: If you *grunt*, you make an involuntary sound caused by making a great effort, or you make a short sound instead of speaking (*grunt when lifting a heavy suitcase/When I asked him if he was annoyed with me, he just grunted*).
D: If you *squeal*, you make a high-pitched sound because you are frightened or excited (*squeal when seeing a huge spider/squeal with delight*).

7 C: **In the absence of something** = because something is missing/lacking/not present.
A: *A scarcity of something* = a shortage of it, a lack of supply of it (*There is a scarcity of cheap housing on the market at the moment*).
B: *The/A lack of something* = none of it/not enough of it (*Lack of interest in the event meant that there was only a small crowd./The lack of goals produced a rather boring match./a lack of facilities in a city*)Note: *In the lack of* is not possible.
D: *For want of something* = because something doesn't exist/is lacking (*She stays in the job for want of a better alternative*).

8 B: If someone **outdoes** someone else, they do better than them at something (*rivals constantly trying to outdo each other*).
A: If someone *excels at something*, they are very good at it or do it very well (*She always excelled at Physics when she was at school*).
C: If one thing *outweighs* another, it has more importance than it (*The interests of her children outweighed all other considerations for her*).
D: If someone *overdoes* something, they exaggerate it or do it to an extent that is not necessary or advisable (*overdo the importance of something trivial/I think I've overdone the spices in this dish*).

9 A: If clothes **shrink**, they get smaller as a result of being washed.
B: If something *is crumpled*, it has lost its shape and is no longer smooth as a result of pressure being applied to it (*a crumpled jacket/piece of paper*).
C: If an account or a piece of writing is *condensed*, a short version of it is given (*a condensed version of a story*).
D: If you *compress something*, you force it to occupy a small or smaller space by applying pressure to it (*compress a great many clothes into a suitcase*).

10 B: If people are **in attendance**, they attend or are present at something.
A: If you are or do something *in company with someone*, you are or do it with them (*In company with most other people there, I was astonished by what happened*).
C: *Someone's/Something's presence* is the fact or act of being there (*Will my presence be required at the meeting?*).
D: *Someone's/something's appearance* is the fact or act of appearing or arriving somewhere (*His unexpected appearance took everyone by surprise*).

11 A: If you **resort to something/to doing something**, you take an unpleasant course of action because every other course of action has failed to achieve the desired result.
B: If you *employ something* to achieve something, you use it in order to achieve an aim (*employ certain technical terms to explain how something works*).
C: If you *apply something to something*, you use it in order to help you to achieve an aim (*apply logic to a problem*).
D: If you *adopt* a particular course of action, you decide to follow it or start following it (*adopt a different method for solving a problem*).

12 D: If someone/something **comes over to someone as something**, they create the impression of being something.
A: If something *is coming along*, it is making progress (*How is dinner coming along?*).
B: If someone/something *comes up to* a certain standard or level, it reaches or achieves it (*His work didn't come up to the required standard*).
C: If an attempt to do something *comes off*, it is successful (*take a risk that comes off*).

13 C: If something is **uppermost in** your mind or thoughts, it is the thing that you are thinking about more than anything else.
A: *supreme* = the greatest possible (*do something with supreme skill/confidence*).
B: *principal* = main/greatest in importance (*my principal reason/concern/wish*).
D: If someone/something is *superior to* someone/something, they are better than or more important than them in some way (*His skills are superior to those of any other player in the team./The Managing Director is superior to the Head of Department*).

14 A: If you **get by**, you manage with some difficulty to survive financially.
B: If you *keep up* a certain level or standard, you succeed in maintaining it (*This is good work. Keep it up!*).
C: If you *live on* a certain amount of money, that is the amount of money that you have and are able to spend in the normal course of your life (*people who have to live on low incomes*).
D: If you *stand for* something, you tolerate it (*I'm not going to stand for any more of her rudeness*).

15 A: If you **remedy** something, you find a solution to it or make it right again.
B: If you *recover* something, you get it back again (*recover losses*).
C: If a doctor or form of medical treatment *cures someone of* an illness, they cause the person to recover completely from it or they end it (*cure a patient/a disease*).
D: If an injury or cut *heals*, it gets better through a natural process (*That cut will heal more quickly if you don't cover it*).

16 B: If something is **modelled on** something, it is mainly copied from or based on it.

A: If something *moulds* something, it causes it to develop in a particular way (*His personality was moulded during his schooldays*).

C: If something is *adapted from* something, it is based on it but changes have been made (*a film adapted from a novel*).

D: If something *shapes* something, it influences the nature of it or the way it develops (*Our attitudes are shaped by the culture we come from*).

17 D: Purely = simply and with nothing else involved.

A: If someone does something *singly*, they do it alone or individually (*guests arriving singly/give out books singly*).

B: If someone does something *fully*, they do it without leaving anything out (*explain fully*).

C: If someone says something *directly*, they say it without trying to be diplomatic or polite (*He told me directly that he was annoyed with me*).

18 B: If you **feel for** someone, you have sympathy for them because they are unhappy.

A: If you *commiserate with* someone who is unhappy, you tell them that you have sympathy with them.

C: If you *sympathize* with someone who is unhappy, you feel sympathy for them or you tell them that you feel sympathy for them.

D: If you *pity* someone, you feel that they are a very unfortunate or inadequate person (*pity someone who is always unlucky/pity yourself because life has treated you badly*).

19 C: If someone/something is **promising**, they are considered likely to be good or successful.

A: *Prospective* = might be or happen in the future (*a prospective customer/law*).

B: *Potential* = might become or develop into (*a potential winner/disaster*).

D: *Thriving* = prospering or developing well (*a thriving trade/economy*).

20 A: If someone **inquires into** something, they try to find out information or details about it.

B: If someone *seeks* something, they try to find it (*people seeking employment*).

C: If someone *investigates something*, they examine it and try to find out details about it (*investigate a crime*).

D: If you *explore something*, you consider it carefully and try to find out about every aspect of it (*explore the possibility of starting a business*).

21 D: If something **crosses your mind**, it suddenly or briefly comes into your mind.

A: If something *hits you*, you suddenly realize or think of it (*It suddenly hit me that I was making an awful mistake*).

B: If something *touches you*, it affects you emotionally because it is something pleasant for you or kind to you personally (*I was touched by all the cards I was sent when I was ill*).

C: If something *strikes you*, you suddenly realize it or it suddenly comes into your mind (*It struck me that something was wrong*).

22 C: If you act in a certain way (*act + adverb*), you behave in a way that suggests a certain feeling, attitude or belief, although this may not really be the case.

A: If you *behave* in a certain way (*behave + adverb*), you act in that way (*behave strangely/nervously/foolishly*).

B: If you *pose as* someone, you pretend to be that person, although you are not (*pose as an expert*).

D: If you *pretend to be something/someone*, you say or act as if you are that thing, although you are not (*pretend to be clever/a policeman*).

23 C: If you *glance* in a certain direction, you look quickly and briefly in that direction.

A: If you *blink*, you open and close your eyes quickly (*stare at something without blinking once*).

B: If you *squint*, you frown and partially close your eyes because of bright light in your eyes or because it is difficult to see something (*squint into the sunshine/squint at small print*).

D: If you *glimpse something*, you see it for a brief moment and then it disappears (*glimpse a figure moving in the distance*).

24 B: Regard for something/someone is respect or consideration for them.

A: *Sensitivity to something* is awareness and understanding of the feelings of others (*show sensitivity to the way someone is feeling*).

C: *Awareness of something* is knowing or realizing that it exists or is the case (*show awareness of a problem*).

D: *Perception of something* is the ability to realize or understand the true nature of something, not only how it appears on the surface (*an analysis that shows considerable perception of the situation*).

25 A: A **deficiency** is something lacking in or wrong with someone/something.

B: A *shortage* is not enough of something (*a shortage of water*).

C: A *disability* is a permanent physical problem that prevents someone from doing certain things (*he gets a pension because of his disability*).

D: A *snag* is a small disadvantage or problem (*It's a good idea but I can see one or two snags*).

FURTHER PRACTICE AND GUIDANCE

p 67–68 PAPER 1 SECTION A

1 a consideration
 b view
 c regard
 d relation

2 a Allowing
 b Assuming
 c Regarding
 d Considering

3 a Seeing as
 b Judging by

 c As for
 d Provided

For explanations of questions 1–3, see ***Paper 1 Section A*** *above.*

4 a turned: If someone *turns up* at a particular time, they arrive at that time.

b getting: If it is *getting on for* a particular time, it is approaching or nearly that time.

c put: If you *put someone up*, you give them temporary accommodation in your home.

d takes: If something *takes up* a particular amount of time, it occupies that amount of time.

e get: If you *get something over with*, you do and complete something unpleasant so that it is not still waiting to be done.

f turns: If someone *turns to someone*, they go to that person for help.

g taken: If someone *takes to doing something*, they start regularly doing something strange or uncharacteristic.

h get: If someone *gets away with doing something*, they do something that they should not be allowed to do but they are not punished or made to stop doing it.

i put: If you *put up with something*, you tolerate it even though you don't like it.

j turned: If you *turn something/someone down*, you refuse an/their offer.

k take: If you *take someone up on* an offer, you accept their offer some time after it has been made.

l put: If something *puts you off doing something*, it makes you not want to do it.

p 69–71 PAPER 1 SECTION B

Two marks per question (Total: 30)

First Passage

26 B: At that point she *just wanted the horses out* (to remove them from where they were because of the possibility of flooding) (line 8).

A: She *wasn't too concerned* (not very worried) (line 7–8), despite the fact that it had *flooded across the road* (line 5) and that people had *said there was flooding* (line 6–7), so she doesn't appear to have thought the flooding would be severe.

C: It had flooded across the road *down where the barn is* (line 5), but she doesn't say that she thought there was a danger of the barn itself flooding.

D: At this point it is already *hailing really bad* (lots of small pieces of ice were coming down heavily like rain) (line 6), so the storm is already happening and seems to have been bad at that time.

27 B: The trees that were in the river were *snarling* (making aggressive sounds) *snapping* (making cracking sounds) and *shoving down that river* (moving very fast and violently down it as if they were pushing their way

down it) (line 11–13). The river was causing them to do this because it was moving fast and violently.
A· It was the trees that were making the noises she describes at this point, not the river. The noise made by the water came a little later (line 15-17) and was not what first struck her.
C: The river wasn't threatening the trees, it had already knocked them over and was carrying them along.
D: It was *so much wider* (line 13) than she had ever seen it before and *fifty times as big as it had ever been* (line 10-11) but she doesn't say that she thought it was getting bigger and wider, she says that it was already bigger and wider than it had ever been.

28 A: She thought that it was following them and *trying to catch* them, as if it knew what it was doing and had a mind of its own (line 18–19).
B: They went down into the ditch and up again out of it to get out of the way of the water. She wasn't worried that it would throw them into the ditch, they went into it of their own accord.
C: She kept stopping because she was fascinated by what she saw (line 20) but she did move – she went into and out of the ditch and she reached *up to the yard* (line 22).
D: She couldn't believe that there was so much water because they normally had little rain there and wanted it very badly – *you pray for it* (line 21), but she did not spend time analysing the danger the water presented, she acted together with the others to get out of its way.

29 B: They were *surrounded* by the water and they couldn't escape by driving along the drive because the road at the bottom of it was flooded (line 24-25). They therefore had no alternative but to drive across the alfalfa field.
A: The water had already reached it – it *went into Kenny's alfalfa field* (line 23).
C: The drive wasn't blocked because they drove to the bottom of it – it was the road at the bottom of the drive that was blocked (line 25).
D: It did lead to higher ground – they went *up the hill to our neighbour's place* (line 27) but that's not why they drove across it. They drove across it because it was the only direction they could go in to escape from the water.

30 D: *Crazy* refers to her apologizing to Kenny for driving across his field, as she thinks that this was a crazy thing to do in such a terrible emergency (line 30-32).
A/B: The whole incident and the drive across the field could be described as crazy, but it's apologizing as they drove in terrible circumstances across the field that she describes as crazy.
C: It is observing local customs of politeness in such an emergency that she describes as crazy, not the customs themselves. In fact, she agrees that it is *not courteous* to drive across a neighbour's field and that you should apologize for it normally (line 28-30).

Second Passage

31 D: He says that it is *growing more difficult* (line 6) to *pinpoint* (identify exactly) *a man's place of origin by his speech* (line 6) because he found that *regional speech is in the process of disappearing* (line 3) and being replaced by *standardized* speech (speech that is common to everyone everywhere) (line 8-11). If speech is like that, it is difficult or impossible to notice any differences in people's speech because such differences do not exist, and this is what he found.
A: The impact of *decades of radio and television* was that regional speech was in the process of disappearing but it *was not gone, but going*, which means that although it was disappearing it had not yet completely disappeared (line 3-4).
B: He *can remember a time* when he could identify almost exactly where someone came from by listening to his speech (line 5-6) but the fact that he finds it much more difficult to do that now is because regional speech is disappearing, not because he has forgotten what local accents sound like.
C: Local accents weren't changing or beginning to sound different, they were disappearing.

32 A: Although bread is now *tasteless* (line 10) and the standard speech that will be used throughout the country will also be *tasteless* (line 15), the bread is also *uniformly good* (line 10) and the standardized radio and television speech is *perhaps better English than we have ever used* (line 8-9).
B: He says that the country's bread is *uniformly good and uniformly tasteless*, which means that it is the same throughout the country but he says that the country's speech *will* become uniform (*become one speech*) which means that this has not yet happened (line 10-11). The process of speech becoming the same throughout the country is taking place but it is not yet complete.
C: He says that *in the many years since I have listened to the land, the change is very great*, which means that he hasn't listened to regional speech for a long time and hasn't observed it changing over a period (line 15-16). Therefore he didn't notice any change in it until he took his trip. He makes no reference to noticing changes in bread, only to the fact that it is now all the same.
D: He refers to the *inevitability* of the changes (the fact that such changes are bound to occur and nothing can be done to prevent this) (line 12-14). He therefore does not think that people have consciously caused these changes because they want progress, but that the changes have been automatic.

33 D: The deep south *holds and treasures some other anachronisms* (keeps and values highly some other things that

are out of date or old-fashioned as well as regional expressions) (line 19-20).
A: Local speech also survives in the Southwest, which has *kept a grasp, but a slipping grasp on localness* (held on to local speech, although it is losing its hold on it and it is disappearing there too) (line 18-19).
B: Other regions are losing their local speech but the deep south is not because it holds on to old-fashioned things, although it may also lose it one day because *no region can hold out for long against* (can resist for a long time being destroyed by) progress (line 20-22).
C: They are similar only in that regional speech is used, to different extents, in both, but they are different in that the deep south has not started to lose its regional speech, whereas the Southwest has.

34 C: He says that the way in which things from the past are viewed is inaccurate because those things weren't really as good as people say they were – *Mother's cooking* was generally poor, *good unpasteurized milk* was contaminated and a danger to health, *the healthy old-time life* was in fact full of ill health and death from diseases about which nothing was known and *sweet local speech* was caused by lack of education (line 25-28).
A: He mentions a number of unpleasant aspects of life in the past but no ways in which it was better than modern life.
B: He says that older people often *protest against change* (line 28–29) but does not agree that life in the past was as good as people say it was. All of his references to the past are to bad aspects, not to things he thinks should have been preserved.
D: Although he thinks that many aspects of life in the past were bad, he says that *we have exchanged corpulence for starvation, and either one will kill us* – instead of having too little to eat, we are now fat – and this is not an improvement on the past because both cause death (line 29-30).

35 B: He describes people who try to *hold it back* (prevent change from taking place) as the *sad ones* because they feel *bitterness* about the loss of old-fashioned things and don't enjoy the things gained from change (line 32-33).
A: The people who suffer do not enjoy the benefits of change but this does not mean that they don't have them. They too gain from it, but they complain about it and try to prevent it (line 32-33).
C: He says that it is impossible to predict what life will be like in 100 or 50 years and that he is sensible enough to realize this (line 30-32). This suggests that some people think they can predict it but he doesn't believe that they can and he doesn't talk about such people's reactions to change.
D: He does not say that it is wrong to be critical of change – he says that it is *in the nature of man* and therefore

natural to do so (line 28–29).Criticizing change is not wrong, trying to prevent it is.

Third Passage

For the questions on this passage, see also the questions in **Further Practice and Guidance** *on pages 72-73 and the answers to them below.*

36 C: The writer refers to the speed of the diver's movements throughout the first paragraph. Strong currents *shoot them rapidly* down and over things (line 3-4); stopping is like *trying to stand in a hurricane* (an extremely strong wind) (line 4-5); it is only just possible to *steady yourself and steer* (line 5-6); it involves *dodging rocks* (taking action to avoid hitting rocks) that suddenly come towards you as you move at great speed (line 6); it is *underwater motorway madness* (like driving much too fast and carelessly and nearly crashing into other vehicles on a motorway) (line 7); and the divers are in *fast currents* (line 7).
A: Divers might be able to catch hold of a sea creature as it passes them if they can react quickly enough (line 8) but this is not the main attraction.
B: The writer talks about diving with a *partner* who the diver holds with one hand *to steady yourself* (line 5-6), but the presence of a partner, although perhaps important, is not presented as why people want to do drift diving.
D: Divers travel *a kilometre or more* (line 4) but it is not suggested that this is an unusually long distance or that it is what makes drift diving attractive.

37 A: The writer refers to the effect on the diver several times in the second paragraph. It is *like night flying* because you cannot see the surface or the bottom (line 9-10); you are *weightless and apparently motionless* (you feel as if you are not moving, although you are) (line 12); pressure has an effect on the lungs, which have to be repeatedly filled with air (line 16); and you are in an environment that is dark, cold and *alien* (unfamiliar and perhaps hostile) (line 16–17).
B: The writer says that when you get to the bottom everything is one colour – *completely blue-green* (line 13-15), and this is the only reference to the colour of what can be seen. By the time you reach the bottom, colours *from the red end of the spectrum* have been absorbed by water and cannot be seen (line 14-15).
C: You *depend on your depth gauge to measure progress* when ascending and descending (line10), so it has to be reliable, and the writer mentions the effect of pressure on various pieces of equipment – *your suit, your mask and your buoyancy regulator* (line 15-16), but the reliability of equipment is not the main point in his description of depth diving, it is simply one aspect of it.
D: Obviously depth diving involves diving a long way down and the writer does describe the journey down

and reaching the bottom but he does not put any emphasis on how far it is from the top to the bottom.
38 B: Most wreck divers *are happy simply to swim* along the *hulls* (the bodies of ships) (line 20-21). The use of *however* in this sentence is to contrast these divers with the ones who take things from the wrecks (line 18-20). Therefore most wreck divers are not looking for things to take with them from inside wrecks, they are content simply to swim along the outside of them.
A: Some, but not most, wreck divers, take a large number of *mementoes* (souvenirs) back with them (line 19).
C: Some, but not most, become *weighed down* by mementoes (take so many of them that they are a heavy weight to get back to the surface). It is a *wonder* (a surprising thing) that they manage to surface at all, which means that they do manage to surface with their mementoes, but these are not the majority of wreck divers (line 19– 20).
D: Many of the more *intact wrecks* (those that have not broken up to a great extent) and the more important ones are *protected* (action has been taken to stop people entering them) (line 22-23). However, most wrecks are not like this, they are *huge chunks* (separate big pieces) of broken steel and there is no suggestion that divers are prevented from going into these.

39 A: Wrecks have *enticing* (very attractive and tempting) *enclosed spaces* but only people who are *foolhardy* (who take foolish risks) or very experienced *venture deep inside them* (go deep inside them despite the danger involved) (line 24-25).
B: The sounds of breathing are *amplified* (made louder) in them and the bubbles produced by a diver breathing have to take an indirect route to get out (line 25-26), but there is no suggestion that breathing itself is difficult.
C: Creatures look out from *crannies* (little spaces) inside the wrecks and they are *grotesquely enlarged* (made to look bigger and ugly) by the water (line 26–28), but there is no suggestion that these creatures are a danger to divers.
D: It is not suggested that it is difficult to move around inside wrecks, only that problems can occur if divers enter enclosed spaces in them.
40 D: One of the reasons why night diving is *the ultimate thrill* (the most exciting thing) for the writer is that *all kinds of creatures* that can't be seen during the day come out and *feed, mate and exercise* (line 29-30).
A: Obviously, it is dark because the diver can only see what is in the light from his torch (line 30-31), but it is not stated that sea creatures cannot see the diver.
B: The colours that can be seen are *more defined* (sharper and clearer) (line 31), but this does not mean that they are different colours from during the day.

C: Different sea creatures, which *are hidden during the day*, can be seen (line 29-30) at night but this does not mean that a greater number of sea creatures can be seen then.

PAPER 1: SECTION A 25 marks
          SECTION B 30 marks
          TOTAL   55 marks

To be converted into a score out of 40 marks.

FURTHER PRACTICE AND GUIDANCE

p 72–73 PAPER 1 SECTION B

For explanations of these questions, see the explanations on the **Third Passage** *in* **Paper 1 Section B** *above.*

Question 36
1 shoot
2 no
3 The diver holds the partner tightly with one hand and this makes it possible to steady yourself.
4 c
5 a
6 yes

Question 37
1 It is the only way they can measure progress.
2 weightless, motionless
3 Everything is the same colour.
4 It is affected by pressure.
5 a and c

Questions 38 and 39
1 They bring a lot of things back to the surface with them.
2 a
3 a
4 Because they are protected.
5 yes
6 a
7 b
8 amplified, enlarged, magnifying
9 c
10 no

Question 40
1 yes
2 yes
3 no
4 no
5 no

FURTHER PRACTICE AND GUIDANCE

p 76 PAPER 2

Assessment of sample composition

1 Content
This composition is all relevant. Although it does not describe the actual journey until the second half, the first half deals with why the writer has chosen this particular journey and there is therefore a very good reason for starting the composition in this way – the first half connects closely with the second.

2 Organization

The organization of the composition is good and there is a clear structure and progression. The first paragraph gives background, describing things that the writer has already done; the second paragraph deals with why this has caused the writer to choose the journey he/she has chosen; the third paragraph desribes the journey.

3 Linking

Good linking does not necessarily have to mean long sentences. In the first paragraph there is effective linking of *ideas* with short sentences: *However, ... Don't understand me wrong ... On the contrary.* There is other good and accurate linking, for example, *during which* (second para). Otherwise the composition contains a number of short sentences, for example, in the third paragraph, where each sentence covers each single part of the journey. In some places, it would be possible to link these to make the composition flow a little better, for example, the part beginning *The train* could easily be linked as follows: *The train would cross the Ural mountains, the dividing line between Europe and Asia, and this itself should be very exciting.*

4 Use of vocabulary

The vocabulary is fairly simple but adequate. It is accurate and appropriate for the subject matter. It is not particularly adventurous but marks would not be lost for this; instead, marks would be gained for more adventurous vocabulary. There are one or two mistakes: *exiting* (first and third paras) should be *exciting*; and *mean* (second para) should be *means* (the noun *means* is both singular and plural).

5 Use of grammar

The composition is mostly correct grammatically, with some errors. It shows a good command of appropriate verb tenses, for example, in the first paragraph, where the present perfect is used for what the writer has done until now and the present simple is used for general truths. There is a tense mistake in the second paragraph, where *I enjoyed* should be *I enjoy*, to link with the verbs in the present simple that follow it and because it does not refer to a specific time in the past. Also *For a long time now I wanted* should be *For a long time now I have wanted*, as it refers to a period up to and including now. In the third paragraph, the writer has varied the modal forms, which is very good. The whole paragraph refers to a hypothetical journey and *would* is therefore obviously appropriate. However, instead of constantly repeating *would*, the writer has also used *should* – with the meaning *probably will/would* – and *could* – with the meaning *I would be able to*. There are some mistakes, however: *In last ten years* (para 1) should be *In the last ten years*; *food* (para 1) should be *the food* because it refers to particular food (the food on

the plane) not to food in general; *a exotic* (para 1) should be *an exotic*; *If only possible* (para 3) should be *If possible*; *spend day or two* and *After couple of days* (para 3) should be *spend a day or two* and *After a couple of days*.

6 Style

The style is appropriate – the composition is serious but not too formal and has a conversational quality that makes it flow well. The use of the question in the first paragraph is an effective way of making a point.

This is a competent and well-expressed composition with some errors, that would be given a score of approximately 12–15 marks out of 20.

p 77 PAPER 3 SECTION A QUESTION 1

*See also the questions in **Further Practice and Guidance** on page 80 and the corresponding answers.*

One mark per question (Total: 20)

1 **that**: *it was then that* something happened = something happened at that time or point in time.
2 **which**: This refers to the word *Pomodoro*.
3 **referring/alluding**: the *-ing* form is used here with the meaning *and this refers possibly to*. If a word or phrase *refers/alludes to* something, it relates to or describes it in some way.
4 **according**: *according to someone* introduces something that someone said or wrote, although it is not necessarily true.
5 **were**: This forms part of a passive verb; people crushed them deliberately (*got* would suggest that it was accidental).
6 **then/afterwards**: This refers to the next part of a process, the next in a sequence of events or actions. *After* would need to be followed by a subject and a verb and cannot precede the last in a sequence or series.
7 **into**: If something *turns into* something else, it changes completely and takes a different form.
8 **way/means/method**: A *way/means/method of doing* something is how it is done.
9 **the/for**: If one thing *allows/allows for* something, it makes it possible. *The preparation/preparation of something* = the act or process of preparing something.
10 **this**: *This product* = the product just described (preserved tomatoes).
11 **where**: This refers to the place just mentioned, markets.
12 **It**: This is the subject of the passive verb here.
13 **full**: If something is *packed full of* something, it contains a very large amount of something.
14 **and**: This links the two *precious qualities contained in the seeds*, not the other *precious qualities* mentioned next.

15 **along/together**: *along/together with* = and/and in addition; *but* is not appropriate here because all the things listed are *precious qualities*.
16 **in**: If something is *in a certain form*, it is of that type.
17 **allowing/enabling**. If something *allows/enables something*, it makes it possible; the *-ing* form here = and it allowed/enabled.
18 **following/next/subsequent**: = in the 150 years after the initial technology for preservation of tomatoes in the forms we now know was created.
19 **only**: If one thing is *second only to something*, only the other thing is ahead of it in some way, in this case in popularity.
20 **as**: This introduces in what way it is second only to the potato.

p 77 PAPER 3 SECTION A QUESTION 2

*See also the questions in **Further Practice and Guidance** on pages 80-81 and the corresponding answers.*

One mark per underlined word or phrase (Total: 12)

a as/though the building was, it wasn't to my taste (1 mark)
= Although the building was impressive/The building was impressive, but ... Sentences with these meanings can begin with an adjective followed by *as/though*.
b something/one (that) I am willing to discuss at the moment (1 mark)
something/one is used instead of repeating *matter*; because *not* is supplied, *I am not willing* has to be changed to *I am willing*.
c the incorrect assumption that I held the same opinions as he did (1 mark)
If you *make an assumption*, you assume that something is the case, although this is not necessarily true; *the assumption* has to be used here because a particular assumption is specified; the adverb *incorrectly* has to be changed to the adjective *incorrect*.
d every/a good/a very good/an excellent(1) chance(1) of succeeding(1) as an actress (3 marks)
If someone *has every/a good/a very good/an excellent chance of doing something*, it is very likely that they will succeed in doing something that they would like to do or are trying to do.
e no attempt/effort to conceal his dislike for me *or* (it) clear that he disliked me (1 mark)
If you *make no effort/attempt to do something*, you do not try to do it; *if you make clear* or *make it clear* that something is the case, you show or say clearly that it is the case.
f did they give me a place to stay, (but/but also) they didn't want any money in return (1 mark)
If a sentence begins with *not only*, the verb that follows it must be in the question form (although the sentence is not, of course, a question).

A sentence of this kind can be linked with *but* or *but also* .

g no point (in)(1) considering (1) such a ridiculous proposal seriously (1) *or* no point (in)(1) seriously (1)considering such a ridiculous proposal (1) *or* no point (in)(1) giving serious consideration(1) to such a ridiculous proposal (1) *or* no point (in)(1) giving such a ridiculous proposal (1) serious consideration (1) (3 marks)
If *there is no point (in) doing something,* it is not worth doing; you can *consider something seriously, seriously consider something, give serious consideration to something* or *give something serious consideration.*

h having been there/to America before, America/it was a whole new experience for her (1 mark)
Not having been/done = because the subject had not been/done.

p 78 PAPER 3 SECTION A QUESTION 3

One mark per underlined word or phrase (Total: 7)

a place of (1): *in place of* = as a replacement for.

b the result that (1): *with the result that* = and the result was that ...

c whichever way/no matter which way/however (1): *whichever way/no matter which way/however you do something* = it makes no difference which way you do it, the same fact is still the case.

d be better off (1): If someone *would be better off doing something,* in the opinion of the speaker there is a better alternative to what they are planning to do or thinking of doing or to something else that has been mentioned.

e must(1) be thinking(1) (2): *must* is used when making an assumption of what the speaker believes to be the case, although there is no proof of this; if you *are thinking of someone,* you have a particular person in your mind; in this sentence the verb must be in the present continuous form because it describes something that is happening at this moment.

f it as an (1): If you *take something as something,* you interpret it as being that thing.

p 79 PAPER 3 SECTION A QUESTION 4

One mark per underlined word or phrase (Total: 14)

a The chances are(1) that the meeting won't/will not end(1) before 8. *or* The chances of the meeting ending(1) before 8 are not high/low.(1)(2 marks)
The chances are that something won't happen = it is very unlikely that something will happen; if *the chances of something happening are not high/low,* it

is very likely that it will not happen.

b There is no such address(1) as(1) the one (that) I sent the parcel to(1). (3 marks)
If there is *no such place/thing, etc as something,* that place/thing, etc does not exist, even though perhaps someone mistakenly thinks it does.

c She keeps a record of everything that is said in the meetings. (1 mark)
If you *keep a record of something,* you write down or store information so that it can be referred to later.

d Are you familiar(1)with (1) this kind of computer?*or* Is this kind of computer familiar(1) to you?(1) (2 marks)
If you are *familiar with something,* or *something is familiar to you,* you have knowledge or experience of it.

e The realization of(1) how much it was going to cost made me change/caused me to change(1) my mind. (2 marks)
The realization of something, is the mental process of becoming aware that it is the case; in this sentence, the realization caused something to happen.

f I tried to impress on them that urgent action was required.*or* I tried to impress the need for urgent action on them. (1 mark)
If you *impress on someone* that something is the case, or if you *impress something on someone,* you make them understand something important by telling them forcefully.

g The company is in the process of reorganizing its departments. *or* The company's departments are in the process of being reorganized. (1 mark)
If someone *is in the process of doing something,* they are doing something that takes a period of time and have not yet completed it.

h Tina is inclined(1) to upset (1)people unintentionally. (2 marks)
If someone *is inclined to do something,* especially something not considered good, they tend to do it.

SECTION A:

QUESTION 1	20 marks
QUESTION 2	12 marks
QUESTION 3	7 marks
QUESTION 4	14 marks
TOTAL	53 marks

FURTHER PRACTICE AND GUIDANCE

1	that	11	where
2	which	12	It
3	referring	13	full
4	according	14	and
5	were	15	along
6	then	16	in
7	into	17	allowing
8	way	18	following
9	the	19	only
10	this	20	as

p 80 PAPER 3 SECTION A QUESTION 1

For explanations, see Section A question 1 above.

p 81 PAPER 3 SECTION A QUESTION 2

*For all the acceptable answers to question 2 of the test and explanations of them, see **Section A question 2** above.*

a	3, 5	e	3, 4, 5
b	2	f	3
c	1	g	3
d	1, 5	h	5

p 82–84 PAPER 3 SECTION B

Answers similar to or covering the same points as those given here are acceptable providing they are phrased accurately.

*See also the questions in **Further Practice and Guidance** on pages 85-86 and the corresponding answers.*

a **remain where she is/not travel** (1 mark)
If you *stay put,* you stay where you are or you don't move.

b **reports about how good the places that travellers have visited are** (1) **which she has not asked for but is given anyway** (1) (2 marks)
A *testimonial* is a description recommending something or someone, especially officially. If something is *unsolicited,* it is given or sent to someone who has not asked for it.

c **They talk about the fact they have travelled a long way with very few belongings/things** (1) **as if it is something to be proud of/ something good** (1) (2 marks)
They *make a virtue of* (claim that it is something good) *the fact that they've traversed* (travelled across) *three continents with hardly anything* (almost nothing) *in the sturdy rucksack* (the strong bag they take with them) (line 13-14).

d **If the places they have been to are so wonderful and the people are so friendly** (1), **why don't they go to live there permanently/why have they come back/why haven't they stayed there permanently** (1)? (2 marks)
The writer asks *if that's the case* – if it's true that *it's all so beautiful out there and the people are so friendly – why come back?* (there is no reason for them not to have stayed there permanently) (line 17-18); she wonders why, if *foreigners are such friendly, hospitable people,* they aren't *summoning the removal men* (calling in a firm to transport all their belongings to a new home, in this case the country they have just visited) (line 19-20).

e **that they have not really enjoyed their trips as much as they say they have** (1 mark)
She implies that they have not really found their trips *all so refreshing* (as refreshing as they say) because they want a bath and a good rest as soon as they return, presumably because they feel dirty and tired rather then healthy and energetic – as they would if the trip had been *refreshing* – (line18–19).

f **that they are not really friendly and hospitable** (1 mark)
She says that if foreigners were really friendly and *hospitable* (welcoming to visitors), the travellers would be getting ready to move permanently to their countries (line 19-20).

g **because they talk continuously in a way that suggests they have not spoken for a long time** (1 mark)
As they are eating a great deal quickly –*stuffing their faces* –, they are *chattering* (talking a great deal) *with relish* (with enjoyment) like *a mute* (a person who is unable to speak) who has suddenly become able to speak (line 20-21).

h **It involves people going to distant places and claiming to own them** (1) **as soon as they arrive there** (1).(2 marks)
She says that she is *not imbued with* (not filled with) *the spirit of imperialism*. The implication of this is that the travellers she describes are filled with it, in that they go to *far-flung corners of the globe* (distant places in the world), *trample a couple of blades of grass underfoot* (walk on a very small part of the land there) and then *claim them as their own* (claim to own them) (line 22-24).

i **She can take as much luggage as she wants to** (1), **be sure that accommodation has been booked for her in a hotel** (1), **know exactly what she's going to get** (1) **and complain if she doesn't get it** (1). (4 marks)
She can take *a full complement of* (everything that should be included in) *luggage*, know that there is a hotel with her name *indelibly etched in its register* (her name is entered in its register and cannot be removed from it because she has firmly booked a room), she knows *precisely what I'm going to get* and she can find out *the reason why I haven't got it* because she can wave the brochure in anger at the manager (show him what the brochure states and demand angrily to know why she hasn't got it) (line 24-28).

j **is something I hate/can't stand, etc** (1 mark)
If something is an *anathema to you*, you detest it or totally disapprove of it.

k **Having to wait a long time for her plane to leave** (1), **the distance to the airport** (1), **the distance within the airport to the check-in** (1), **and the difficulty of carrying suitcases such a long distance** (1). (4 marks)
She says that planes are *invariably* (always or almost always) late and that she has felt herself *growing old in departure lounges* – an ironic reference to the amount of time she has had to wait there; she says that people who talk about *just hopping onto a plane* (simply and quickly getting onto a plane without any difficulty) are talking *rot* (rubbish) and she describes getting to the airport as a *trek* (a long and difficult journey) *of no mean significance* (of considerable scope or dimensions); she says that there are *at least three miles of walkways* to the check-in – *at least* implies that this is a

long way; and she says that you have to do several *involuntary work-outs* (periods of physical fitness training that you don't want to do) as you *juggle your suitcases* (move them from hand to hand so that you can manage to carry them) to the check-in (line 31-35).

l **because she fears that it will crash** (1 mark)
She is *doom-laden* (fearing disaster) when she travels because she thinks that her flight number will be part of the newspaper headlines the next day, where it will be described as *ill-fated* (destined to end in tragedy or disaster).

m **a complicated process involving officials/bureaucracy/rules and regulations which it is difficult to find your way through/easy to get lost in** (1 mark)
A *labyrinth* is a complicated system of passages, paths, corridors, etc, which it is difficult to find your way through or easy to get lost in – here the word is used figuratively; *officialdom* = officials of many kinds or the rules and regulations involved in bureaucracy.

n **the fact that there is always a child crying/shouting loudly in the seat behind her** (1), **the loud noise of the engines** (1) **and the fact that the food is always standard/the same** (1) (3 marks)
If a child is *screaming*, he/she is crying or shouting very loudly; she says that the *roar* (loud noise of the engines) and the *regulation* (standard) mass-produced food are reasons why being on a plane is *a misery* (something that causes her suffering) (line 38-42).

Questions a–n: Total: 26 marks

PAPER 3 SECTION B – SUMMARY

o *One mark each for inclusion of the following points or points similar to them:*
1 **they damage the places they visit**: they have *destroyed vast acres* (large areas) *of its natural resources* (line 4).
2 **they make other people listen to long stories about their trips**: they *regale the stay-at-homes with their travelogues* (line 4- 5); they have also *harangued her with* (forced her to listen to) *long, unsolicited testimonials* (see question b).
3 **they are not really interested in the places they visit or the people there**: their *main pre-occupation* (interest/ concern) is *not with the places they've seen or the people they've met*, despite the fact that *they feign interest in* (pretend to be interested in) some of the people they came across (line 8-10).
4 **they dress in an awful way and they all dress in the same way**: they dress *appallingly* (very badly) and they *all wear the same uniform*, which she then describes (line 11–12).
5 **they think it's good that they travelled a long way with very little**: (line 13-14, see question c).
6 **they say how much they have enjoyed their trips but they do not**

act as if this is really the case/do not seem to be telling the truth: (fourth paragraph, see questions d, e, f, g).
7 **they act like imperialists/as if they own the places they visit**: (line 22-24, see question h).
8 **they have a casual attitude to their trips and don't plan them carefully**: she plans her holidays *with the precision of a military campaign* and their casual attitude is *anathema* to her for this reason (line 29-30 and see question j).

Total: 8 marks
Plus a maximum of 3 marks for general impression, based on the following criteria:
– relevance
– general level of fluency
– accuracy of language
– absence of copying from passage
– length

SUMMARY:	TOTAL:	11 marks
SECTION B	TOTAL:	37 marks
PAPER 3	SECTION A:	53 marks
	SECTION B:	37 marks
	TOTAL	90 marks

To be converted into a score out of 40 marks.

FURTHER PRACTICE AND GUIDANCE

p 85–86 PAPER 3 SECTION B

*For explanations, see the explanations for the answers to **Paper 3 Section B** above.*

Question c
1 hardly anything
2 d

Questions d, e, f and g
1 that they were *fun* (very enjoyable)
2 a bath and a good rest
3 that they were friendly
4 A eat a lot   B talk a lot
5 A that they didn't eat well B that they didn't have anyone to talk to
6 because they were moving to another place to live

Question i tick 1, 4, 5 and 7

Question k tick 1, 3, 4, 5 and 6

Question n three

p 87 PAPER 3 SECTION B SAMPLE SUMMARY

See Paper 3 Section B – Summary above
1 Nothing that is irrelevant is included. The following relevant points from above are included and partly included: 1/2: first sentence; 3: second sentence; 4: third sentence; 5: (third sentence) This point is not completely included because the writer's criticism is not just that the travellers take little with them but that they boast about doing this (½ point); 6: (fourth sentence)

Again, this point is not completely included because it is not simply the travellers' enthusiasm about their trips that the writer criticizes but the fact that she thinks this is false and that the travellers are pretending to have enjoyed their trips more than they really did (½ point); 7: and 8: are not included.

For the points included, this summary scores 5 out of 8.

2 There are no language mistakes and the summary is generally quite fluent.

3 No sentences or phrases have simply been copied from the passage and the summary is not too long or too short.

For general impression, the summary scores 2 out of 3.

This summary therefore scores 7 out of 11.

p 88 PAPER 4 PART ONE

The line references are to the tape transcripts on pages 171-173.

One mark per question (Total: 8 marks)

1 **E**: Their kitchens come with *free plan and design* (line 16-17). A free trial for a product (line 9– 10) is not work but free use of it to see if you want to buy it.

2 **C**: They don't have the *something for nothing* offers that other companies have, they have *incredibly low prices* (line 64-67).

3 **E**: They guarantee that they can *beat* (in this context, charge less than) *anyone else's price for the same quality* (line 17-19). The Curtain Mill does not compare its prices with anyone else's.

4 **M**: They want you to make an *informed decision* (one based on real knowledge of the subject) and so they *place so much emphasis on the expert advice* they offer (line 45-50).

5 **S**: They offer *a fourteen day cooling-off period*, which means that you can decide not to go ahead with an agreement to buy something during the fourteen days after making that agreement (line 34-35). If you *cool off*, you become less enthusiastic about something.

6 **S**: They are *still setting the standards for the copier industry* (still establishing the high levels of quality that others in the same kind of business try to reach) (line 32-33).

7 **M**: They give *impartial advice* (advice that is completely objective and not based on favouring one thing or another) on which phone to buy so that customers get an arrangement that *suits your individual needs* (line 51-55).

8 **T**: They offer *a ten-day free trial* (line 9-10).

p 88 PAPER 4 PART TWO

One mark per question (Total: 10 marks)

9 **no**: The presenter is surprised that 20% of all coffee sold in Britain is real coffee because that is *a higher proportion than I imagined* – he thought that most people were too *lazy* to *percolate* (to make real coffee in a machine) (line 8-18).

10 **yes**: George says that the idea that making real coffee requires a lot of effort, which leads people to be too lazy to do it, *is a bit of a myth* (something that people widely believe but is not actually true) because with machines such as the one he has brought with him – the cafetière, or plunger pot – *it's very simple indeed* (line 19-27).

11 **no**: George says that making real coffee in a cafetière is *no worse than making tea* and *no more of a chore* (not a more unpleasant or boring task) *than making tea*, but he does not say that it is easier than making tea (line 38-42).

12 **no**: George says that *there is nothing to indicate that it's going to damage your health* and that organizations in Britain and the US would confirm that this is so (line 62-69). This means that there is no evidence that drinking real coffee damages your health but it does not mean that there is proof that it doesn't.

13 **no**: line 70-80; George says that the *scares* (widespread fears among the public about something that might affect them) and stories about what happens to people who drink too much coffee are *frequently taken out of context*. This means that people hear the stories but are not told all the details and circumstances connected with them and so get the wrong impression. For example, stories about the harmful effects of coffee may concern people who boil beans, which can be harmful, but not many people do that and so not many people run the risk of harmful effects from coffee. George is therefore not saying that the stories are not true or that people have made them up but that people get the wrong impression from them.

14 **yes**: George doesn't think that instant coffees can *come anywhere near touching real coffee* (cannot even nearly reach the same standard as real coffee because they're completely different, have a *tell-tale flatness* (have a dull taste that reveals that they are instant and not real) and differ in texture (line 91-97).

15 **yes**: George says that it is *much safer to buy it ready ground* than to *grind it yourself* because a lot of care has been taken to make sure that ready ground coffee is of high quality (line 111-119).

16 **yes**: George at first says that boiling water should be used and then corrects himself and says *just off boiling water* (water that is not quite boiling) should be used (line 125-127).

17 **yes**: George tells the presenter in answer to his question that you can get *branded coffees* (coffees sold with a manufacturer's or other name on the label) that achieve *very high standards* in supermarkets as well as in specialist shops (line149-156).

18 **yes**: George says that *you really need to know what you're doing* (you have to know a lot about beans) if you're buying beans, so that you can choose the best ones for you or choose good ones (line 157-161).

p 89 PAPER 4 PART THREE

One mark per question (Total: 12 marks)

19 **an unmarked path/a glacier**: line 1-4

20 **an (ancient) axe**: line 12-13

21 **(a couple of) ski poles**: line 20-22; They released the body with these, they failed to release it earlier with a pneumatic drill (line 10-11).

22 **completely dry/dried**: line 26-30; It had been dried and then covered with snow and ice. Together, these two things add up to the process of the body being *mummified* – it had therefore not been mummified **before** being covered with snow and ice.

23 **made of wood and stone**: line 36-37; The fact that it was made of wood and stone led the team to believe that the body was *very, very old*.

24/25 a marble bead/a leather pouch (in any order): line 48–49

26 **Bronze Age**: line 53–54; An archaeological period is an Age.

27 **internal organs**: line 62–65; Since this body was more well-preserved than other bodies, it must have been less fragile than them and, unlike them, its internal organs must have survived.

28 **not as old**: line 65–70: The oldest bodies previously found are *half the age* of the Iceman and the best preserved are only 500 years old, whereas the Iceman is thousands of years old.

29 **cut their hair**: line 80-82; The hair had been *clearly cut*.

30 **hidden from/shielded from/concealed from/invisible to**: line 87-94; It had *miraculously* (by incredibly good fortune) not been attacked by animals because a light covering of snow had *shielded* (covered or hidden it) *from the view of these predators* (animals that look for other animals to kill and eat could not see it).

p 90 PAPER 4 PART FOUR

*The letters in brackets after each explanation refer to the choices for each of the five questions in **Further Practice and Guidance** on page 91-92 and the corresponding answers.*

One mark per question (Total: 5 marks)

31 **C**: She says that a soap is a story about *either a related family or a group of people who work together* – they should therefore have the fact that they are members of the same family or the fact that they work in the same place in common (line 9-11). (C)
A: She says that viewers should feel *as if* the characters are living on *some special fictional island somewhere* so that they can feel that the characters are living their lives even when the programme is not on (line 13-18). This is the impression that viewers should

have and does not suggest that the programmes should actually be set in a fictional place. (B, F)

B: She says that soaps take place in *a sort of never-ending middle*, in that there is no beginning or end to the story (line 19-20) but, although soaps do try to make viewers wonder what will happen next, she does not say that a soap has to do this to be called a soap. (A)

D: A soap should be *a continuing story* (a story that is continued in each episode) (line 8) and it has *no beginning, no end* (line 20) but she does not suggest that only soaps that have been on television for a long time can really be called soaps. (D, E)

32 A: The *bigger dramas* were and *still are really* about men *escaping from difficult situations*, whereas soaps are about *women coping with everyday situations* (line 38-44). She then amends this and says that they are about both *women and men* doing this. She contrasts *difficult situations* with *everyday situations* and the implication is that the *difficult situations* in other dramas are not common ones for most people, as *everyday situations* are. (A,B, C, D)

B: She says that soaps haven't changed much since they started (line 24-28) but she says that other dramas haven't changed much either because they *still are really* about the same things (line 38-40), so this is not a way in which soaps differ from other dramas. (A, D)

C: Women *are the most important characters* (47-48) and men are the most important characters in other dramas because they are *about men* (line 40-41), but this does not necessarily mean that there are more women than men in soaps. (B, C)

D: The intention of the first soaps was *to attract housewives* so that they would *stay glued to their radios* (remain giving their full attention to them) and household products could then be sold to them in the advertisements (line 30-34). Soaps were therefore meant to be popular with women and Hilary prefers them because the most important characters are women (line 45-48). However, she does not suggest that soaps are popular with housewives and that other dramas are not – there is no suggestion that other dramas are not also popular with housewives. (E, F)

33 B: Nobody *will admit to watching soap opera* (line 51-52) and *we feel guilty about admitting that we watch soap* (line 56-58). (B,C)

A: Critics *don't help* (are one of the reasons why we don't like to admit to watching soaps) because they imply that viewers of soaps are victims of a *con trick* (a planned act of deception) because they don't realize that they are watching fiction (line 58-63). However, people still watch them – they say they prefer reading a good book or going to the theatre but the audience figures do not correspond with this (line 52-56). (B, C, D, E, F)

C: Although there are some unfortunate people who believe that soaps are real, the presenter implies

that it is not right that *we're all presented* as being like them by critics *just because* (simply because) there are some people like that (line 63-69). In other words, such people are not typical and form a minority of soap watchers. (A)

D: We pretend that – *apparently* – we prefer reading and going to the theatre (line 52-54) but there is no suggestion that people who watch soaps really preferred these things before they started watching soaps or that watching soaps has stopped them from pursuing such activities. (B, D, E)

34 A: She says that although *a fair proportion of* (quite a lot of) men watch soaps, *a larger proportion of the viewing population watching soap opera regularly are female* (line 85–93). In other words, plenty of men watch them but more women watch them regularly. Her son and daughter are an example of this – her son's interest *fluctuates* (the amount of interest he has in them frequently changes) whereas her daughter is *loyal* to the programmes and watches them very regularly (line 94-97). (B, E, F)

B: The presenter says that young women with families are *always a good target for condescension* (always spoken of as inferior with regard to viewing habits) (line 72-74), but Hilary thinks this is not fair and is just a fact of our *sexist world* (of our world, which regards women as inferior) (line 84-85). Hilary therefore thinks that what is regrettable is that women are criticized for watching soaps, not the fact that they do so or that there is anything wrong with soaps. (A).

C: They are watched by a *fair proportion of men* (line 86-88). (B, E)

D: She says that watching soaps is seen *as a sign of mental deficiency* (lack of intelligence) but she disagrees with this view. She thinks it is unfair and because of *our sexist world* that programmes more likely to appeal to men are seen as *fine*, whereas magazines or programmes aimed at women are not (line 76-83). In other words, some people say that soaps are for people who are not very intelligent but she disagrees and does not state that they deal only with unimportant things. (A, C, D)

35 C: We find it *reassuring* (it comforts us) that *the setbacks* (the problems or events that stop people's lives from going on happily) *come round like the seasons* (happen again and again at regular intervals) (line 103-105); soaps *provide lonely people with friends* (line 115-117) and show us *there's somebody out there worse off than ourselves* (there are people with worse problems than ours) (line 119-121). (C,D, E)

A: They show us *problems similar to our own* and *help us solve those problems* (line 121-124) but he doesn't say that the characters in them always solve their problems. (D, F)

B: They are different from formal dramas because of their *open-endedness* (they have no end, whereas formal dramas have to have a beginning, a

middle and an end) (line 110-112), but there is no reference to how easy or difficult either of them are to follow. (A)

D: It is stated that they are set in closed communities, *which is increasingly unlike the world we live in today,*(line 113–115) but this does not mean that they are totally unlike real life, and they have *naturalism* (line 109–110) – they show life as it really is and show *problems similar to our own* (line 122). (B)

PAPER 4	PART ONE	8 marks
	PART TWO	10 marks
	PART THREE	12 marks
	PART FOUR	5 marks
	TOTAL	35 marks

To be converted into a score out of 20 marks.

FURTHER PRACTICE AND GUIDANCE

p 91–92 PAPER 4

*For explanations, see **Part Four** above.*

31 Tick C, D and F
32 Tick A, B, C, D and E
33 Tick A, B, C and D
34 Tick B and F
35 Tick C, D and E

FURTHER PRACTICE AND GUIDANCE

p 95–96 PAPER 5

Talking About Pictures

Examples of possible remarks:
1 *It looks as if* they're all rather busy.
The man at the front *might* be the boss.
It would appear that the woman is listening to what the younger man is saying.

2 *I'd say* they're commuters going to or coming home from work.
If you ask me, they all look rather unhappy.
I expect the photo was taken in a city.

3 *He seems to be throwing* away the contents of his briefcase.
Judging by the expression on his face, *I reckon* he's rather happy.
He must have just given up his job.

TALKING ABOUT THE TOPIC

1	are/get promoted; get promotion	**7**	freelance/ a freelance(r) /self-employed
2	get the sack/ are sacked get sacked/ get fired/ are fired are dismissed	**8**	livelihood
		9	living
		10	manual
		11	trade
		12	profession
3	made redundant	**13**	management
		14	workload
4	hand in/give your notice	**15**	deadline
		16	overtime
5	resign (from it)	**17**	backlog
6	unemployed/ jobless; out of	**18**	retire
		19	deductions
		20	workforce

TEST FOUR

p 97–98 PAPER 1 SECTION A

Note that all explanations in this part refer to the meaning or use of each option most closely related to the question, not necessarily to the only meaning or use of these options.

For questions 1–4, see also the questions in **Further Practice and Guidance** *on pages 99-100 and the corresponding answers.*

One mark per question (Total: 25)

1 **A:** *LOOK OUT!* In this type of question, more than one of the options fits the meaning, but only one fits the structure of the sentence (*disagreeing* also fits the meaning but would have to be followed by *with*).

2 **C:** *LOOK OUT!* In this type of question, all the choices belong to a set of words related to one thing – walking – but only one fits the precise context.

3 **A:** *LOOK OUT!* The choices are all similar or related in meaning – subjects or parts of subjects – but only one fits the meaning of the sentence.

4 **C:** *LOOK OUT!* Again, the choices all have similar meanings – to a small extent – but only one can form the collocation required.

5 **D:** If you are **on your guard**, you are being very careful because you fear there might be danger or because you are anxious not to make a mistake.
A: If you are *on the defence*, you are being attacked or criticized and you are defending yourself (*be on the defence in a discussion*).
B: If you are *on the lookout for something*, you are watching carefully so that you will notice it if it appears (*be on the lookout for a better job*).
C: If you act with *caution*, you are very careful not to do something too quickly because it might have bad consequences (*treat an offer with caution*).

6 **B:** **Instead** can go at the end of a sentence to refer to an alternative.
A: *Otherwise* = if not (*I might see you tonight. Otherwise I'll definitely see you tomorrow* / *I trusted him. I wouldn't have told him all my secrets otherwise*).
C: *Or else* = or (*Press this button or else the machine won't work*).
D: *In place of* = as a replacement for (*get a new computer system in place of an older one*).

7 **A:** If you **pluck up the courage to do** something, you force yourself to be brave enough to do it.
B: If you *grab* an opportunity or chance, you take it eagerly (*grab the opportunity to travel free of charge*).
C: If you *grasp* information, you understand it (*I couldn't grasp the plot*).
D: If you *snatch* an opportunity for something, you take it quickly (*snatch a few hours' sleep while you can*).

8 **A:** If something **makes for** something, it helps to create it.

B: If someone is *getting at* something, they are trying to say it or suggesting it indirectly (*What exactly are you getting at?*)
C: If you *head for* a place, you go in the direction of that place (*head for the exit*).
D: If you *run into* someone, you meet them by chance (*run into an old friend at a party*).

9 **A:** **It remains to be seen** = it will not be known until later. This type of question tests an idiom.

10 **D:** If you can **conceive of** something, you can imagine it.
A: If you *visualize something/something happening*, you form a mental picture of it or imagine it (*visualize a scene/I could visualize them sitting there and wondering where I was*).
B: If you *wouldn't dream of doing* something, you wouldn't even consider doing it (*I wouldn't dream of doing anything illegal*).
C: If you *picture something/something happening*, you form a mental picture of it or have a clear idea of what it would look like (*I can just picture his face!/He had pictured himself collecting the trophy at the end of the match*).

11 **D:** If you do something **in anticipation of** something else you do it because you think the second thing is likely to happen.
A: *Forethought* is consideration in advance of what might happen and planning done accordingly (*Lack of forethought made the scheme a failure*).
B: *Foresight* is the ability to realize what might happen and act accordingly (*It's lucky that I had the foresight to book in advance*).
D: *The prospect of something/something happening* is the thought or expectation of it happening or being the case in the future or the mental picture of it (*The prospect of having to be in hospital made him miserable*).

12 **D:** What you are **letting yourself in for** is something unpleasant that you are getting involved in as a result of agreeing to do something.
B: If you *put in for* something, you apply for it (*put in for a transfer at work*). A and C are not possible.

13 **C:** If you **keep a straight face**, you continue to look serious and do not smile or laugh.
A: If something is *plain*, it is simple and without decoration or pattern (*plain furnishing*).
B: If a surface is *smooth*, it is even and has no bumps or holes (*a smooth road surface*).
D: If something is *level*, it is not at an angle (*The picture on that wall over there isn't level*).

14 **A:** If you **discount** something, you decide that it is not worth considering and dismiss it.
B: If you *skip* something, you miss it out and go on (*skip a chapter/meal*).
C: If someone is *ejected* from a place, they are removed from it or forced to leave it because they shouldn't be there or are behaving badly (*eject hooligans from a stadium*).

D: If you *snub* someone, you ignore them with the intention of insulting them (*After our argument, she snubbed me every time we met*).

15 **D:** If you **content yourself with** something, you are satisfied with it, although often it is not as good as what you really want.
A: If you *settle for* something, you accept it even though it is not as good as what you really want because you have no choice (*We had to settle for a cheaper one because we couldn't afford the one we wanted*).
B: If you *please yourself*, you do what you want to do and are not told what to do ('*What time would you like me to come?*' '*Please yourself. It doesn't matter to me*').
C: If you are *reduced to something/doing something*, you are forced by circumstances into the embarrassing position of having to do something you consider inferior (*As his debts grew, he was reduced to taking any work he could get*).

16 **B:** If a group is **formed**, it is started by getting people together.
A: If something is *composed of* something, it consists of it (*The exam is composed of five papers*).
C: If one thing is *associated with* another, it is connected with it (*the paperwork associated with starting a business*).
D: If something is *compiled*, it is produced by collecting various things together (*The report was compiled from interviews with everyone concerned*).

17 **C:** **Granted (that)** = Accepting or knowing that it is true that ...
A: *To accept* is not possible here, but *accepting* would be. *Accepting that* = admitting or agreeing that something is the case (*Accepting that he couldn't win, he stopped trying*).
B: *Truly* = It is absolutely true that ... (*Truly, this is the most amazing thing that's ever happened to me*).
C: If you *take something for granted*, you assume that it is the case without having to check (*She took it for granted that I knew what she was talking about but I didn't*).

18 **C:** If you **question** something, you say that you have doubts about whether it is right.
A: If you *disbelieve* someone/something, you do not believe that they are telling the truth or that what they say is true (*She seemed to disbelieve me/what I told her, even though it was true*).
B: If you *suspect someone (of something/of doing something)*, you think that they might be guilty of something (*She suspects him of plotting against her*). If you *suspect something*, you doubt whether it is honest or can be trusted (*I suspect her motives*).
D: If you *wonder about something/(about) whether, why, etc*, you are not sure about it, have doubts about it and are thinking about it (*I've been wondering about his suitability for the job ever since he started it./I'm still wondering (about) whether I made the right decision*).

19 D: **Supposing (that)** = Based on the belief that/If it is considered certain or likely that.
A: *In case* = Because it might happen (*I left early in case I was delayed on the way*).
B: *Except for something/doing something* = apart from/with the exception of (*Except for public holidays, this train ticket is valid at all times/Except for making a couple of phone calls, he's done very little all day*).
C: *Presumed* could not be used here, but *Presuming* could. *Presuming (that)* = Believing that something is certain to happen or be the case (*Presuming (that) everything goes according to plan, I'll get there at about 10*).

20 A: If something **moves someone to do** something, it causes them to do it by having a powerful influence on them.
B: If someone *originates* something, they create or invent it or cause it to exist (*Who originated this idea?*); when something *originates*, it starts to happen or exist (*a custom that originated centuries ago*).
C: If one thing *results in* another, it leads to it or has it as a result (*Heavy rains have resulted in flooding*).
D: If you *draw a conclusion*, you reach a decision or make a judgement based on what you know about something (*It's difficult to draw any conclusions from such little evidence*).

21 A: **Isolated incidents, instances**, etc are individual ones that are not connected with each other and do not form part of a general pattern.
B: If someone/something is described as *solitary*, they are a single one and there are no others (*I was the solitary person who disagreed./ A solitary voice broke the silence*).
C: If a house is *detached*, it is not joined to any other house on either side.
D: If something is *unique*, it is the only one of its kind or it is unlike any other (*a unique work of art/opportunity*).

22 A: **With hindsight** = being able to look back with the benefit of now knowing what happened later, and what could have changed the present situation.
B: *In retrospect* = looking back to something in the past and viewing it differently; (*In retrospect, it was one of the most enjoyable periods of my life*).
C: *An afterthought* is something extra that is said, thought or done after the main thing (*'Oh, and thanks for helping me', he added as an afterthought*).
D: A *review* of something is an examination of it to see what, if any, changes should be made to it (*a policy review/a review of the rules*).

23 D: If you **look someone up**, you visit them after not seeing them for a long time or in a place where you have not been before.
A: If you *look out for someone/something*, you pay careful attention with the intention of noticing or finding them (*look out for a friend in a crowd/police looking out for clues*).
B: If you *look round a place*, you move round it, looking at what is there (*look round a city and see the sights*).
C: If you *look on someone/something as something*, you regard or view them in that way or you have that attitude towards them (*I look on her as a very good friend./I don't look on the problem as particularly serious*).

24 D: If someone **professes to be/do** something, they say that they are/do it, although this is not true or is unlikely to be true.
A: If someone *asserts something/that* ..., they state it forcefully (*He asserted his case./She asserted that she had never said anything of the kind*).
B: If someone *alleges that* ..., they say that it is true or is the case, without proving this (*A newspaper has alleged that he is involved in corruption*).
C: If you *declare something/that* ..., you say it firmly or formally or you announce it (*She declared her intention never to speak to him again./He declared that he was in complete agreement with the proposal*).

25 D: If something happens **abruptly**, it happens suddenly and often unexpectedly.
A: If someone does something *impulsively*, they do it suddenly and without having thought about it first (*buy clothes/decide impulsively*).
B: If you say something *briefly*, you say it in a few words rather than saying a lot or you do not give details (*explain briefly what someone has to do*); if something happens or is done *briefly*, it happens or is done for only a short time (*I was briefly annoyed./She briefly led the race*).
C: If something will happen *shortly*, it will happen soon or a short time later (*I'll let you know shortly*).

FURTHER PRACTICE AND GUIDANCE

P 99 –100 PAPER 1 SECTION A

1 a disapprove: If someone *disapproves of something/of someone doing something*, they think that it is morally wrong or that it is not acceptable.
b differ: If people *differ*, they disagree about something; if things *differ*, they are different from each other.
c dispute: If someone *disputes* something, they say that they believe that it is not correct or not true.
d oppose: If someone *opposes* something, they disagree with it or are against it and show this in some way.
e object: If someone *objects to something/to doing something*, they say or feel that they don't like, agree with or approve of it.
f contradict: If one person or statement *contradicts* another, they say the opposite of the other.
g disagree: If someone *disagrees with something*, they don't agree with or approve of it.

2 a limped: If you *limp*, you walk with difficulty and with one leg stiff because it hurts or is injured.
b stumbled: If you *stumble*, you almost fall when walking or running because you hit something or put your foot down wrongly.
c ambled: If you *amble*, you walk very slowly, because you are not in a hurry.
d sprinted: If you *sprint*, you run as fast as you possibly can.
e paced: If you *pace up and down/round* a place, you walk up and down/round it in an anxious, nervous or impatient way.
f crept: If you *creep*, you move very quietly or secretly because you do not want to be heard or seen.
g crawled: If you *crawl*, you move on your hands and knees or stomach.

3 a topic: The *topic* of a conversation, composition, lesson, etc is the subject of it, what it is about.
b case: A *case* is one particular instance or example or one thing or person considered separately from others.
c factor: If something is a *factor in* something, it contributes to or is part of the cause of a situation or action.
d point: A person's *point* is the opinion or idea they are expressing.
e question: A *question* is something that is discussed or has to be decided.
f aspect: An *aspect of* something is one of the parts that it consists of.
g theme: The *theme* of a book, film, play, speech, etc, is a subject that appears throughout it or keeps appearing in it.

4 a modestly: If something *improves/increases modestly*, it increases/improves but not to a very great extent.
b weakly: If someone *smiles weakly*, they smile only a little because they are not really pleased or happy.
c remotely: If you are *not remotely interested/concerned*, etc, you are not at all interested/concerned, etc.
d narrowly: If someone is *narrowly defeated* or *loses narrowly*, they lose but by only a small margin.
e mildly: If you are *mildly surprised/worried/annoyed*, etc you are a little surprised/worried/annoyed, etc.
f barely: If something is *barely audible/visible/comprehensible*, etc, it is almost impossible to hear/see/understand, etc.
g softly: If someone is *softly spoken*, they have a quiet voice.

p 101-104 PAPER 1 SECTION B

Two marks per question (Total: 30)

First Passage

26 D: The wind had been blowing very strongly before she woke up. As a result the iron gate had *rattled loose* (been shaken loose) and it *cringed and banged* (made a frightened noise and a noise of hitting something) (line 2), but this was before she woke up. The writer has given the gate human characteristics which is why he has

used the word *cringed* (to move back or down in fear). However, we know that she noticed the strong bursts of wind because when she woke up, the windows were *shaking in their heavy frames*.(line 7). Since the frames were heavy, the wind must have been very strong to make the windows shake.
A: She was in a room above the dog (line 5–6). The dog *scratched at the door* but this was the door in the hall, not of her room (line 4-5).
B: The gate had been made loose by the wind and therefore it had not fallen down and was still attached to its posts, although it was not firmly attached.
C: The dog gave *a muffled growl* (made a quiet sound of displeasure) and *padded about* (walked softly)(line 3–4).

27 C: She was amazed that he could still be asleep on such a stormy night because anyone would imagine – *you'd think* – that he would have been worried about his journey and about being away from her for six weeks, and therefore unable to enter such a deep sleep that the storm didn't wake him up. She asks herself *what kind of a man was he?* to be able to do this in the circumstances, and therefore thinks that the fact that he can do it indicates that he isn't concerned about being away from her for such a long time (line 8-11).
A: She may well have been annoyed with him but this is not because she wanted him to deal with the dog, it is because she thinks it is wrong that he can continue being in a deep sleep in the circumstances, when he should have been unable to sleep deeply because of worrying about his journey and about being away from her for so long.
B: She finds it amazing that he can continue to sleep in the circumstances – *How on earth anyone could sleep through something that would waken the dead* amazes her – but there is no suggestion that she envies him for this – she is disappointed or annoyed about it. (line 8-11).
D: She may well have realized this but it is not what she thought when she woke up and saw him still asleep.

28 B: He thought *it was tidy* to put used matches back into the box but she found this *exasperating* (it made her very angry or frustrated) (line 15). He therefore thought it was right to keep them and she presumably thought they should be thrown away.
A: He never *heeded her* (paid attention to her or did as she told him) but this doesn't mean that he did it unintentionally. In fact, he did it deliberately, because he thought it was tidy to do so (line 14–15).
C: She knew why he kept them because he told her that it was tidy to do so.
D: The problem was that he put used matches back into the box and she didn't like this, but there is no suggestion that they didn't have enough matches they could use.

29 A: Mrs O'Brien was sure that *this time* she had packed everything that he wanted and that *she had forgotten nothing* (line 25-26). This trip was different from previous ones in that on previous trips that Tom took she *was always sure to forget something* (line 22-23).
B: She had made a list and *ticked each item off* (checked that each item was there one by one) (line 26), and a number of items that she packed are mentioned (line 23), but there is no suggestion that he wanted to take more with him than he usually took. On previous trips she had forgotten to pack certain things he had wanted and he had complained about the fact that she hadn't packed them (line 23-25), so she hadn't packed more than he had previously wanted, she had packed what he had always wanted.
C: He was *sure to bring it up with her* (to raise with her the subject of what she had forgotten to pack) *as soon as he stepped ashore for his two-weeks leave* (line 23-24), which makes it clear that two-weeks leave was a regular occurrence for him and not simply something that would happen this time.
D: He *wouldn't be able to launch any of his ill-humour on her this time* (be able to direct his anger at her for forgetting to pack certain things this time because she had packed everything) (line 27), but he directed his anger at her for this when he returned, not before he left (line 23–24). We are not told anything about his mood before leaving.

30 D: He could sleep deeply despite the fact that he was about to be away from her for a long time, he paid no attention to what she said about the matches and he got annoyed if she forgot to pack something for him when he was going away.
A: Obviously, there were things that she didn't like about him – the fact that he could sleep when he should have been worried about being away from her for so long, his habit with used matches and his complaints when she forgot to pack something – but there is no suggestion that she was glad when he wasn't there.
B: She always packed his case for him when he went away and he complained if she forgot something, but there is no suggestion that he wanted to do it for himself and disliked her doing it for him.
C: She knew that he got angry every time he came back and she had forgotten something and she had always forgotten something on every trip, so it was not difficult for her to predict this.

Second Passage

*For the questions on this passage, see also the questions in **Further Practice and Guidance** on pages 105–106 and the corresponding answers.*

31 D: The writer says that it is possible that you are *triggering* (causing) *a behaviour pattern that is for you a problem* (line 6-7). The implication is that this behaviour is a problem for you but may not be for others. The fact that you might be causing this behaviour and that therefore the problem may only affect you is something that *hasn't really dawned on a lot of people* (that a lot of people haven't realized); readers are told to *think again* if they have come to the conclusion that *the situation is beyond your control* because this is not the right conclusion (if you are causing it, you may be able to do something about it) (line 3-5).
A: Problem people include *uncooperative colleagues and underlings* (employees of much lower status) *who fail to do things as well as you do* (line 2) but there is no suggestion that the colleagues are uncooperative because they are ambitious or that the underlings would like to improve their status.
B: Problem people include bosses who *keep moving the goal-posts* (keep changing what those who work for them are told they have to achieve) (line 1–2) and it may well be that they lack clear purpose, but they are only one example of problem people and there is no suggestion that the behaviour of *uncooperative colleagues or underlings who fail to do things as well as you do* is due to a lack of clear purpose.
C: The mistake people make is to think that the situation is beyond their control – since they may be causing the problem behaviour, they may be able to do something about it by changing their own behaviour. The writer is therefore saying that it is possible to control the behaviour of problem people. However, he doesn't imply that their behaviour will get worse if you don't do anything to control it, only that it will continue.

32 C: Authoritarians are said to have *feelings of inadequacy* (lack of confidence in their own personalities and abilities) (line 14-15). This is hidden by the forceful way in which they behave – talking too much and not listening enough, acting as if everyone else is lazy or untrustworthy, not allowing others to make any decisions and expecting people to obey them all the time (line 8–11).
A: They certainly act as if they are better at their jobs than everyone else is at theirs and think that others are inefficient, but there is no suggestion that they are in fact less efficient than they think they are, even though they are said to really lack confidence in their abilities.

B: They are only a problem for people *with ideas and initiative* (people who want to make decisions themselves) because they don't let anyone else make decisions. However, if it *suits you to have someone taking all the decisions and telling you what to do*, they are not a problem and the implication is that there are people who don't mind this at all and for whom, therefore, doing nothing about the behaviour of authoritarians is *a good idea* (line 11-13).

D: They expect *unswerving obedience* (to be obeyed at all times and without question), they don't trust others and they don't let others make decisions because they think they would make the wrong ones, but it is not suggested by the writer that they think others are rivals or trying to get their jobs, even though this may be so (2nd paragraph).

33 B: You should be *compliant on the issues that are sacrosanct and non-negotiable* (you should be obedient concerning matters that the authoritarian considers can never be changed or discussed) (line 20-21). These issues include anything that has the *risk of chaos* because authoritarians *loathe* (hate) this (line 18–19) *insubordination by a junior* (disobedience from someone lower in rank) (line 20) and anything that might *jeopardize the orderliness which the authoritarian holds so dear* (be a danger to the sense of order that authoritarians value so highly) (line 23-24). You should therefore obey every order without arguing. However, you should be *assertive* (act firmly and independently) with regard to other matters and *assume that it's all right to do things until told otherwise* (believe that you can act as you think best with regard to things about which you have not been given any orders). You should do this *until told otherwise*, which means that you should do as you are told if orders are later given to you about these matters (line 21-22).

A: If you could make them realize that they are being unreasonable, it is highly likely that they would change their behaviour, but the writer states that *there is little point in trying* (it is not really worth trying) to *persuade authoritarians to change* (line 15-16).

C: The writer states that they are sometimes less *bossy* than usual (sometimes they are not giving orders and demanding that other people do things as much as they usually do) (line 16-17). It may well be that they are more tolerant at these times, but you are not advised to discuss anything with them at any time (you are advised that some things cannot be discussed at any time and that you can use your own initiative when no orders have been given, but there is no suggestion that you should talk to them).

D: You are not advised to challenge them at all – confronting them, arguing or putting your point of view are not advised. Instead, you are advised that showing initiative may enable you to *win their trust slowly* (their trust may result from your use of initiative) (line 22–23).

34 B: You should *start by asking their advice ... about what you should do differently* – suggest to them that you make mistakes as well as them, even though this may not be true – before turning the conversation to how they can improve (line 30-31).

A: Defensive people always give explanations that are *seemingly plausible* (appear to be possibly true) (line 27) when they have done something wrong. You are not advised to say that you don't believe them, you are advised to adopt a *softly-softly approach* (a very gentle one) because otherwise there is the likelihood of *the defensive barriers being raised* (of the person defending themselves and refusing to admit that they have done something wrong) (line 29-30).

C: You shouldn't blame them for anything, you should approach them gently and invite them *to join you in analysing why it happened* (line 28-29).

D: You should *choose a time when he has made a mistake* (line 27-28), but there is no suggestion that it has to have been a particularly bad mistake – it is simply another of the mistakes he makes and will not admit to, because as far as people like this are concerned *nothing is ever their fault* and they have explanations which sound possible but are not true for all of them(26-27).

35 B: You are advised that the best way of dealing with defensive people is to make them *learn that defensiveness doesn't pay* (that there are no advantages to being defensive) (line 34). They learn this because you *ease up on them* (stop putting pressure on them) (line 34) once they have stopped being defensive and admitted responsibility (line 32-34).

A: You are advised to make them *accept responsibility for their part in the mistake*, which indicates that they were not completely responsible for it, others were too (line 33).

C: Although the *softly-softly approach* will stop them becoming defensive because it involves asking them how you can do better, once the conversation turns to how they can change *this will provoke more defensiveness* (it will cause them to react by becoming defensive again, as they usually are) (line 29-32). It is therefore not possible to prevent them from becoming defensive.

D: You *must not let them off the hook* (you must keep putting pressure on them to admit responsibility) while they are being defensive and you should *keep repeating your challenge* – to admit responsibility – until they finally do admit responsibility (line 32-33). You are not advised to agree that some of their denials are acceptable. Although they may be only responsible *for their part in the mistake* and others may also be partly

responsible, it is not stated that you should agree with them that they are not responsible for certain things.

Third Passage

36 A: The writer thought when Shawn started to apologize that he was going to tell him that he had not got the job, but he then found out that Shawn was really apologizing for not giving him an office on the 18th floor (line 6-8).

B: Shawn asked him questions for 40 minutes but he doesn't say that he thought this was a longer time than he had been expecting the interview to last (line 5-6).

C: He was told that most reporters worked on the 18th floor but he would have to work on the 16th floor because there were no free offices on the 18th, but he doesn't say that he had had any expectations regarding the floor he would work on if he got the job (line 7-8).

D: He describes Shawn's physical appearance (line 4-5) but doesn't say that it surprised him.

37 C: Shawn had an *apologetic tone* (he spoke as if he was always apologizing for something) and a *diffident* (shy, lacking in self-confidence) *almost whisper of a voice* (a very quiet voice, as though he were trying not to be heard) but this was *camouflage* (it concealed) his *very firm notions of what he was doing* (his strong ideas of what he was trying to achieve and the fact that he believed that he was the only person who could do this) (line 9-11).

A: He had an *immensely determined curiosity about the world that his writers could put him in touch with* (he was keen to find out about things he didn't know from his writers) (line 13-14). He therefore wasn't pretending that he didn't know about certain things, he genuinely didn't know about them.

B: His way of speaking to people suggested that he was not very confident or determined, whereas in fact he was very determined (line 9-11), but there is no suggestion that he deliberately spoke in this way to deceive people.

D: His *timidity* (lack of confidence or courage) (line 13) meant that he travelled little – he *never flew in a plane*, presumably because he was afraid of flying (line 11-12). However, since he relied on his writers to *put him in touch with* the world he was curious about, he did not know very much about the places that they went to and he had not been to.

38 A: He didn't feel the need to *demonstrate greater knowledge and acquaintance*, a need that other editors felt (line 14-16). The writer wanted to do an article about the Iron Curtain (the imaginary division that used to exist between Western and Communist Europe) and Shawn's question indicated that he didn't know where this was, so he was obviously willing to admit that he didn't know something that the writer knew (line 16-18).

B: Shawn *wanted to know all about* the place that the writer was going to write his article about, so it is likely that articles his writers wrote entertained him personally. The writer thought about what Shawn would think when reading his article while he was writing it, because he saw Shawn as his *first, expectant reader* and therefore wanted to entertain him, but this does not mean that Shawn expected this (line 18-19).

C: He was different from other editors because he didn't feel the need to show that he knew more than his writers; there is no suggestion that he should have known more than he did, only that many editors are keen to show that they know more than their writers (line 14-16).

D: He took a personal interest in the writer's article about the Iron Curtain but other editors also took a personal interest in what their writers were doing, in that they seemed to *compete with their staff* in terms of knowledge (line 14-15).

39 C: The magazine was *writer-driven* (influenced entirely by its writers, not anyone else) *at Shawn's behest* (because that is the way he wanted it to be) (line 22).

A: He had fixed ideas about what it should **not** include – he was against *the sensational, the sordid and the self-seeking* – but he was *open to* (had no fixed ideas about) anything else that could be in the magazine.(line 20–21)

B: He allowed writers to *probe the depths of a subject, where truth may reside* (examine a subject carefully to find out the truth about it) (line 23-24), and it is therefore likely that many articles in the magazine were serious, but this does not mean that he insisted that every article should be serious.

D: When he was editor of it, the magazine *eschewed topicality* (rejected what was only of interest at the time and for a short time) (line 21-22).

40 C: The writer states that he *never had such praise* (was never praised so highly) as when Shawn indicated that what he had written was *wonderful or beautiful*. He feels this because Shawn rarely – *once in a rare while* – gave such praise, because he was very careful about the language used by his writers. If the writer didn't think that Shawn was a good judge of writing, he wouldn't have felt that praise from him was so important(line 28–30).

A: The writer says that Shawn *had precise ideas about language* and these included punctuation (line 26-28), but he does not say that he thinks that Shawn treated this as more important than he should have done.

B: The writer rarely – *once in a rare while* – received praise from Shawn and when he did he valued it greatly – *I've never had such praise*. He does not suggest that Shawn should have given more praise, only that he valued praise from Shawn (line 28-30).

D: If writers were *excited about the project being proposed* and he *sensed enthusiasm* from writers, Shawn would give the *go-ahead* (allow them to proceed and write the article) (line 25-26), but the writer does not indicate that he disapproves of this and he does state that Shawn was very strict when editing what his writers wrote.

PAPER 1: SECTION A 25 marks
SECTION B 30 marks
TOTAL 55 marks

To be converted into a score out of 40 marks.

FURTHER PRACTICE AND GUIDANCE

p 105–106 PAPER 1 SECTION B

*For explanations of the answers to these questions, see the answers to the **Second Passage in Paper 1 Section B** above.*

Question 31
1 c
2 a
3 a
4 b

Questions 32 and 33
1 no
2 b
3 people who don't like someone taking all the decisions and telling them what to do/people with ideas and initiative.
4 yourself
5 b
6 yes
7 b
8 b
9 c
10 orderliness

Questions 34 and 35
1 a
2 c
3 c
4 b
5 a

FURTHER PRACTICE AND GUIDANCE

p 109 PAPER 2

Assessment of sample composition

1 Content
The letter is relevant at all times and deals only with the matter to be addressed. There is no repetition and it comes to the point straight away with no unnecessary background information or introductory sentences.

2 Organization
The letter is well organized, with good paragraphing – each paragraph deals with a separate issue. The first clearly explains what the letter is about; the second explains one problem; the third explains another problem; the fourth explains what the writer has so far done; the fifth explains what the

writer wants; the sixth explains what the writer will do if he/she doesn't get what he/she wants. The final two sentences effectively and accurately end a formal letter of this kind.

3 Linking
There is good linking in the letter, for example: *with reference to* and *Indeed* (first paragraph); *Firstly, so that* and *considering* (second paragraph); *However* and *inspite of the fact that* (third paragraph); *besides* (fourth paragraph); *Consequently* and *either ... or* (fifth paragraph). In addition, *which* effectively links sentences in the first and fifth paragraphs. However, the sentence in paragraph 3 beginning *On the other hand* could be more appropriately expressed. As the purpose of the letter is to complain, the introduction of a positive point is a little awkward, especially because it comes between two negative points. This sentence would be better expressed as follows: *Although/Though/While the tape deck is functional, the play button on desk A has come off and ...*

4 Use of vocabulary
There is plenty of appropriate and accurate vocabulary that is more than basic, for example: *dissatisfaction* and *on several counts* (in several ways) (first paragraph); *rotate* (second paragraph); *functional, came off* and *shoddy workmanship* (careless or poor quality work done in the production of something) (third paragraph); *gain ... satisfaction* (fourth paragraph); *refunding, take necessary measures* (fifth paragraph); *take further steps, court action* (sixth paragraph); *in anticipation* (final sentence). There are a few mistakes: *not polite at all with me* should be *not at all polite to me* (para 4); *a shame* (para 4) is not strong enough in the context of a letter of complaint – if you say that something is a shame you feel sad or sorry about it – and something indicating more annoyance, such as *which is unacceptable/disgusting/disgraceful* would be more appropriate; *with the hope* should be *in the hope* (para 5); *If my desires are not fulfilled* (para 6) is an inappropriate phrase – it is used for referring to deep emotions – and this would be better expressed as, for example, *If my complaint is not satisfactorily dealt with* or *If my requests are not met*, etc; *lead to* in para 6 is incorrect – one thing leads to another = one thing causes/results in another, but a person cannot lead to an action – and this phrase should be changed, for example, to *and even take consumer court action* or *and even resort to court action* (do it because all other actions have failed to produce the desired result).

5 Use of grammar
The letter is generally fluent with regard to sentence structure and includes more than short, simple sentences. In addition, it is well punctuated, with effective use of dashes (–) to explain

or add to points that have been made (paras 4 and 5). The verb tenses are all appropriate (although *came off* in para 3 perhaps should be *has come off* since there is no reference to when this happened). There are one or two grammatical mistakes: *which I would really like to let you know* should be *which I would really like to let you know about* – you *let someone know about something*; the sentence near the end, beginning *I expect* is incorrect – it should read *I expect to hear from you concerning these matters and that you will take my complaint seriously* because the verbs *hear* and *take* have different subjects (*I expect to hear; you will take my complaint seriously*) and therefore the second subject (*you*) must be included in the second structure for the sentence to be correct.

6 Style

The letter is appropriately formal and observes very well the conventions of such letter-writing – it opens with the purpose of the letter, explains the writer's situation and purpose clearly and concludes with a well-phrased request for a reply. *I thank you in anticipation* is an appropriate way of ending such a letter – *I look forward to hearing from you/receiving your reply*, etc is perhaps more appropriate for a letter requesting something than one complaining about something, because it is more polite.

This is a very good formal letter of complaint which conforms with the style appropriate to such writing and contains few mistakes. It would be given a score of approximately 14–17 marks out of 20.

p 110 PAPER 3 SECTION A QUESTION 1

One mark per question (Total: 20)

1 **less**: *less than* + adjective = not + adjective. It was a *less than auspicious occasion* = it was not an occasion that showed signs of future success.

2 **which**: This refers to the story and gives further information about it.

3 **until/before**: This refers to what ended the period of the story being rejected.

4 **it**: = the story.

5 **attracted/got**: If something *attracts/gets attention*, people pay attention to it.

6 **appeared**: If something *appears* in a publication, it is printed or published in it.

7 **last**: *at last* is used with something that happens after a long period of waiting, trying or wanting it to happen.

8 **however**: This is used because a disadvantage produced by what has just been mentioned is being described – *This fame, however, grew ...* = But this fame grew ...

9 **extent**: *to such an extent that* = so much/so greatly that.

10 **have**: *Doyle is reported to have said* = It is reported that Doyle said.

11 **rather/sooner**: If someone *would rather/sooner do something*, they would prefer to do it.

12 **point/time**: *at one point/time* = there was one occasion when.

13 **further**: *a further thing* = an additional thing, one that comes after another or others previously mentioned.

14 **Although/Though**: *Although/Though* is used for stating that what might be expected to be the case isn't the case. Sherlock Holmes first appeared over a century ago and it might be expected that he wouldn't still be popular after all that time, but he is.

15 **most**: *the most ... of all time* = the most ... that has ever existed.

16 **up**: If you *take up residence somewhere*, you move into a home and start living there.

17 **really/actually/truly**: If something *doesn't really/actually/truly exist*, it doesn't exist, although some people say or think that it does.

18 **on**: If something *lives on*, it continues to exist or be remembered for a long time after it starts or happens.

19 **powers**: Someone's *powers of something* are their mental or physical abilities at something; *powers of deduction* are the ability to solve or find the reason for something by using logic and intelligence.

20 **at**: you *live*, etc at an address.

p 110 PAPER 3 SECTION A QUESTION 2

One mark per underlined word or phrase (Total: 13)

a <u>a performance that/which</u>(1) <u>delighted the audience/the audience were delighted by/the audience found delightful</u>(1). (2 marks)
Someone *gives a performance*; *that/which* must be used to link *performance* with the description of it; if someone *is delighted by something*, it *delights them*, it is *something that/which they are delighted by* or *is something that/which they find delightful*.

b <u>(to me) to be enjoying</u> her new job a great deal (1 mark)
The pattern *seem (to someone)* + infinitive must be used here; *It is my impression that she* = it seems (to me) that she = she seems (to me) to; because the verb in the original sentence is in the present continuous form to refer to a current situation, *seem* must be followed by the present continuous form of the infinitive (*to be -ing*).

c <u>had I solved one problem</u> (1) <u>than I was faced with another</u> (1)(2 marks)
If one thing happens a short time after another, *hardly* can be used with the meaning *only just, only a short time before*. It can be used in two patterns: subject + *had hardly done* + *than* + *when* (*I had hardly solved one problem when I was faced with another*) or *Hardly* + *had* + subject + *done* + *than*, as here. If the sentence begins with *Hardly*, the first

verb must be in the question form, although this is of course not a question.

d <u>(that) the crimes had been/were committed</u> by the same person (1 mark)
If something *suggests that something is the case*, it indicates that it is the case; *they seemed to have been committed* = it seemed that they had been/were committed.

e <u>take much/a lot</u>(1) <u>for Jack to lose</u>(1) his temper (2 marks)
If it *doesn't take much/a lot for someone to do something*, exceptional circumstances are not required for them to do it, they do it regularly and in ordinary circumstances because it is a habit of theirs or part of their nature.

f <u>an enormous contribution</u> (1)<u>to</u> (1)<u>the team's success</u> (2 marks)
If someone/something *contributes to* or *makes a contribution to something*, they are involved in it and have an influence on it; the adverb *enormously* is linked to the verb *contributed* and has to be changed to the adjective *enormous*, which is linked to the noun *contribution*.

g <u>people at work gossiping about him/being gossiped about by people at work/it/the fact that people at work gossip about him</u> (1 mark)
If you *don't like someone doing something/don't like something happening/don't like it that something happens/don't like the fact that something happens*, it happens and you don't like it.

h <u>to</u> (1) <u>expectation/what was expected, he decided not to stand for election</u>(1) (2 marks)
Contrary to something = opposite from/completely different from/ despite something; *contrary* to must be followed by *something*, not by a subject, verb, etc.

p 111 PAPER 3 SECTION A QUESTION 3

*See also the questions in **Further Practice and Guidance** on page 113 and the corresponding answers.*

One mark per underlined word or phrase (Total: 7)

a <u>for which</u> (1): *for which we had paid* = that/which we had paid for; you *pay for* something that you receive or should receive.

b <u>as/though it is</u> or <u>as/though it may/ might be</u> (1): = although it is/may be/ might be boring to do it.

c <u>on the grounds/basis that</u> (1): If something is done or thought *on the grounds/basis that something is the case*, it is done because that is the case or a decision to do it is made with that reason.

d <u>shouldn't have/needn't have made</u> or <u>didn't need to/were wrong to make</u> (1): If someone *shouldn't have done* or *was wrong to do* something, in the opinion of the speaker, they did something bad or wrong; if someone *needn't have done* something, it wasn't necessary for them to do it but they did it; if someone *didn't need to do* something, it wasn't necessary for them to do it. If you *make something obvious*, you show it very clearly.

e without having to/needing to/being forced to (1): = because I knew the speech so well, I didn't have to/didn't need to/wasn't forced to look at my notes.

f choice/option/alternative(1) but to (1)(2): If you *have no choice/option /alternative but to do something*, you have to do it because there is nothing else that you can choose to do.

p 112 PAPER 3 SECTION A QUESTION 4

The numbers in brackets in the explanations to these questions refer to the options in Further Practice and Guidance on page 114. See also the corresponding answers.

One mark per underlined word or phrase (Total: 13)

a It is/will be in your interests(1) to get/ that you get (1) a specialized qualification. (2 marks)
If *it is in your interests to do/that you do something*, doing it will benefit you; *your interests are ...* (1, 4) is used to describe the things that you are interested in (*my interests are reading, cycling, etc*); if *something interests you* (2), you find it interesting.

b Their refusal to give (1)me my money back made me furious/infuriated me.(1)*or* I was infuriated by (1)their refusal to give(1) me my money back. (2 marks)
A *refusal to do something* is a statement in which the speaker refuses to do something; *make + someone + adjective describing feeling* = cause someone to have that feeling; if something *infuriates you* or you are *infuriated by something*, it makes you furious; in 1, the preposition is incorrect – you are *furious with someone*, you are *furious at/about something*; in 3, *of giving* is incorrect, it should be *to give* and *had* is incorrect, it should be *made*; in 4, *of giving* should be *to give*.

c What I'm not sure about is whether we'll be able to afford it or not.*or* Whether we'll be able to afford it or not is what I'm not sure about. (1 mark)
What I'm not sure about = the thing that I'm not sure about; in 1, *about it* should be *about* – the subject of *is* is *what I'm not sure about* and *it* is an incorrect addition; in 2, *it's* should be *is* – again *it* is an incorrect addition because the subject of the verb *is* is *whether we'll be able to afford it or not*; in 3, a correct sentence could begin *The thing that I'm not sure about* or *The thing I'm not sure about* and *what* is incorrect. However, these sentences would not include *what*.

d The latest sales figures are/show an improvement on the previous ones (1 mark)
If something *is/shows an improvement on something*, it is better than it; in 2,

the sentence could be partially re-written as *There has been an improvement in the sales figures*, but this does not permit the comparison between the latest figures and the previous ones which the original sentence has; in 3 *make* should be *are/show* and *to* should be *on*; 4, though grammatically correct, makes no sense – where is *there*? and *the latest sales figures* have to be the subject of the sentence because they are *an improvement*.

e Nobody/No one who comes/coming to this city(1) fails to notice the beauty of its architecture.(1)*or* Nobody/No one comes to this city(1) and fails to notice the beauty of its architecture. (1)*or*There is nobody/no one who comes to this city (1) and/who fails to notice the beauty of its architecture.(1) (2 marks)
Everyone who comes notices it = nobody, etc who comes fails to notice it/nobody, etc comes and fails to notice it/there is nobody, etc who comes and/who fails to notice it; in 1 *it is* should be *there is*; in 2, the order is wrong – *who comes to this city* should follow *nobody* because together they form the subject of this sentence (*nobody who comes to this city* is the subject, not simply *nobody*); in 4 *nobody comes* should be *nobody who comes* because this defines *nobody*.

f Theories about the causes of the disease have changed(1) in the light of recent research(1).*or* In the light of recent research,(1) theories about the causes of the disease have changed(1).*or* Recent research has cast/shed/ thrown new light (1) on the causes of the disease.(1)(2 marks)
If something is thought or decided *in the light of* something else, it is thought or decided as a result of considering certain information or events that have taken place; if something *casts/ sheds/throws new light on something*, a discovery or new information changes views on it and makes it more clearly understood; in 1, it is not possible to use *the light of* something as a subject to express the meaning of the original sentence; in 2 *put* should be *cast/ shed/ thrown*; in 4 *with light from* should be *in the light of*.

g I was reluctant to commit myself(1) to buying/to buy(1) more goods from the same company. (2 marks)
If you *commit yourself to doing/to do something*, you make a firm promise or agreement to do it; in 1, 2 and 3 the patterns after *commit* are incorrect.

h Payment will be made on receipt of the order.*or* On receipt of the order, payment will be made. (1 mark)
On in this context = when/as soon as something happens/has happened; *on receipt of something* = when/as soon as something is/has been received; *receipt of something* is the act of receiving it; in 1, *with* should be *on*; in 2, *at* should be *on*, *the* should not be included and the phrase *order receipt* is not possible; in 4, *once* must be followed by a subject, verb, etc. – the sentence could correctly be phrased *once the order is/has been*

received but this does not include *receipt*.

SECTION A

QUESTION 1	20 marks
QUESTION 2	13 marks
QUESTION 3	7 marks
QUESTION 4	13 marks
TOTAL	53 marks

FURTHER PRACTICE AND GUIDANCE

p 113 PAPER 3 SECTION A QUESTION 3

For explanations, see Section A Question 3 above.

a 4   b 2   c 1   d 4   e 2   f 3

p 114 PAPER 3 SECTION A QUESTION 4

For all the acceptable answers to Question 4 of the test and explanations, see Section A Question 4 above.

a 3   b 2   c 4   d 1   e 3   f 3
g 4   h 3

p 115–117 PAPER 3 SECTION B

Answers similar to or covering the same points as those given here are acceptable providing they are phrased accurately.

See also the questions in Further Practice and Guidance on pages 118-119 and the corresponding answers.

a **that it was unnecessary for her to have so many racquets to play only one game** (1 mark)
He says that five or six racquets *are now required to play one game of tennis* and the implication is that so many were not necessary before and so are not necessary now (line 2–3).

b **that the officials would come/run after her and beg her to come back and continue the game** (1 mark)
She hadn't *quit* (given up/stopped completely); she was *just biding her time* (waiting until what she wanted to happen happened) until the officials *came running*, or kneeling (asked her on their knees, *begging her to return* (asking her desperately to return) (line 5–6).

c **if you agree to do something graciously, you agree in a pleasant way** (1) **but the player did not apologize for her behaviour/did not accept that she was wrong/was rude throughout the incident** (1) **(2 marks)**
If you accept/agree to do/refuse something *graciously*, you do so politely and pleasantly; since she had behaved badly, and only returned because she got what she wanted – the officials begging her to do so – and there is no suggestion that she apologized or accepted that she was wrong, her agreement to return was certainly not gracious (line 6-7).

d **they felt that she had shown courage/ been brave in punishing/humiliating the umpire for acting badly/doing something wrong** (1 mark)
The crowd *came to their feet to pay tribute to* (stood to applaud/honour) *her act of bravery* (her brave/courageous act) in *giving the umpire his come-uppance* (punishing/humiliating the umpire for something he deserved to be punished/humiliated for) (line 7–8).

e **He didn't get angry** (1), **he looked embarrassed** (1) **and frightened** (1) **because he accepted that he had done something wrong and was sorry about it** (1) (4 marks)
If you *fume*, you feel or get very angry; if you *blush*, your face goes red because you are embarrassed; if you *cower*, you move your body backwards or bend it forwards because you are frightened; the umpire *knew he had behaved badly* and *seemed truly sorry* (line 8-9).

f **an excellent game** (1) **and bad behaviour by the players** (1)(2 marks)
The fans expect to see a game *superlatively* (brilliantly) played and they also expect to see *high jinks* (naughty, excited but harmless behaviour) and *low jinks* – this is the writer's own invented phrase and must indicate that while high jinks are harmless, low jinks are bad behaviour (line 13–14). That the crowd expects to see bad behaviour is also indicated by the fact that they applaud the player when she returns in the first paragraph and therefore support the way she behaved.

g **because they are afraid of what the crowd's reaction would be/afraid that the crowd would get violent/riot/ cause trouble/afraid that public order could not be maintained if they did so** (1 mark)
Sports officials know that a sports crowd *spurned* (rejected, not given what it wishes) is dangerous and they therefore seem *cowed* (frightened by somene's threats or aggressive behaviour) because they have to *have in mind* (consider) *the maintenance of public order* (making sure that people do not get out of control and behave violently) (line 14–17).

h **they were the children of wealthy people and didn't have to earn money/ had plenty of money** (1) **and therefore didn't take the game so seriously/ played for pleasure** (1) (2 marks)
The players of the past were *upper-middle-class offspring* (the children of wealthy people) who *didn't have to work for a living* (didn't have to work in order to earn money to live on) (line 21–22) and therefore had a *nonchalant code of behaviour* (a way of behaving that showed they did not care very much about what they were doing) (line 24).

i **the children of company directors who will inherit from their parents** (1) **and who have no particular aim in life** (1) (2 marks)
If someone is *loitering*, they are in a place with no particular purpose and doing nothing in particular; an *heir* is someone who will inherit money from a parent or other relative.

j **badly paid professional sportsmen** (1 mark) *footballers being the worst example* = footballers were the worst example of professionals and professionals were being paid in the past *at the going rate of plumbers' assistants* (the average wage for plumbers' assistants, which it is implied, was low) (line 25–26).

k **an acceptable/morally good** (1) **set of rules for behaviour/code of behaviour** (1) (2 marks)
If something is *decent*, it is morally correct or acceptable; an *ethic* is a rule/moral principle or set of rules/ moral principles regarding right and wrong behaviour.

l **they want to be adored/worshipped/ loved** (1), **they want all the comforts of wealth/luxury** (1) **and they want to behave exactly as they wish** (1) **both when playing and in private** (1) (4 marks)
They think they are *entitled to adoration* and *the pamperings of luxury* – if someone is *pampered*, they are given all the comforts they want and don't have to do anything for themselves; they think that there should be *no questions asked about* (no criticism of) their behaviour *on or off the course*, etc (when they are playing or when they are not) (line 33-36).

m **the top players realize that the organizers of events shown all over the world will make a great deal of money from them** (1) **and they want a share of that money** (1) (2 marks)
The best players know that *by virtue of* (because of/as a result of) *world-wide exposure* (being seen by people all over the world) the organizers will *take in many millions* (gain an enormous amount of money) and they *don't pause for long* before saying that they should have some of that enormous amount (line 36-38).

n **when a linesman's decision has gone against them/when a linesman has made a bad decision** (1) **because this affects their income greatly/because this can make a big difference to how much money they get** (1) (2 marks)
If you *blow up*, you suddenly and violently lose your temper; it takes *considerable character* (you have to be a person who can react calmly to difficult or unpleasant situations) not to do this if whether you earn a hundred or fifty thousand *turns on* (depends on, is governed by) the linesman's call. You are only likely to *blow up* if such a call is against you or wrong(line 38–40).

*Questions **a–n**: Total 27 marks*

PAPER 3 SECTION B – SUMMARY

o *One mark each for inclusion of the following points or points similar to them:*

1 **sports stars behave badly when they are playing** (first and second paragraphs)

2 **crowds encourage players to behave badly** (first and second paragraphs); in these paragraphs he does not blame the officials for not being severe enough with players, he says that this is because they are afraid of the crowd's reaction. (see questions f and g).

3 **players are motivated chiefly by the desire to become wealthy** (third paragraph); the writer is not criticizing them for being well-paid or for taking the game very seriously; he compares them with the sportsmen of the past who didn't need to earn money and therefore didn't need to take the game seriously but he believes that it is *unjust* and *absurd* (ridiculous) to expect them to have the same carefree attitude as those who didn't need money, and to be paid as badly as professionals were in the past, and states that he approves of sport now being a profitable career, like any other form of entertainment. However, in line 29-30, he states that players are now motivated to take up sport by the desire to become wealthy and that is what is wrong.

4 **sport hasn't developed a code of principles concerning good behaviour that can keep the behaviour of players under control** (there is no decent *ethic that can discipline the game* (line 31 and see question k).

5 **the media encourage young stars to think that they should be adored, have everything they want and be able to behave as badly as they like** (line 33-36 and see question l).

6 **young stars lack the character/are too childish/have not been brought up well enough to keep themselves under control when an official's decision goes against them** (they *blow up* because they were not *taught when young the definition of a brat*. A *brat* is a badly-behaved and annoying child and the writer is saying that he thinks the sports stars of today are brats because they weren't stopped from being brats when they were children (line 38-42).

Total: 6 marks

Plus maximum of 4 marks for general impression, based on the following criteria:
– *relevance*
– *general level of fluency*
– *accuracy of language*
– *absence of copying from passage*
– *length*

SUMMARY:	TOTAL	10 marks
SECTION B	TOTAL:	37 marks
PAPER 3	SECTION A	53 marks
	SECTION B	37 marks
	TOTAL	90 marks

To be converted into a score out of 40 marks.

FURTHER PRACTICE AND GUIDANCE

p 118-119 PAPER 3 SECTION B

For explanations, see the explanations for the answers to Paper 3 Section B above.

Question a: They now use five or six racquets to play just one game.
Question b: no
Question d: c
Question g: The crowd might cause trouble/become violent/riot, etc.
Question h: A: They had good manners.
B: They were the children of the upper-middle-class.
Question l: Tick 2, 3 and 4.
Question c: a
Question i: c
Question j: c
Question n: c

FURTHER PRACTICE AND GUIDANCE

p 119 SAMPLE SUMMARY

See Paper 3 Section B – Summary above.

1 Nothing that is irrelevant is included – the whole summary refers to different criticisms the writer makes of sport today. The following relevant points from above are included or not included: 1: first sentence; 2: This point is not included; 3: This point is partly included because the effect of earning large sums of money is mentioned (second sentence) but the idea that this is why some young people take up sport today is not included (½ mark); 4: third sentence; 5: This idea is included in the second sentence but the fact that it is caused by the media is not included (½ mark); 6: last sentence

For the points included, this summary scores 4 out of 6.

2 The general level of fluency here is reasonable, with some language errors:(first sentence) *the sports stars behaviour* should be *sports stars' behaviour* or *the behaviour of sports stars* (it refers to sports stars in general, not particular ones; in the first alternative, there should be an apostrophe after 's' to indicate a plural possessive); (second sentence) *entitled of* should be *entitled to*; (fourth sentence) *refers to* is not appropriate here because it means *mentions* – it should be *concerns/relates to/is associated with*, etc – *backgroung* should be *background* and *behaviour* is an uncountable noun in this context, so it should be *what bad behaviour is*.

3 Nothing has been completely copied from the passage – the third sentence is very similar to what is in the passage but it has been rephrased, indicating real understanding of that part of the passage; the summary is of the right length.

For general impression, the summary scores 2 out of 4.

This summary therefore scores 6 out of 10.

p 120 PAPER 4 PART ONE

The line references are to the tape transcripts on pages 173-175.

One mark per question (Total: 10 marks)

1 **herbal pills and teas**: line 3–4
2 **tins of salmon**: line 5-9; He *dropped this* (gave up selling herbal pills and teas) because he thought it more sensible to *buy in bulk* (buy things in large quantities) and sell things more cheaply than other shops did.
3 **open (the) tin(s)/open them**: line 16-20
4 **(little) libraries**: line 27-32; He realized that people had to go to chemists to get their *prescriptions* (the medicines doctors told them to get for treatment) and that while they were there, they might get something else too.
5 **records**: line 38-40; They now sell sandwiches but then they sold records, and shop managers had to learn how to operate the gramophones on which they were played then.
6 **circulate them/give them to other people/lend them to other people**: line 52-58; There were some books they wouldn't get for people at all because they considered them indecent and there were others that were *borderline* (considered quite indecent but not so indecent that they wouldn't supply them), that customers were obliged only to read themselves and not to lend to anyone else.
7 **a red label/red labels**: line 58–60; Ordinary books had a green shield on them, *these books* (the ones that could not be circulated) had red labels.
8/9 **the (purely) chemist business/the chemists; the gift side/gifts/the sale of gifts (in any order)**: line 72-76; The *number one side* was the chemist business and the *number two side*, that Jesse's wife took over, was the gift side.
10 **chairman**: line 91-94; Jesse sold the company but his son John continued to work there, bought the company back and became chairman.

p 120 PAPER 4 PART TWO

One mark per question (Total: 10 marks)

11 **yes**: Penny says that what people remember depends on what goes into their minds at the time when it happens and that the *selectivity of* what you remember (the choice made by the mind regarding what it takes in and remembers and what it does not) is *different for men and women* – men's minds select different things to remember from what women's minds select (line 8-18).
12 **no**: Penny says that reports show that women allow themselves to be responsible for remembering things like birthdays, with the result that men can relax and not worry with regard to such things. Men therefore, it is implied, do not remember things like birthdays as well as women do, because they are not required to (line 18-23).
13 **no**: Penny uses arguments as an example of the way that men and women remember things differently, but she says that a man might consider that there was an argument about a certain issue, whereas a woman might say that there was no argument about it. Her point is therefore not that women remember arguments more clearly than men, but that men and women may disagree about whether something was an argument or not (line 30-34).
14 **yes**: Martin does not agree that you can say that men's and women's memories differ or that any other two groups of people have different kinds of memory (line 41–45)but he does agree that it is a question of *perception* – that *different kinds of things mean different things to different people* (line 35-38). He says that people in general tend to remember things that matter to them personally. He talks about people in general and says that they remember things if they interpret them as being *personally significant to them* (line 45–50).
15 **no**: Martin is *dubious about that* – he doubts whether it is true that women *feel the emotions of an event or conversation better than a man does*. He thinks this idea is based on a *stereotypical belief* (a belief that is based on an incorrect idea of what a whole group of people are like in general that is commonly held) that women are *more emotional beings than men* and he doesn't *subscribe to* (agree with) this view (line 57-61). He believes it is possible that a strong emotional reaction to an event will make you remember that event in more detail, but that this is equally true of both men and women (line 61-65). He says that *emotion does influence memory* but not by *interacting with gender* (by being associated with the sex of the person involved) (line 70-73).
16 **yes**: Penny says that it can be *problematic* (lead to problems) if people's memories are too good because then they might *always operate on the past* (be focused on the past all the time). A lot of couples *get locked into* this (become permanently fixed in focusing on the past) and this can cause a *slide* (a decline in the relationship) and *separate camps* (couples divided into opposing sides) (line 81-92).
17 **yes**: The presenter says that to argue about the past is a *futile thing to do* (a useless thing to do because it won't change or achieve anything), even though a lot of couples do it, and Penny agrees with this (line 93-101).
18 **yes**: Martin says that people *can reach a new interpretation of events* and they can *find a new memory* for experiences

they shared (line 110-114). He says this in relation to the question of whether it is a waste of time for couples to disagree about who is *remembering more correctly than the other one* because the past can't be changed – *you can't alter it* – (line 95–99), which is the point that he says he is returning to. He is therefore saying that disagreements about what actually happened in the past can result in the people who disagree reaching an agreement on a new interpretation of it that is different from the two interpretations they each had and argued about.

19 no: Martin says that they *do work* but only for certain things such as items on a list or names and *aren't much use* (don't work well) for remembering the *meaningful events of one's life* (things that happen and matter to you personally) (line 124-132).

20 yes: Martin says that the techniques for improving your memory don't work if you want to keep *a photographic record* (a memory of every single detail) *of everyday events* but that anyway *it would be strange* if someone tried to do that and *it would be unusual if somebody tried to use them in that way* (line 132-139). He therefore believes that most people don't try to remember every single detail of everyday events.

p 121 PAPER 4 PART THREE

One mark per question (Total: 5 marks)

21 C: When asked how he works out who the publicity for a film should be aimed at, he says that *sometimes it's really difficult* and gives an example of an occasion when he *wasn't quite ready for* (wasn't expecting or prepared for) *how many kids enjoyed* a certain film. He had expected it to have *wide audience appeal* (appeal to all kinds of people) but he was surprised by the high number of children that enjoyed it (line 36-41). This is an example of the kind of thing he has discovered.
A: They don't get *stuck into* (start working very hard on) the marketing until the film is finished and they've seen it but he does not say that they change their publicity after they've prepared it (line 21-25).
B: He says that you know who *kids' movies* (movies for children) are going to appeal to – children and some parents. This does not mean that they appeal more to parents than to children (line 33-36).
D: He says that you know that action movies are going to appeal to more people than any other kind of movie, but he expects this and does not say that he is often surprised by how popular they are (line 29-32).

22 A: They are cutting down the budget for advertising and publicity (reducing the money they spend on it) and they are *figuring* (calculating) that since people find out about films

anyway, there is no point in spending so much on advertising them (line 44-52). Most of their publicity is therefore free in that they don't have to pay for articles in magazines and newspapers or items on TV about films, although they spend *quite a lot of money* on the material that is sent to these places for them to put into their articles or programmes. This material is then *placed* (put in) for free (line 57-61).
B: They spend money on what they send out and they don't make journalists pay to see the films; as a result, the films are reviewed. There is no suggestion, however, that the material they send is likely to lead to good reviews or that the more they spend on it, the more likely it is to lead to good reviews (line 62-68).
C: Giving publicity material away enables them to get free publicity in the media and they have decided that it is better to do this and to spend less on advertising (line 57-61).
D: They spend quite a lot of money on material that results in publicity in the media and feel that this enables them to reduce spending on advertising, but it is not stated that they are thinking of spending more money on such material (line 44–68).

23 A: If the film companies give radio stations *something to give away* – a prize –, they will mention the film (line 68–72) because this enables the radio stations to feel they are *getting the appearance of being generous to their listeners* (line 90-92). The implication is that they might not mention the films if there wasn't this advantage to them.
B: The film companies give radio stations *heaps of* (a lot of) free goods (line 75-76) but in exchange they get *coverage for the movie* (mentions of it in the media) (line 89-90) and there is no suggestion that they mind supplying so many goods, because it is worth it to them. Furthermore, the radio stations don't demand the goods, they get *inundated with* them (they are sent more than they have asked for or want) (line 76–77).
C: Radio stations will mention the film, *even if they don't review it*, if the film company gives them something (line 68-72). The film companies therefore expect coverage for their films in the form of them being mentioned on the radio but they don't expect that the films will always be reviewed.
D: Although they may not review the films, they are useful because they give them coverage.

24 C: Film companies *don't force people to cover the film* – if journalists who have been invited to a free screening don't like the film, *they don't have to cover it* (line 132-134).
A: The film companies choose people to interview the stars who will do the kind of interview they want (one that will be favourable to the star and in which they will not try to expose the private life of the star) but it is not stated that the film companies actually

tell them what questions to ask (line 98-108).
B: The journalist says that they may feel they are being *bribed* (offered something in exchange for favours) and be suspicious of the motives of film publicists if film publicists suddenly offer them *lavish* (very expensive) gifts. However, a lot of this *comes down to* (depends on) the relationship that journalists have with film publicists, so not all journalists are suspicious of all film publicists (line 114-123).
D: They may think they are being bribed if they are offered gifts, but it is not stated that they are not allowed to accept them.

25 C: Some films have generally bad reviews but *it doesn't make any difference to the box office* – to how many people pay to go and see them at cinemas (line 137-142).
A: Bad reviews mean that *potentially* (it is possible that) *groups of people out there* don't go to see a film who would do so if the reviews were good (line 142-146) but most people *make up their own minds about whether they want to see it or not*, so they are not influenced by reviews (line 148-151).
B: Bad reviews *may pick up heavily on the negative aspects* of a film – may concentrate mostly on what the critic dislikes about the film, but no comment is made about the abilities or knowledge of the critics who write these (line 137-140).
D: He says that *the more coverage you get, the more aware people are of the film* – so even bad publicity is good because it increases public awareness of the film.(line 146–148) However, he does not say that it can be better to have bad reviews than good reviews – bad reviews may stop some people from seeing the film who otherwise would (line 142-146).

p 122 PAPER 4 PART FOUR

*The letters in brackets in these explanations refer to the questions about each of the people in **Further Practice and Guidance** on page 123–124. See also the corresponding answers to these questions.*

One mark per question (Total: 9 marks)

26/27T/P (in any order): When Trowser started making his trousers, *he was thought to be completely mad* (line 102–103) and *the whole thing was regarded as a bit of a joke* before trousers became fashionable (line 108-109) (B). Pocket *was thought to be fairly silly and all kinds of jokes were made about him* when he first invented pockets (line 126-128) (A). There is no mention of the initial reaction to Gusset's invention (C), to how long Coffin's invention took to become popular (E) or to people finding Walkman's invention amusing (D).

28 T: He put his invention *on the market* (advertised it and tried to sell it) *as* *economical* – he said that it would not involve a lot of expenditure once it had been bought, presumably because it would last a long time (line 104-105) (E). There is no reference to the cost of Gusset's invention (E).

29 W: His invention was *a bit cumbersome* (too large to be carried or handled easily); he couldn't put it in his pocket or carry it on his belt because the technology didn't exist to make this possible. More recently the technology arrived that made this possible (that enabled his invention to be smaller) (line 142-152) (E). Gusset's invention created something bigger than what previously existed but we are not told that this caused it to fail (D); Trowser's product *came all the way down to the ankle* and was therefore longer than garments worn at the time, but it did succeed after a while (A); Pocket's invention was considered *silly* but we are not told that had anything to do with the size of it (C).

30 K: The sauce that he started selling and *put into commercial production* was one *that his wife had been making for years* before he did so (line 78-82); it was therefore his wife's invention and what he did was to start selling it (C, D). In the case of Coffin, boxes for people to be buried in already existed but he invented boxes made of wood and that is what he gave his name to (C). Trowser's name was spelt differently from the way his invention is now spelt but he did not take his idea from someone with a similar name (line 95-97) (C).

31 C: He *made a considerable fortune out of this* (earned a great deal of money) from selling his boxes because they were commercially successful in the City of London (line 63-65) (B). Ketchup's product was successful too but he *actually didn't really make any money out of it* (line 82-84) (B). Fashionable young men started to wear Trowser's invention and of course it became enormously successful, but it is not stated that he became wealthy from it (line 111-113) (D). Pocket's invention *caught on* (became popular) because people realized that it *made sense, especially in winter* (line 128-131), but there is no reference to whether he made any money out of it or not, and no suggestion that he successfully advertised it or that it was successful in his lifetime (D, E).

32/33 G/C: Underpants already existed; what Gusset did was to invent something that joined together the two separate legs that they consisted of at that time, therefore creating one larger garment when previously there had been two (line 40–47) (A, B, D). People were already buried in boxes; what Coffin did was to change the material these boxes were made of from stone to wood (line 51-58) (A, D). There is no suggestion that when Pocket had his idea any form of pocket had already been thought of (B). Walkman was *one of those people who are born before their time* (his ideas were in advance of the

period in which he lived) (line 137-139), and so no form of his invention existed then (A, B).

34 K: Although it is not suggested that he had previously invented unsuccessful things, Ketchup *had various business failures* until he started selling his wife's sauce *as a last resort* – because he had tried everything else and could think of nothing else to do (line 76–81) (A, E). The *portable recording and playback device* (line 140-141) is the Walkman and there is no suggestion that he invented more than one thing (C).

35 W: He did succeed in making a portable recording and playback device, but he wanted it to be *truly portable* (line 150-151). However, the *technology of his day* (at that time) was not advanced enough for this idea to be carried out (B). Coffin's invention was not too advanced for the time, his boxes were considered not to be *theologically correct* (line 57–59) by the monks he worked for because of what they were made of (D).

PAPER 4	PART ONE	10 marks
	PART TWO	10 marks
	PART THREE	5 marks
	PART FOUR	9 marks
	TOTAL	34 marks

To be converted into a score out of 20 marks.

FURTHER PRACTICE AND GUIDANCE

p 123-124 PAPER 4 PART FOUR

*For details on these answers, see the explanations for **Part Four** above.*

Gusset: Tick A and D
Coffin: Tick B and D
Ketchup: Tick A, B and C
Trowser: Tick A, B and E
Pocket: Tick A and E
Walkman: Tick B and E

FURTHER PRACTICE AND GUIDANCE

p 127 PAPER 5

Talking About Passages

1 b
2 It seems to be promoting the attractions of theme parks and it is likely that it will then give details about different ones.
3 The excitement of theme parks. They are *giant fun farms*, they are for *thrill-and-spill seekers* – people looking for excitement and danger –, and people are *bounced, dropped, swirled round and round and turned upside down*, all of which emphasizes the exciting, fast and violent movement involved in taking the rides.
4 a
5 Changes regarding concerts given by big stars because of new technology.
6 Ticket prices have risen because the

cost of staging concerts has risen; stars make their profits from souvenirs, not from ticket sales.
7 a newspaper report
8 How wonderful the game was and the scenes at the end of it were/What a wonderful occasion it was/The high quality of the game and the atmosphere at the end of it.
9 The players played extremely well – they played with *class* (great skill) and *pace* (great speed) and they had *persistent bloody-minded guts* (they kept trying hard because they were determined not to lose and they were brave). The applause at the end *was wholly merited* (the players completely deserved it). They were sportsmanlike at the end, congratulating each other.

Talking About the Topic

1 audience
2 spectators/ crowd
3 band
4 cheer
5 clap/applaud
6 orchestra
7 boo/jeer
8 interval/intermission
9 plot
10 exhibit
11 characters
12 best-seller/blockbuster
13 box-office
14 hit
15 subtitles
16 set
17 main/leading
18 scene

LISTENING SCRIPTS

TEST 1 PART 1

You will hear a local radio station's morning traffic and weather reports. For questions 1-10, fill in the information given in the reports.

You will hear the piece twice.

ANNOUNCER: ... and now it's over to Shirley Smith for the latest traffic information and Philip Burrows with the weather forecast.

TRAFFIC: The M3 approaching the city is 5 extremely slow because of an earlier accident that hasn't been cleared yet and the rest of the motorways are all busy and all rather slow moving. There's a broken-down coach on the 10 A40 eastbound, where there are lane closures anyway, so there are quite a few delays there coming into town. The M1 southbound, that's very slow this morning, because Junction 2, 15 which was supposed to re-open this week is still closed. On the A50 westbound there's a lot of congestion – that's due to a broken-down bus outside the station and the A406 is 20 closed due to an accident so there's a lot of congestion there. The M4 eastbound, approaching junction 5, roadworks there are causing long tailbacks now and on the A20 a lorry 25 has shed its load, causing severe delays. On the A107 there are faulty traffic lights at the junction with the A70 and the A374, that's closed because of a fire, with serious 30 congestion over a wide area. This is Shirley Smith. Traffic news, every ten minutes.

WEATHER: According to our weather station, the temperature's now 8 35 degrees, there's a breeze from a west-south-westerly direction and air quality is good. It's one of those mornings when you might say that it's too good to be true and indeed 40 it's not going to stay brilliantly sunny all day long – there'll be a build-up of cloud during the course of the morning. Nevertheless, there'll continue to be sunshine at times from 45 late morning onwards, with occasional interruptions during the afternoon. One or two of the clouds could be big enough for there to be an outside chance of a localized 50 shower, though in any given place there is little likelihood of this. It will also be fairly cool later in the day, with a blustery wind from the west and a top temperature this afternoon 55 of ten degrees – that's three degrees higher than we had yesterday and about the same amount lower than the seasonal average. Weather updates, every half hour. 60

Now listen to the piece again.

TEST 1 PART 2

You will hear a discussion about violence in films and on television. For questions 11-18, write YES in the boxes next to those views which are expressed in the discussion and NO in the boxes next to those views which are not expressed.

You will hear the piece twice.

PRESENTER: Does violence in films and on television play a part in causing violence in society? There has been an argument raging in the newspapers about this and I have 5 with me the film director Carrie Spielmann to discuss it. Carrie, there have been some fine performances, marvellous performances, and these films have been beautifully directed 10 with great cinematography, but at the same time at the nub of them there are some dreadful things going on and we have a series of these films doing well at the box office ... 15

CARRIE: Well you know, you can't only make films about cute and lovely people doing cute and lovely things. What dramatists have done throughout history is to take stories 20 from life and encapsulate them in stories and plays, and life includes nice things and it includes conflict and it includes evil, and of course evil existed long before the advent of 25 cinema and television. It was far less safe to walk the streets of America in the nineteenth century than it is today. In those times, you couldn't walk across Central Park during the 30 day – people were being murdered there, men carried special cudgels to stave off attack ...

PRESENTER: .... and people were dying of all sorts of diseases they don't die of 35 now, so that's no reason for not trying to stamp it out, is it?

CARRIE: That's really a pathetic argument, that is. No one can suggest that the people who did that in 40 earlier days were encouraged by films or television because it wasn't there, so if you seriously believe that you can take certain programmes off or if certain films hadn't been made, 45 muggers would get up in the morning and say 'we're not going to do any mugging today because that programme isn't on television, we'll go and help little old ladies across the 50 street' – it's nothing to do with conquering disease, that is the most ridiculous comparison.

PRESENTER: I take your point about films having to reflect different ways of 55 life, and of course you're quite right to say that violence does exist in society – I think some people's fear, though, is that sometimes the intellectual argument is being used 60 by some of today's film-makers,that is imposed on something that is really just tapping into man's worst excesses, you know.

CARRIE: Well man's worst excesses have 65

always been there and they've always received publicity. Are you suggesting that this radio station will stop reporting violence, that the newspapers will stop reporting it, the 70 television will stop reporting it – you can't hide from people what they know is going on. And the recent, or comparatively recent government report, which they themselves 75 commissioned, two of the most distinguished academics in this country went into this very deeply, it took many years to produce, it stated unequivocally that they could find no 80 link between violence as depicted on the screen or television and violence in people. Most people, if they wish to see those sorts of films, distinguish the good guy from the bad guy and 85 come out and go and have dinner, they don't go out and knock anybody about.

PRESENTER: Carrie, thank you very much indeed for joining me this afternoon. 90 Carrie Spielmann there, film director, destroying my arguments anyway (laughs). Worth making, nevertheless, I thought. What are your views on that – if you care to 95 counter what Carrie said there, if you've got your own opinions, call us now on...

Now listen to the piece again.

TEST 1 PART 3

You will hear an interview with someone who collects certain objects. For questions 19-23, choose the most appropriate answer, A,B,C or D and write your choice in the box provided below each question.

You will hear the piece twice.

INTERVIEWER: Well, even I used to keep a few stamps in an album for a while, but my rather feeble attempt to be a collector was put to shame when I went to meet Robert Opie. He's 5 dedicated his whole life to his collection, most of which is housed in the Museum of Packaging and Advertising. Robert, what exactly do you collect? 10

ROBERT: That's very difficult to explain. It's the whole story of an enormous social revolution that's happened over the last hundred years and the main thing I'm interested in within 15 that is the story of shopping and products and brands. I collect everything that one puts into today's shopping basket, everything that's in today's supermarket, but looking 20 back at it over the last hundred, hundred and fifty years and the evidence of this is now the packs that have survived, the advertisements, the promotions ... 25

INTERVIEWER: How much stuff have you got?

ROBERT: Well, more than I really want but it probably amounts to

something like about three hundred 30
thousand items at the moment.

INTERVIEWER: How do you decide what
to collect?

ROBERT: Um, it can become quite tricky
when I suddenly find I'm running 35
out of money, er, because when I'm
shopping, you see, first of all I go
round and think, what do I need for
the collection, what new products
have arrived, what new designs have 40
come along to update the previous
design and then I go around and
think, what am I going to eat tonight,
you know, so it's mainly made up of
those things and I get very 45
disappointed when there's a product
I want but I've already got the
packaging, you see, because I have to
wait till the next change comes along.

INTERVIEWER: When did you begin 50
collecting and why?

ROBERT: About the age of three, I think it
was, when I found this wonderful
stone in the path at home and came
back and actually discovered then – 55
my mother told me – it was a
fossilized sea urchin. Well, that began
my stone collection and then I went,
like many other schoolchildren, onto
other things like stamps and coins 60
but I was always trying to find things
that other people hadn't collected
because to my mind what was the
point of collecting things that
everyone else had done and that 65
everyone else was going to have a
better collection than me? So then at
the age of sixteen I suddenly thought,
well, you know, here's something,
packaging, that everybody's literally 70
throwing away and something is
always happening and changing in it,
so from that moment I've saved all
the packages I've ever eaten the
contents of. 75

INTERVIEWER: Do you feel that your
collecting is an obsession?

ROBERT: Er, I'm sure some people
probably think it is but I tend to find
that I'm driven by this commitment 80
that I'm saving the nation's heritage,
even though a lot of people think that
the rubbish aspect is not really
someone's heritage. I have to put in a
certain number of hours every day to 85
save something which I think should
be saved. You may have watched the
Olympics and you see these people
doing four or five hours' training
every day and I find that, I mean, 90
that may be called an obsession but
it's really a dedication to a particular
thing and I think I'm probably
dedicated in that kind of way.

INTERVIEWER: Do you ever wish you 95
could stop collecting?

ROBERT: Um, I think I'd find it difficult,
it's in the blood I'm afraid and um, I
mean, it's terrific fun but it's almost
like getting a million-piece jigsaw 100
and then slowly putting these pieces
together but with the big
disadvantage that the number of
pieces is always growing, so I've got
to add endlessly, endlessly, 105
endlessly, it's just terrible (laughs).

Now listen to the piece again.

TEST 1 PART 4

*You will hear a professional photographer
talking about his work. For questions 24-33,
complete the notes.*

You will hear the piece twice.

ANNOUNCER: Peter McDairmid, aged 25,
is a freelance photographer. In this
programme he describes his work.

PETER: It's a good idea to be on top of
what's happening around, I mean 5
I've always been interested in that
anyway, which is, I think, what led
me to news photography. My
working day, there's no such thing as
a typical working day, every day's 10
different, that's what's good about
the job. I'm one of five freelance
photographers used regularly by *The
Independent*. Because I'm freelance I
might not work at all – I may not 15
work tomorrow, I may not work the
day after or I may work seven days.
There are probably safer ways of
making a living but they wouldn't be
so much fun. 20

The Picture Desk at the
newspaper gets going at about ten
o'clock usually, so I may get a phone
call after ten and that would be to
come into the office to do something 25
nearby or it could be to drive
somewhere a long way away, you
just never know. The Picture Editor
gives me a brief – well, I say a brief,
you don't get that much of a brief, 30
you get told what the story is and
what you're going to cover but they
don't tell you how to cover it, that's
up to you. I mean, I really don't
know much about the job until I get 35
there, I just have to play it by ear.

The best way to learn is to do the
job and I'm still learning now. You
pick up things from other
photographers, you see what's going 40
on and how they're doing it. You
have to get yourself so familiar with
your equipment, so that the technical
things you hardly have to think
about because you really have to 45
concentrate your whole mind on the
composition of the picture.

My interest in photography really
came from when I was at school. We
had a dark room and we learnt basic 50
printing and photography. When I
left school first of all I worked in a
restaurant and I did some of their
publicity photos. I had a portfolio
which was pretty useless really, stuff 55
I'd been doing at school and I took
that to every local paper in the area,
and I didn't get anywhere at all but
the second time around when I tried
again I was more successful. After a 60
year on local papers, followed by a
year at a picture agency, I went
freelance.

When you're actually out on a job,
you don't really know what picture 65
you're going to get and you can
spend the whole day feeling totally
unsatisfied and think you've got
nothing and come back and think
'maybe this works'. It can be exciting, 70
you're right there, you can be at some
event and the focus of the whole
country is there, everyone's looking.
Once I've gone out and taken the

photographs, I've got a lot of
freedom when I come back to the 75
office to process and print them how
I like. I process the negatives myself
and I print them myself – I can also
ask the printers to do it, the printers
are very good – and that freedom is 80
all part of the freedom of how I work
and how the paper trusts the
photographers.

I have a school qualification in
photography and that's my only 85
formal qualification and in fact there
aren't any in particular. However,
there are courses in press
photography at Linford College in
Manchester. For the addresses of 90
local and regional papers, you can
look in the Press Directory or the
Press Guide and you can get help
and advice from the Bureau of
Freelance Photographers. 95

You have to be motivated, you
have to want to do it because nobody
else is going to push you to be a
photographer. You just have to push
yourself or you'll never get 100
anywhere. And you need a technical
knowledge of photography and a
good visual sense. And you need
luck – you can go home and not
know what's going to make the 105
paper, what's going to be published.

Now listen to the piece again.

TEST 2 PART 1

You will hear an extract from a radio programme about the early days of popular songwriting in the USA. For questions 1-10, write T next to those statements which are true and F next to those statements which are false.

You will hear the piece twice.

ANNOUNCER: And now we visit the first home of American popular music, Tin Pan Alley on New York's Broadway. Three veteran songwriters who started their careers there in the 1920s and 30s take us with them – Mitchell Parish, Ann Rennell and Gerald Marks.

MITCHELL: The music business was always there but the name Tin Pan Alley wasn't heard of until sometime in the late 1800s when a reporter by the name of Rosenthal was asked by his paper to go to the music industry district and it was summer and as he was walking along the street the windows were open and the pianos were going, all of them, maybe 25 or 30 pianos going at one time, and when he went into a publishers' office he said 'My, walking along this street is like walking along where they're playing a bunch of tin pans' and Tin Pan Alley got its name from that and it stuck, nobody has come up with a better description of it.

I have the highest respect for Tin Pan Alley writers and songs because many great writers started as Tin Pan Alley writers. Well, you know, they didn't go and say 'Well, I'm going to be a Tin Pan Alley writer' but they wound up there.

ANN: It goes up to 49th and Broadway where there's a building called the Brill Building and this was, in my day, when I first came around in the late 1920s, this was the music business, in the Brill Building. You could go through the Brill Building with a song, demonstrating it for publishers and you would probably demonstrate it for oh, anywhere from fifteen to twenty publishers right in that one building, you didn't have to move off the spot.

They never told you what they were looking for because they didn't know, they were just hopeful it would arrive, whatever it was that appealed to their sense of marketing a commodity, so there was no criterion for writing a hit song that you knew would be a hit ahead of time. There was no way, because there were many wonderful songs, you know, published that never made hits and yet they were wonderful songs, so they were not properly exploited. That was the difference too, so if you went, um, to one publisher, got a hearing and he said no, you still went on to the next one and tried with him because there was no model to follow, except what was popular at the time and if you followed that too closely, then that wasn't good either, you see, because it wouldn't be individual enough to stand out from other songs. And it didn't depend on what you thought was a marketable song, it only depended on the publisher. So there you were, you went from one to the other, seeking the mind that thought as you did, who would hear your song and agree that it was marketable.

GERALD: I remember having late coffee in Lindy's, which was the big restaurant at that time for the entertainment industry in New York, and there were always about six or eight songwriters there every night in a corner of the restaurant – it was sort of reserved for songwriters and there were about six or eight. And if you're talking about a community, that was the community. There was no big social life, it was mostly writing – if you made a date with someone it was mostly to write and nothing else and that was the entire life of the songwriter, he wrote, wrote, wrote. It was his living, he paid his rent with that, he tried to keep his family going with that, pay his expenses and er, sure there were friendships but the talk was always Tin Pan Alley, the talk was always your latest song, the talk was always a new idea or 'listen to this tune, I'm gonna hum it for you on the street and see if you like it' – it was always talk like that.

Well, it started to decline, if you call it declining, with the advent of television and radio. You see, then the publishers didn't have to be in one location and a lot of them moved to California, that's where the action was, in California and Tin Pan Alley moved where the action was, because in California they were producing musical movies and New York was secondary after that.

Now listen to the piece again.

TEST 2 PART 2

You will hear a report on fires in a National Park in the USA. For questions 11-15, choose the most appropriate answer, A, B, C or D and write your choice in the box provided below each question.

You will hear the piece twice.

PRESENTER: The firefighters of Yellowstone Park in the USA were a strange breed of firefighter. They responded instantly to any fire but only fought fires caused by people. If it was a lightning fire, the chances were that they would just fly out and watch it burn. The policy was arrived at in the 1970s when they found that lightning fires burnt themselves out in a fairly small area of land. The bulk of the park remained untouched, enjoyed by thousands of visitors.

The policy made sense until 1988, when the American public was enraged when a series of unfought fires engulfed Yellowstone. The 'natural fire management policy' was suspended and the fires were fought. But by then nearly half the park had burned away. Today the results of the fires are still all too clear.

So was the policy of letting fires burn wrong? Ironically, the year when the policy ended also marked the end of a study of the history of fires in the park. This showed that huge fires had burned away large parts of the park regularly every few hundred years. Bill Romme is one of the researchers.

BILL: By counting the rings in the trees, we found that there was a huge area across the park where the forests all began to grow in the same year – 1704 – and that indicates to us that there was a massive forest fire then that destroyed all those trees' predecessors.

PRESENTER: That fire burnt down 40% of the park. Another fire was traced to the 1870s, when some trees survived but still bear the scars. Ash dredged from lakes testified to further periodic fires, dating back over a thousand years.

The policy of allowing lightning fires to burn sprang from a general philosophy of letting nature deal with its own problems. Tracing so many massive fires suggested that they weren't a problem but were actually an essential part of shaping the nature of the park. The fires a few years ago gave an opportunity to test out that theory. Bill Romme is now carefully analysing which plant species are re-establishing themselves in different areas of the park.

BILL: On one site, we found that the lodge pole pine, the predominant tree in the park, is having a tough time fighting back. You'll only find one or two of them around there, while in other parts of the park it's thick with saplings. We've traced that to a difference in the pine cones on the trees before the fire. In other parts they were closed up tight and able to withstand fire, while on that particular site they were open and burned easily. Why's that? Well, the other difference is that the sites where they are growing back well burned in the fire in the 1870s, while the last fire on that particular site was a hundred and fifty years earlier. It's almost as if more recent memories prepared some trees for the latest fires.

Every site under study that burned in the fires a few years ago is growing back in a slightly different way. We've found some aspen tree seedlings which are a bit of a surprise because there weren't any aspens in that area before the last fires. We still don't know exactly how they got there but they wouldn't have got there if it hadn't been for the large size of those fires.

PRESENTER: And that seems to be the important thing. Fire creates opportunities and differences. In one place the pines grow straight back, in another something different grows. The nature of Yellowstone has always been diverse and it now appears that fire is a cornerstone of that diversity. All that destruction is actually preserving nature. The natural fire policy seems to have been right.

Now listen to the piece again.

TEST 2 PART 3

You will hear an extract from a TV programme about Ocho Rios. For questions 16-23, complete the notes.

You will hear the piece twice.

Ocho Rios is very popular because everybody has a dream and when you go on vacation what you try to do is to live that dream that you can't live every day. It is situated on the north coast of Jamaica, is protected by coral reefs and has calm seas which are good for fishing and for swimming. Twenty-five years ago, when the government decided to develop it into a tourist resort, it was just a quiet fishing village, with one main street, only one policeman and no more than three or four electric light bulbs in the street. So what effects have the changes had on the place and the people?
The builders constructed an artificial bay to enclose part of the sea. The population at the time was just about 650 people, today it is nearly 13,000. Sandwiched between the new hotels lies the one part of Ocho Rios that has changed very little, Fisherman's Beach. Most of the fishermen there have given up fishing and now take tourists out to sea. For the fishermen who still work, the catches are smaller and they have to go further out to get them. Most of the fish caught go to the hotels and restaurants.
Just down the coast from Ocho Rios is Jamaica's famous attraction, Downs River Falls. It's one of the only waterfalls in the entire world that you can actually climb. Everything has been done there for the tourist. Even the rocks have been made secure so they're safe to climb. A major development in Ocho Rios was the building of a new pier. The cruise ships that start from the US and tour the Caribbean islands can now call here too. The passengers have eight hours on shore. In the centre of the town lies the craft market. Its 120 stall holders belong to the Craft Association but they all compete when it comes to selling to visitors.
There has been tourism in Ocho Rios for a long time but the hotels were small and hidden away along the coast. With the government decision to develop the town, more and more hotels have been built and they now employ more than 8,000 people. But what have the local people lost in developing their town for tourists?
Ocho Rios has lost a lot of its local life, and by local life what I mean is things for the people who live there to do. Most things are geared for the tourists to do – there's a lot for the tourists to do – but very little for the people to do. The cinema which was here before and which locals used to go to, has been torn down and a new shopping centre built. A lot of places where Jamaicans used to hang out have been torn down and in their place have been put famous attractions or places for tourists.

Now listen to the piece again.

TEST 2 PART 4

You will hear an interview with someone who started a business with her husband. For questions 24-33, write YES next to the feelings which she mentions they have or had, and NO next to the feelings which she does not mention.

You will hear the piece twice.

PRESENTER: I have with me Sarah Williams. Let me introduce her and say what we're going to talk about. She and her husband, some ten years ago, gave up their careers with established business organizations and set about creating their own business. Hence the title of the book she's written, called 'Breakout – Life Beyond The Corporation'. And she says they've been elated by their successes, often driven to tears by near failure, but never have they wanted to return to work in someone else's large company. Sarah, welcome.
SARAH: Nice to be here.
PRESENTER: Not a single glance back?
SARAH: Not a glance backwards. Occasionally a glance sideways, thinking I wish I was over there, but never backwards. No, I don't think either of us has ever wanted to go back to working for employers. I think, gradually, as you do your own thing, you actually become more and more arrogant and I'm not sure we're employable any more.
PRESENTER: So you've no wish to go back and rest your head on the bosom of somebody else's company?
SARAH: No, not at all ... in fact, in the book I did talk to a fair number of entrepreneurs, about 35, 36, something like that, a lot of people, and they didn't all succeed, a few of them did fail and that's obviously sad, but of the ones that have failed some have actually gone off and started new ventures, so I think it's like a drug actually, I think once you're on it, I'm not sure you can ever get off it.
PRESENTER: Now why did you decide to break out, because you had comfortable jobs, secure jobs, did you not?
SARAH: Yes. It's very much a desire just to do your own thing and perhaps not necessarily fitting in and not particularly liking to be told what to do and always feeling, well maybe you could do it slightly better yourself, and wanting, just really, independence. And people have very different motives for wanting to break out. For some people it's money, which of course is attractive and I'm not saying no to the money, um.. but independence was the key thing.
PRESENTER: Now as you presumably sat down ten years ago and discussed it – I don't know quite how the circumstances arose – what, did you ... you sat down with your husband and you said 'what are we going to do?' – what considerations were there, what were the arguments you had about whether or not to?
SARAH: It really hinged on whether or

not we were going to be happy carrying on doing what we were doing, working for large companies, and if we weren't going to be happy doing that, we should try the other, which was start up a business ourselves. So it was really a question of happiness and being interested and enjoying what we were doing, and once we'd got that far and decided we were just going to do our own thing, then it came down to real nitty gritty practicalities like, you know, how would we find the money, would we be able to survive while we were doing it, would we be able to raise the money, and obviously really really important, what were we going to do, what was the business we were going to start?
PRESENTER: And how did that resolve itself, the last question?
SARAH: The last question resolved itself, I mean, we were looking for a particular sort of business, looking for a business that we had some sort of experience in because that's very important, I think. If I'm giving advice to other people, it's to try and do something you know about.
PRESENTER: Mmm, I was going to ask you that. The jobs that you were in gave you some preparation for what you were going to do by yourselves, so you weren't completely branching into totally alien territory.
SARAH: No, no, my husband had been working in the computer industry, which is in fact where the business is that we started, so he was very knowledgeable about distribution structures, about the way the business worked ... um ... so there was a lot of experience already there.
PRESENTER: So you made your decision, bearing all these things in mind and you decided to go ahead. Was there a sense of danger, a sense of fear, a sense of the unknown?
SARAH: Oh yes, and well, it wouldn't have been any fun if there hadn't been, would it?
PRESENTER: So clearly you like a challenge.
SARAH: We don't like being bored, that's quite true. If life is boring and going along in a very humdrum fashion, I think the temptation is for us to say, 'well let's throw all the cards up in the air again and see what happens when they fall down'. So perhaps we have a low boredom threshold, I'm not quite sure.
PRESENTER: OK, well we have to take an ad break just at the moment. If you want to join in this discussion and talk to Sarah, the number is 6523476. We'll be back in a moment.

Now listen to the piece again.

TEST 3 PART 1

You will hear a series of advertisements on a radio station. For questions 1–8, write in the box the first letter of the company whose advertisement matches each statement

You will hear the piece twice.

Are you fed up and frustrated with motorway traffic? Jams cost you time and money. Avoid motorway congestion using Trafficmaster. Real time information is beamed from motorway sensors into your own portable display unit in your own car. So why not phone now on 0878–54536 to find out more and apply for a ten-day free trial? You'll receive a Trafficmaster brochure and a free map showing alternative routes around motorway jams. Phone us now!

My Eurokitchen, isn't it divine – so stylish, so smooth, yet so robust. My Eurokitchen came with free plan and design, ten-year guarantee and a guarantee they could beat anyone else's price for the same quality. I love my Eurokitchen so much that I had them come back and fit the bedroom. And from the 25th to the 28th, top chefs will be cooking in the Eurokitchen at the Food Exhibition. See masterchefs and mastercraftsmen brought together in the Eurokitchen.

A very special thank you to all those who have actively criticized the photocopier industry for playing an important part in helping create the Southern difference. We listened, we responded and we're still setting the standards for the copier industry. Here's what makes the Southern difference: a fourteen-day cooling off period, guaranteed quality and reliability, agreements from 90 days to 108 months and our own finance – you don't deal with a bank or leasing company. Customer choice and customer care is built into everything we do. That is the Southern difference. Southern Business Group, the much copied copier company.

At the Mobile Phone Warehouse we believe that, to make the informed decision about buying a mobile phone, you need all the facts. Which is why we place so much emphasis on the expert advice offered by our sales consultants. We believe in giving you impartial advice on all aspects of buying a mobile phone so that you end up with the package that suits your individual needs. We stock a wide range of mobile phones and offer a choice of networks and tariffs so that you can be sure of an impartial view. We've now produced a catalogue which puts this philosophy down on paper. For a free copy, call us on 657689.

Hello there! You know all those so-called something for nothing offers of flights, holidays and cruises? Well you won't get any from the Curtain Mill. We've decided you'd rather have incredibly low prices. There's a stock of over a thousand rolls of material to choose from, the very best quality designer fabrics and no gimmicks! So for a good old-fashioned value-for-money offer on curtaining, visit your nearest Curtain Mill, or call 765435.

Now listen to the piece again.

TEST 3 PART 2

You will hear an extract from a programme about coffee drinking in Britain. For questions 9–18, write YES next to those views which are expressed in the discussion, and NO next to those views which are not expressed.

You will hear the piece twice.

PRESENTER: Right, in this part of the show I'm going to be talking about coffee, and I have with me George Docker, from the Real Coffee Association. George, what's the proportion of real coffee drunk to instant coffee in this country?

GEORGE: Um, the size of the market, which is probably one of the best ways of measuring it is six hundred million pounds, and a hundred million of that is real coffee and five hundred is instant coffee, so it's quite surprising.

PRESENTER: About 20%. It's a higher proportion than I imagined, I imagined most people to be far too lazy to percolate most of the time.

GEORGE: Well, that's a bit of a myth I think, I mean, there is a belief that real coffee's much more difficult to make and also that it's more expensive but certainly with the advent of this thing which you see here, the cafetière – the plunger pot – it's really very simple to make indeed.

PRESENTER: The coffee companies spend a lot of money trying to persuade us you can get real coffee from an instant coffee jar – we see people not being able to tell the difference …

GEORGE: No, of course you can tell the difference, it's extremely obvious.

PRESENTER: So does this cafetière effectively allow you to make proper coffee instantly?

GEORGE: It does – well, you've got to leave it a couple of minutes or longer maybe, to infuse, but that's no worse than making tea, it's no more of a chore than making tea I find.

PRESENTER: You've mentioned tea. We always talk about the national drink being 'a nice cup of tea'. What's the balance between tea and coffee drinking in this country?

GEORGE: That's quite interesting. Roughly 59% of our population drink coffee each day and when they drink it, they drink 3.6 cups, would you believe, and 81% of people drink 2 cups a day and interestingly 15% of the roast and ground coffee drunk in the UK is drunk on a Wednesday.

PRESENTER: Is it supposed to be good for you now, coffee, because periodically we have all these horror stories about how it's desperately bad for you and then it goes into a cycle and then it's apparently very good for you.

GEORGE: Well, put it this way, if you like drinking roast and ground coffee, there's nothing to indicate that it's going to damage your health. Um, the British Heart Foundation, I think would agree with that and there are various societies concerned with health in America who confirm it.

PRESENTER: But there have been these sort of scares and these stories that people drink too much coffee, people who sit in their office all day like I do, consuming cup after cup …

GEORGE: Yes, I have to say I think those are frequently taken out of context. For instance, if you boil beans, you certainly do get a few harmful extracts coming out of coffee, but most people don't boil beans.

PRESENTER: How much do you drink, George?

GEORGE: I drink increasing amounts as I get older, I think. I drink probably five cups a day.

PRESENTER: Should it be drunk black to appreciate it properly?

GEORGE: I think it's as you like. The true experts would probably drink it black, I drink it black.

PRESENTER: Can instant coffees come anywhere near touching real coffee?

GEORGE: I don't think they can, everything about them's different, they always have a sort of tell-tale flatness and the texture's not the same.

PRESENTER: Tell people exactly how to use the cafetière, how should you do it, what temperature should the water be, and things like that.

GEORGE: I think there are a number of very basic and simple rules that start for instance with always use fresh water, make sure that the cafetière is clean, very importantly make sure that you've got the right ground for a cafetière – it's slightly coarser than you would normally have for a filter machine.

PRESENTER: And you can buy it ready ground – you don't have to grind it yourself?

GEORGE: Oh no, no, in fact personally I think you're much safer to buy it ready ground because then all the care that goes into making it is preserved to give you a really good cup of coffee. We in the Real Coffee Association have started a system of symbols which go on packs to indicate very clearly which is the right grind for particular types of brewing and it's very important to get that right. Then pour the boiling water on it – sorry, just off boiling water. One other important thing is to put the right amount of coffee into the cafetière and that normally would be one tablespoon per normal cup.

PRESENTER: That's quite a large amount for one cup of coffee, whereas with instant coffee you just put a teaspoon in, don't you? Now, what's the shelf life of real coffee?

GEORGE: Well, if you don't open the pack you'll find that it'll keep for a very long time, but once you've opened it you really should keep it in the fridge, or in fact people say the freezer sometimes, and try to get through it, it's best if used within a week. Yes, the biggest enemy of ground coffee is oxygen – therefore one wants to shut it away in an air-tight tin if you can and keep it in the freezer. 145

PRESENTER: And finally, you can get this stuff from a supermarket as well as a specialist shop? 150

GEORGE: Um yes, I think the branded coffees are all achieving very high standards these days – high standards of blends, of using the right beans, of processing and so on, whereas if you're buying beans you really do need to know what you're doing to get the bean that you expect and know that it's been treated properly and so on. 155 160

PRESENTER: George Docker from the Real Coffee Association, thank you for being my guest this morning.

GEORGE: My pleasure. 165

PRESENTER: We've got a lot still to come on the programme but for the time being we must take a break ...

Now listen to the piece again.

TEST 3 PART 3

You will hear a report about a discovery in the Alps. For questions 19-30, complete the sentences below.

You will hear the piece twice.

On the last day of their climbing holiday in the Alps, Helmut and Erika Simon took an unmarked path across a glacier on the Austrian–Italian border. With the last shot in his camera, Helmut photographed what was to become an archaeological sensation. At the time, no one realized its significance. Herr Simon reported the finding of a dead body to the police, who tried to free it from the ice with a pneumatic drill. They failed, but were surprised to find an ancient axe near it. This led to rumours that the corpse might be something unusual. Four days later an Austrian team arrived on the mountain to take the body to Innsbruck. Believing the corpse to have been freed from the ice, they had brought no special equipment. Fortunately, a passing mountaineer lent a couple of ski poles. As they released the corpse from the glacier, it dawned on them that the body was different from others they had recovered from the mountains. 5 10 15 20 25

The strange thing about the body was that it had been completely mummified, which means that it had been dried and then completely covered with snow and ice. Normally when a body is frozen, the flesh turns to a white, waxy substance called adipocere but this body had been mummified instead. Soon there was to be another hint that there was something unusual about it, because shortly afterwards a knife made of wood and stone was found nearby. The team investigating got the idea that this body must be very very old. 30 35

It was taken by helicopter from the mountain to the Institute of Forensic Medicine at Innsbruck University, where an autopsy was carried out. In the autopsy room it was laid out together with some of the extraordinary 40 45

implements that had been found with it. There was not just the knife and the axe, which had a metal blade, but also a marble bead and a small leather pouch. Here was a man from the distant past. But how distant? 50

Archaeologists quickly decided that the find dated from the Central European Bronze Age. They had no doubt about this dating, which they gave as approximately 2000 BC. So the body found by chance 10,000 feet up in the Alps was that of a man who'd lived 4,000 years ago. The media alerted scientists around the world to the find. Never before had scientists seen a body of this age in this condition. Most other bodies are much less well-preserved – they are either very fragile or their internal organs have not survived. The oldest frozen bodies, found in the Siberian permafrost, are half the age of the Iceman, while the best preserved, a group of Greenland Eskimos, are only 500 years old. This unique find, the body of a prehistoric European, holds thousands of clues to his life and death. His possessions and clothing hold thousands more. 55 60 65 70

Two weeks after the find, archaeologists carried out a small excavation of the site. Although a foot of snow had fallen in the meantime, they found more artefacts, including a small cape. In it were hairs from the Iceman's head – black, about 9 inches long and clearly cut. Scientists concluded that the man may have died of hypothermia. Perhaps the weather had changed unexpectedly, with poor visibility, strong wind and snow and he had died. Then the wind may have dried his body and miraculously it had not been attacked by animals – the flies, birds, bears and foxes that would have been up there. The only explanation they could think of for this was that a light covering of snow had shielded the body from the view of these predators. 75 80 85 90

Subsequent research led to the dating of the body being amended. Archaeologists concluded that it was indeed older than they had previously thought. They decided that he had lain there for over 5,000 years and was from the Stone Age. 95 100

Now listen to the piece again.

TEST 3 PART 4

You will hear an extract from a radio programme about soap operas. For questions 31-35, choose the most appropriate answer, A, B, C or D, and write your choice in the box provided below each question.

You will hear the piece twice

PRESENTER: I have with me Hilary Kingsley, a TV columnist and the author of 'Soap Box – The Paperback Guide to Soap Opera' and we're going to discuss that phenomenon of television. Hilary, how would you define a soap? 5

HILARY: I think it's a continuing story about a group of characters, either a related family or a group of people who work together and it's a story 10

that you know is not going to end, it's as if those characters are sort of living on some special fictional island somewhere so that even when you don't listen to them or watch them or when the soap has ended, you know that life there is going on somehow. So it's a sort of never-ending middle, you know, no beginning and no end. 15 20

PRESENTER: How do you think the soap genre has developed since the early days?

HILARY: Well, I don't think that it has changed very much, I mean I don't think it's changed since the 30s and 40s when it started on, er American radio – I mean, I think everyone knows now that it came into being when radio went national in the US and they needed some running stories to attract housewives, keep them glued to their radios and sell products to them, and the products they were selling first of all were soap powders. They were always stories about families, about relationships, about the things that the bigger dramas were not about – those were, and still are really, about men escaping from difficult situations, whereas soap operas are basically about women coping with everyday situations – women and men, of course. But one reason I think why I've always liked soap operas is that the women are the most important characters, they are the moral centre of any story. 25 30 35 40 45

PRESENTER: But few of us are as brazen as Hilary. Ask around, nobody will admit to watching soap opera, we'd all apparently rather be reading a good book or else in the stalls at the theatre. Funny how the audience figures never quite match up. So why do we feel guilty about admitting that we watch soap? Certainly the critics don't help. They imply that by watching soaps, somehow we're the victims of an aesthetic con trick, that we don't know that what we're watching is actually fiction. We're all presented as these passive consumers just because there are people, admittedly sad people, out there who apply for jobs at the shop in the programme or send wreaths for the funeral if a character dies. Soaps have always been patronized, and of course it doesn't help that their largest audience is young women with families, always a good target for condescension, aren't they, Hilary? 50 55 60 65 70 75

HILARY: It's the same thing with women's magazines really, and all women's programmes. I mean somehow, if something's about sport or mountain climbing this is fine, going to a football match is fine, but staying home to watch a soap is somehow a sign of mental deficiency. This is just a fact, I think, of our sexist world. Also it's quite interesting that although I'm sure it's true that there's a fair proportion of men who watch soap opera – the men in my family watch soap opera – I think it's true that there's a larger proportion of the viewing population watching soap opera regularly who are female, girls 80 85 90 and women, girls and their mums. I've noticed that my son's interest in soap operas sort of fluctuates, whereas my daughter is loyal to them.

PRESENTER: So why do we watch? Why do we care what happens to the characters? Well, it's partly down to the conventions of serial drama, and the narcotic effect must have something to do with habit. It's reassuring that the setbacks come round like the seasons. It's an ongoing saga which becomes part of your life and which you know is not going to end and that open-endedness actually helps the naturalism. In an ordinary play the formal structure requires a beginning, a middle and an end. Soaps are also set in a closed community, increasingly unlike the world we live in today. Soaps provide lonely people with friends and a family, they provide gregarious types with an escape from friends and family. They usually show us that there's somebody out there worse off than ourselves and by showing us problems similar to our own, soaps help us solve those problems. Whatever the reason, watch them we do.

Now listen to the piece again.

TEST 4 PART 1

You will hear an extract from a radio programme about Boots the chemist, a well known chain of shops in Britain. For questions 1 10, answer each of the questions below.

You will hear the piece twice.

As a child, Jesse Boot, who was born in 1850, had walked with his father, picking herbs, for Boots the Chemist started off selling herbal pills and teas. But Jesse's success with Boots came when he dropped this – it was for the few, the aristocrats, and Jesse saw more common sense in buying in bulk anything popular and selling it cheaper. When he took charge of what had been his parents' botanical remedy shop in Nottingham, he put the herbs to one side to fill the window spectacularly with tins of salmon. He bought a boatload, special offer, cut the price, advertised, and for the many whose terraced houses were too poor to possess a tin opener, Boots had a man in the shop window who'd open the tin for you. He learnt to sell whatever the public wanted, including all sorts of medicines. His skilled pharmacists would try and make their own and he would sell them a little cheaper than everyone else's. And that's how Boots grew.

And, oh, how cunning he was! Just as you don't shop for prescriptions, you have to go, and on the way may pick up something else, the same principle applied to the little libraries Boots branches had at the back. For the staff it meant changing skills. The rising pharmacists had soon moved on from making up pills to being managers. That meant having to wind up the gramophone.

Boots sold records, just as they are now the second largest purveyor in the country of sandwiches. Then they had the Book-Lovers Library, which the branch manager had to supervise to see that the standards set were conformed to. Their books were safe, they wouldn't upset anyone. They had an on-demand service, they could get you any book you wanted up to a value limit. The company had a very strict policy. Jesse Boot and his successor, his son John, had a strict moral code and there were some books they wouldn't get you if they considered them indecent. Occasionally there was a borderline area where the on-demand customer could get a special order and he or she was under an obligation to read it himself or herself and return it forthwith, not to circulate it. Whereas the ordinary library books had a green shield on them, these books had a red label. The libraries closed some years ago, went the way of the herbal pills, but in the 1940s Boots were purchasing more than one and a quarter million books a year.

The work wore Jesse out. It was his sister in 1885 who suggested he take a holiday in the Channel Islands. There he fell in love with Florence, a stationer's daughter. He took her back to Nottingham to be his wife and though women didn't have a vote then, she took a full part in the business. She took over the number two side of the business. The number one was the purely chemist business and the number two was the gift side. It was a wonderful partnership, they complemented each other. And so they became multi-millionaires, with over 500 branches by 1914 and over ten thousand employees. But Jesse held the shares that mattered and as he saw his son John develop, he disinherited him overnight. Everyone woke up and Jesse had sold the company. Incredible. Very ill, but still in control, Jesse had sold out, the whole lot to a US company. Everyone was incensed, the staff, the whole nation. Jesse thought his son was much too frivolous and that's why he sold the business. But his son John stayed on and after thirteen years he used his friends to buy Boots back into British hands with him as chairman. John Boot, oddly, proved himself a model employer – enlightened, loved and trusted – and by 1933 Boots had expanded to over a thousand branches.

If you go to Nottingham now, Boots are there, manufacturing for the shops, bigger than ever. But the Boots family connection has gone, all gone.

Now listen to the piece again.

TEST 4 PART 2

You will hear an extract from a radio programme about memory. For questions 11-20, write YES next to those views which are expressed in the discussion, and NO next to those views which are not expressed.

You will hear the piece twice.

PRESENTER: A recent study has concluded that women have better memories than men. With me in the studio to discuss memory is Penny Marshall, who's the Deputy Director of a research centre and Martin Conway, who's a professor of psychology. Penny, from your experience, do you agree that women do have better memories than men?

PENNY: Um, I don't know whether you'd call it a better memory or a different one. I think the thing is that what you remember depends on the kinds of information you take in at the time, and I think the selectivity of what you remember is different for men and women. Perhaps because, as reports show, women take responsibility for remembering things like birthdays – it's become a stereotype, I mean men can almost relax and not have to worry about it. But I also think that we found when we asked questions in our own research – and we interviewed husbands and wives separately but at the same time so there was no conferring – we found that the kinds of things, I mean for example arguments, a woman might not consider some issue as being one in which they had an argument, whereas the husband might. It's perceptions – I mean different kinds of things mean different things to different people and therefore what's remembered will also be different.

PRESENTER: Is that something you'd agree with, Martin? 40

MARTIN: Yes, I think I would. I think the important thing with memory is not that memory differs between men and women or between any other two groups you can think of but that 45 people make different interpretations of events. They interpret events according to what's personally significant to them and that's what they tend to remember. 50

PRESENTER: And does emotion come into it? That with women, perhaps their better memory is because they perhaps feel the emotions of an event or a conversation better than a man 55 does?

MARTIN: Well, I'm dubious about that, it seems to be based on a stereotypical belief in women being more emotional beings than men, which I 60 don't subscribe to. There is evidence that if people do have a strong emotional experience, then whether they're a man or a woman they'll remember the event in detail. An 65 extreme clinical case of that is in cases of trauma, perhaps in train crashes, people will have detailed memories of the few moments, just as the train crashed. So emotion does 70 influence memory but it doesn't seem to influence it by interacting with gender.

PRESENTER: How important is it for us, Penny, to have a good memory? 75 Does it matter that much whether you're good or bad at remembering things?

PENNY: I think it's fairly important if you want to be able to operate in the 80 world as it is today. I would think in marriage having too good a memory could actually sometimes be problematic. I think if you always operate on the past, which is what a 85 lot of couples get locked into, they're not talking about what's happening now, they're talking about what happened two years ago and why something didn't happen. Then you 90 start to see a slide into, you know, separate camps really.

PRESENTER: The thing is that it's a futile thing to do, isn't it, argue about the past? I mean, you can't alter it but it's 95 amazing how many arguments are couples disagreeing as to who is remembering more correctly than the other one.

PENNY: Yes, I think that's probably 100 futile, although it's interesting and it can be funny. I think more important is to understand just how differently you do see things, I think.

PRESENTER: That's an interesting point, 105 Martin ...

MARTIN: Yes, if I could return to that point you were making that the past can't be changed, I think there is an important point here and that is that 110 people can reach a new interpretation of shared memories, they can find a new memory for what events meant that they experienced.

PRESENTER: And for somebody who'd 115 like to improve their memory, there's always those small ads in the newspapers about buy this book or

whatever and you hear about ways of forming exaggerated pictures in 120 your mind to remember certain things and these sort of techniques. Do you go along with any of that?

MARTIN: Well they do work but what they work for is, they work for 125 isolated lists of items, perhaps the items that make up a shopping list or the names of a group of people you've just met, but they wouldn't be much use, indeed they aren't much 130 use for remembering the meaningful events of one's life. Indeed, it would be very strange I think, actually trying to as it were keep a photographic record of everyday 135 events. So these techniques don't work in that area and it would be unusual if somebody tried to use them in that way, I think.

PRESENTER: And any advice to end on, 140 Penny, for couples?

PENNY: I think to value the differences and to find they're really a good source of conversation, to find out how you can have been in the same 145 situation, on the same holiday, and how differently you experienced it – it's quite good fun.

PRESENTER: All right, thank you for joining me. 150

Now listen to the piece again.

TEST 4 PART 3

You will hear an extract from a programme about publicity for new films. For questions 21-25, choose the most appropriate answer A,B,C, or D and write your choice in the box provided below each question.

You will hear the piece twice.

PRESENTER: What makes us go to the cinema? People go to films for all sorts of reasons but there's one thing that holds all of those reasons together and that's the film's 5 publicity. It's the work of the Publicity Department of the major film companies, and the small ones as well, to make audiences aware that a film is about to arrive in the 10 cinemas. They're only going to make money if people turn up at the box office and pay for their tickets. It's no use having a brilliant film if nobody knows about it and therefore doesn't 15 go to the cinema to see it. So how does a film get publicized? I talked to Jon Anderson, Director of Advertising and Publicity at Columbia Tristar. 20

JON: It's not until we've actually seen the film that we can get stuck into the marketing and work out who the target audience may be and how we think we're going to sell a film. 25

PRESENTER: So how do you work out who the target audience is going to be?

JON: If you've got a very heavy, hard action movie, then you know it's 30 going to appeal to a much greater percentage of the population. Um, kids movies, again you know who they're going to appeal to – and a certain amount of the mums and 35

dads as well. Sometimes it's really difficult, I mean with one film, for instance, we knew it was going to have a wide audience appeal but we weren't quite ready for how many 40 kids enjoyed it.

PRESENTER: How much money gets spent on publicizing a film?

JON: There's sort of a move on now to be a bit more cautious with spending 45 on the advertising and publicity side, so we're cutting the budget down and figuring, well, you know, a lot of people will find out about the film through the various magazines and 50 newspapers and TV, so why spend so much on the advertising side?

PRESENTER: So, although the film company has to pay for advertising, you can get a lot of free publicity 55 from the rest of the media?

JON: The publicity we get for free is most of it ... I mean, when I say 'free', we do spend quite a lot of money on the material that we send out to be 60 placed for free.

PRESENTER: The film company sends out information to journalists and invites them to see the films for free before anyone else. That results in reviews 65 and articles, perhaps in hundreds of magazines, newspapers and TV and radio programmes. Even if they don't review the film, radio stations will mention it if the film company gives 70 them something to give away on the programmes. What do radio stations get from film companies? Malcolm Bird, radio producer.

MALCOLM: Heaps and heaps and heaps 75 of stuff. When somebody's releasing a film we get inundated with offers – the most usual things to have would be T-shirts, sweatshirts, jogging bottoms, jackets, baseball hats – you 80 can be sent in excess of twenty items per film.

PRESENTER: So what do the film companies get out of this? Jon Anderson again. 85

JON: When radio stations offer their listeners the opportunity to see a film by ringing the station and answering a simple question, we're getting the coverage for the movie and they're 90 getting the appearance of being generous to their listeners.

PRESENTER: Of course another way of publicizing a film is through interviews with the stars. How does 95 the film company go about this?

JON: It's not as simple as just saying yes to everyone. You have to really make sure that you know who you want to interview them, who's going to 100 present the person in the best light, give the most suitable interview. You've got to be very careful because a lot of the newspapers are after stories to expose the private life of 105 the person, which may have nothing to do with what you're trying to promote.

PRESENTER: Apart from interviews, film companies invite journalists to press 110 conferences and screenings and offer newspapers prizes for competitions. I spoke to Mandy Dougan of the Glasgow Times. Did journalists ever feel they were being bribed? 115

MANDY: I know what you mean, um... I

think a lot of that comes down to the relationship that you have with the film publicists. There are some, whose um, motives you would [120] suspect if they suddenly turned around and started offering you lavish gifts.

PRESENTER: Jon Anderson.

JON: Funnily enough, a lot of people are [125] suspicious when they're invited to a free screening of a film. They feel there's a catch and they're going to have to pay in some way. Well, that's not true, I mean, we put on [130] screenings basically to get coverage – we don't force people to cover the film. If they don't like it, they don't have to cover it.

PRESENTER: So, is there such a thing as [135] bad publicity?

JON: Um, it's difficult to say. I mean the reviews of some films can be generally bad, they can pick up quite heavily on the negative aspects of it [140] and yet it doesn't make any difference to the box office. You know, potentially there might be groups of people out there who would have gone if all the reviews [145] had been good. But the more coverage you get, the more aware people are of the film and I think as a general rule they'll make up their own minds about whether they want [150] to see it or not.

Now listen to the piece again.

TEST 4 PART 4

You will hear an interview about things that are named after real people. For questions 26-35, write the first letter of the correct person's name or names in the space or spaces next to each question.

You will hear the piece twice.

PRESENTER: I have with me Eric Sidcup who has written a book about eponyms, all actual people who gave their names to the English language. Eric, what made you begin this [5] search?

ERIC: Well it all started years and years ago when I just happened to stumble on the name of Captain Fred Doldrum, who gave his name to [10] those spells of windless calm that are the, or used to be the blight of sailors in the age when one relied on wind. And I just happened to look in the dictionary and sure enough, the [15] word doldrums is there but there was no mention of the unfortunate captain. And then, I don't know whether it was coincidence or fate but I began to notice other names like [20] this and I started this little hobby of checking whether the dictionary knew about them and time and time again I found that the dictionary didn't know about them, so I made a [25] kind of oath to myself that I would find out as much as possible about those people and do them justice, you might say, delayed justice. And that's what this book does, I think. [30]

PRESENTER: Now we don't know much about Gusset, for example.

ERIC: No, Gusset was actually a London woman in the late eighteenth century, 1779 she was born, and she [35] was, as you might suspect, a seamstress and she belongs to the history of underclothing, I suppose, because what people perhaps don't realize was that until her time [40] underpants consisted of two separate legs which were attached to the waist by tapes. She came up with the marvellously simple idea of joining the legs together with the simple [45] insertion of some fabric, eventually called after her, a gusset.

PRESENTER: Coffin is another one we know nothing about.

ERIC: Yes, you see we take these things [50] for granted. It was only in the sixteenth century that people began to have themselves buried in wooden boxes, which were originally built by this carpenter whose name was [55] Coffin. He originally worked for monks but they preferred to be buried in stone boxes – they thought that was theologically more correct – so he had to move out of the [60] monastery and he began selling his boxes to tradesmen in the City of London. He made a considerable fortune out of this and eventually was Mayor of London. [65]

PRESENTER: Everyone knows that the Earl of Sandwich invented the sandwich but very few people know about ketchup.

ERIC: Yes, there you are. Ketchup was [70] invented, if that's the right word, was made by this couple called Noah and Martha Ketchup, who lived in the US. He was an American Indian and he tried various things in the course [75] of his life and had various business failures until almost as a last resort he started selling this very good mushroom and tomato sauce, or relish, that his wife had been making [80] for years. He put it into commercial production and it became immensely successful, although actually he didn't really make any money out of it.

PRESENTER: Of course some of the [85] figures we've been talking about wouldn't have dressed as we do today. It's only in the last two or three hundred years that we've started wearing trousers. What was [90] the origin of the word 'trouser'?

ERIC: Well people have forgotten – if they ever knew – that they were invented by a tailor called Jacob Trowser, except he spelt it with a 'w' [95] – it's only recently that it's been spelt with a 'u' in the middle. Jacob Trowser was a tailor who for some reason, difficult to understand, started making these trousers which [100] were tubular in design and came all the way down to the ankle and he was thought to be completely mad. He put them on the market as hygienic and economical and the [105] whole thing was a complete failure until the Duke of Wellington actually wore a pair for a bet – the whole thing was regarded as a bit of a joke – but in the way of these things, [110] fashionable young men took the whole thing seriously and began to wear trousers.

PRESENTER: With their hands in their pockets. [115]

ERIC: With their hands in their pockets. That's another thing. We take it for granted that in our trousers we have these things but it never occurs to us to wonder why they're called [120] pockets. What my researches reveal is that there was a gentleman called Henry Pocket, born in 1589, who had the idea of having little pouches sewn into the sides of his breeches. [125] And he was thought to be fairly silly too and all kinds of jokes were made about him, but the thing caught on because it made sense, especially in winter when you could keep your [130] hands in your pockets.

PRESENTER: And Walkman – a relatively recent thing but again much earlier origins.

ERIC: Yes indeed, he was American – [135] Otis P. Walkman – I don't know what the P stands for – and he was one of these people who are born before their time. He had the notion of having some kind of portable [140] recording and playback device, which is a brilliant idea but unfortunately the technology of his day didn't allow him to put the machine in his pocket or carry it on [145] his belt and his was pulled behind him on a little trolley, which was I suppose a bit cumbersome. It wasn't until quite recent times that the technology that made the truly [150] portable Walkman possible was invented.

PRESENTER: It's been great talking to you, Eric, thank you for being my guest. [155]

ASSESSMENT CRITERIA

PAPER 2 COMPOSITION

Marks are given out of 20 for each composition, according to:

- the relevance of the composition to the question set
- the organization of the composition, including paragraph structure and linking
- the range, level and appropriacy of vocabulary, including spelling
- the range, level and appropriacy of grammatical structure, including punctuation
- the appropriacy of style

Individual mistakes do not lose marks. There are no 'right or wrong' opinions and lack of knowledge of a subject is not penalised. However, marks are lost for compositions that are too short or perhaps too long. The following provides a general guide to the marking of compositions.

16–20
- approaching or achieving a high level of native-speaker fluency
- no irrelevance, padding or waffle; task fully addressed
- substantial proportion of sophisticated structure and vocabulary, including varied and appropriate linking and accurate spelling and punctuation
- well-controlled organization and appropriate style
- few if any errors of the kind unlikely to be made by a native speaker; no basic errors and little if any totally inapproptiate vocabulary

11–15
- natural and flowing well with some errors resulting from attempts to use sophisticated structure and vocabulary but not quite getting it right
- little or no irrelevance, with task fully addressed
- some accurate sophisticated structure and vocabulary: good linking and generally accurate spelling and punctuation
- coherent organization and appropriate style
- not many errors and few, if any, basic ones

8–10
- competent and clear but limited and unadventurous
- task reasonably addressed with some irrelevance and/or repetition
- accurate structure, vocabulary and linking, although much of it basic; few basic errors that impede understanding
- clear organization; style not wholly inappropriate

5–7
- errors substantially impede communication
- task not addressed to any significant extent, with much irrelevance and/or repetition
- structure, vocabulary and linking too basic and with many errors
- poorly organized

0–4
- composition rendered incoherent by number and nature of errors
- mostly irrelevant and/or too short for any real assessment to be made
- basic structures inaccurate; no attempt at linking;
- vocabulary only very basic; many basic errors
- no coherent organization

PAPER 5 INTERVIEW

The interview, which lasts 12-15 minutes, uses a combination of visual and verbal stimuli, and ranges from simple identification of material to discussion of related topics and theme-related communicative activities. It is marked according to the candidate's performance regarding the following:

a) fluency
b) grammatical accuracy
c) pronunciation of sentences
d) pronunciation of individual sounds
e) ability to communicate effectively with others
f) range and appropriacy of vocabulary

Marks are awarded out of 5 for each of these categories, giving a maximum of 30 marks, which is then converted into a mark out of 40. The following provides a general guide to the marking of the interview.

5 approaching or achieving native-speaker level in all categories

4 a) little hesitation; b) few errors even in sophisticated structrues and no basic errors; c/d) clear and easy to listen to and understand; e) communicating mostly with ease and effectively with only the occasional minor difficulty; f) few occasions when appropriate vocabulary cannot readily be produced and these only in specialised areas

3 a) little hesitation when talking about everyday matters, some when talking about abstract matters; b) competent and accurate use of more than basic structure with few if any basic errors; c/d) competent with understanding not impeded; e) communicating effectively or adequately in all contexts; f) adequate if limited vocabulary in all but specialised areas

2 a) some hesitation when talking about everyday matters and too much when discussing abstract ideas; b) adequate structures for everyday contexts but significant number of basic errors; c/d) pronunciation making understanding difficult; e) communicating adequately in everyday contexts but significant difficulty when discussing abstract ideas; f) adequate vocabulary but too much of it basic

1 a) constant hesitation; b) many basic errors; c/d) pronunciation making understanding almost impossible; e) poor communication even in everyday contexts; f) inadequate vocabulary even for everyday contexts

0 a) no connected speech; b) not even basic structures correct; c/d) impossible to understand; e) failing to communicate at all; f) only the most basic vocabulary produced